Educating Global Citizens
Colleges and Universities

D0205781

This book provides distinctive analysis of the full range of expressions in global education at a crucial time, when international competition is rising, tensions with American foreign policy both complicate and motivate new activity, and a variety of innovations are taking shape. Citing best practices at a variety of institutions, the book provides practical coverage and guidance in the major aspects of global education, including curriculum, study abroad, international students, and collaborations and branch campuses, while dealing as well with management issues and options. The book is intended to guide academic administrators and students in higher education at a point when international education issues increasingly impinge on all aspects of college or university operation. The book also deals with core principles that must guide global educational endeavors and with problems and issues in the field in general as well as in specific functional areas. Challenges of assessment also win attention. Higher education professionals will find that this book serves as a manageable and provocative guide, in one of the most challenging and exciting areas of American higher education today.

Peter N. Stearns is Provost and Professor of History at George Mason University. He has taught at Harvard, the University of Chicago, Rutgers, and Carnegie Mellon. He has published widely and, under his leadership, George Mason was awarded the 2006 Andrew Heiskell Award for Innovation in International Education.

Educating Global Citizens in Colleges and Universities

Challenges and Opportunities

Peter N. Stearns
George Mason University

Routledge
Taylor & Francis Group

NEW YORK AND LONDON

First published 2009
by Routledge
2 Park Square, Milton Park, Abingdon, Oxon OX14 4RN

Simultaneously published in the USA and Canada
by Routledge
711 Third Avenue Avenue, New York, NY 10017

Routledge is an imprint of the Taylor & Francis Group, an informa business

© 2009 Taylor & Francis

Typeset in Minion by
RefineCatch Limited, Bungay, Suffolk

Library of Congress Cataloging-in-Publication Data
Stearns, Peter N.
    Educating global citizens in colleges and universities : challenges and opportunities / Peter N. Stearns.
      p. cm.
    Includes bibliographical references and index.
    1. International education—United States.   2. Education, Higher—Curricula—United States.
I. Title
    LC1090.S74 2009
    370.1160973—dc22   2008025836

ISBN10: 0–415–99023–8 (hbk)
ISBN10: 0–415–99024–6 (pbk)
ISBN10: 0–203–88518–X (ebk)

ISBN13: 978–0–415–99023–3 (hbk)
ISBN13: 978–0–415–99024–0 (pbk)
ISBN13: 978–0–203–88518–5 (ebk)

Dedication

For Chloe Lavinia,
wishing her a global life

Contents

Acknowledgements

I owe a great deal to many people who have helped, directly and indirectly, in the preparation of this book. Most directly, my thanks to Michelle Woodford for tremendous assistance with the research. I've had important advice and suggestions as well from Alan Merten, Yehuda Lukacs, Cordelia Stearns, Rick Davis, Mark Kamlet, Kathy Trump, Curtis Porter, Tom Hennessey, Kris Smith, Madeline Ross, Karen Gentemann, Geoff Feis, Susan Graziano, John O'Connor, Julie Christensen, Larry Czarda, John Paden, and Nance Lucas. Christa Olson's insights and evaluation were extremely helpful, well beyond the call of duty. Sarah Burrows of Routledge provided guidance and encouragement, and I also must thank the readers of my original prospectus, whose advice was on point. Much appreciation to Laura Bell for assistance on the manuscript; her combination of diligence, imagination and good humor is unusual. My wife, Donna Kidd, provided important suggestions and tolerated at least the usual amount of authorial obsession.

Preface

Turning American colleges and universities into global institutions, or at least making global education one of their top priorities, will surely be one of the leading demands of the 21st century in the nation's higher education. Whatever one's personal level of commitment to global interests, there's no escaping the fact that the United States is enmeshed increasingly in global processes and in interactions with a diverse array of foreign regions and cultures. Understanding the global context better will be a fundamental challenge for effective citizenship, for a diverse array of careers, and for meaningful leisure—for a major slice of personal and social life, in other words.

Yet despite some important traditional commitments to international study, American institutions are not always well equipped to handle the global challenge—or even to recognize it. They operate in a measurably parochial cultural context. Certain types of institutions face particular difficulties in responding to global needs: liberal arts schools have traditionally been the most agile, but they are increasingly atypical, and small, within the larger institutional mix. American faculties are, collectively, less interested in global education than their counterparts in other regions, because some elements share a national disdain for the non-American and often maintain a dubious sense of national educational separateness and superiority. American students come into college with growing interests in global issues but, usually, with scant concrete preparation. And there is little help from the outside—most notably, from state and federal government—to aid colleges and universities in meeting a global agenda.

The need, clearly, is for innovation. Over the past fifteen years, a wide variety of American institutions, from community colleges to ivy-encrusted research leaders, have been responding with impressive imagination, expanding established international programs and adding real new substance. But change is uneven, predictably enough. Even bellwether institutions often struggle to adjust administrative structures and to apply assessment procedures to their new efforts. The question of funding looms large in many aspects of the global endeavor.

The need to develop a global educational agenda, but also the challenges in doing so, underscore the importance of the commitment and understanding of academic administrators—not just at the top, but throughout the staffing of higher education. Global education will continue to depend on particularly eager advocates and specialists, in such fields as study abroad. But it also needs awareness by, and ideas from, a wider array of administrative faculty—in student affairs, most obviously, but also in admissions, budget and other areas. The issues involved in shaping a fuller and more responsive global education are interesting. They need wider currency in the training and routine of academic administration, and in the links between administrators and faculty (and students).

This book is designed to present a picture of the current state of play, to help both specialists and higher education personnel more generally develop a sense of looming challenges, recent achievements, common problems, and probable future trajectories. It emerges from a career in international research and education and from a perspective as provost of a globally ambitious university. Global education needs its place within the standard array of academic topics—right alongside diversity, development activities, or student retention. This book is designed to increase the comfort level with the global agenda, while encouraging further contributions from people devoted to the advancement of higher education in the United States—an advancement increasingly impossible without an effective global component.

1
Defining the Challenge

It would be hard to find an American community college, college or university that has not devoted serious new thought, in recent years, to some aspect—often, to many aspects—of global education. The need to adjust curricula and educational arrangements to the increasingly global context in which Americans operate is impossible to avoid. The idea of "preparing global citizens" may seem a bit grandiose or hollow (or to some, even threatening; the term global is not always neutral). But the notion that educational business as usual matches the many changes in the international environment is hard to defend as well. New global components relate not only to contemporary citizenship, though the linkage is quite real, but also to many workplace opportunities—again, reflecting the wider environment.

This surge of talk, and much action, means that there are a number of quite recent best practices that can be widely shared and discussed. It means, by the same token, that different institutions are at quite different stages in their global efforts—some building on an elaborate existing commitment, others just getting into the game—which is where best practices and explicit discussion can be particularly helpful. The surge also invites more systematic analysis: excitement and even faddishness sometimes outstrip clarity of goals. Innovation may misfire, or encounter unexpected difficulties—and this applies to familiar strategies, like study abroad, as well as the newer rash of efforts to form international partnerships. Here too, an up-to-date survey can help advance the field and minimize (though never eliminate) pitfalls. The sheer administration of global programs, with options ranging from specialized units to efforts to diffuse across the institution, merits assessment as well. Even accreditation procedures come into play, in an atmosphere of innovation: the delicate balance between preserving appropriate standards and developing some trust in international partners and novel arrangements is not easy to strike.

There are also, admittedly, important anomalies in the field, despite the wide discussion. As we will see, there's a troubling American lag in some aspects of the global educational arena that must be addressed. While almost all institutions now have study abroad programs (some of them quite new), in 2005 27% of all schools had no students actually studying abroad. Foreign language attainments have sagged, and requirements of courses with a global or international focus in general education programs have dropped (from 41% in 2001 to 37% in 2006). Few institutions have a global coordinator, and fewer than 40% feature a reference to international in their mission statement (though this has increased from 28% in 2001). Wide variation in degrees of commitment and some lingering uncertainties about commitment of any sort make a new handbook all the more desirable—even as it aims at improving general awareness of what global education entails for active participants and neophytes alike.[1]

For heavily involved institutions, as well as those new to the arena, the additional demands on training are obvious: though important professional associations provide guidance for international specialists, many would-be administrators are schooled on the job, and many higher education officials are called upon to deal with international issues for which their own preparation— even if honed in formal degree programs for higher education administration —provided little or no discussion. Explicit international courses are just beginning to creep into the higher education curriculum: they need encourage- ment, but there is also a place for materials that will address relevant topics in a format applicable to more general issues-in-education courses. There is real benefit in discussing the various facets of international or global education, their interrelationships, and their basic purposes, at a time when new issues and new enthusiasms intertwine.

This book has three basic aims, which are happily reasonably compatible. First is to provide an overview of the main facets of international education, with the goal to serve as part of formal or informal training for academic administrators who, regardless of ultimate specialty, need a sense of the key issues and opportunities in the global arena. Increasingly, it is part of the scen- ery in higher education administration. In the process, the book also seeks to provide guidance for the institutions that seem hesitant to commit to a global agenda, offering reasons for engagement and indications of how to get started—beyond the now virtually obligatory study abroad office. Second, as noted, is to deal with the various aspects of global education and ultimately, their interrelationships, rather than honing in on one facet alone. And third, we will seek to address basic questions of purpose in relationship to the larger American and global contexts. While it is possible, even desirable, for some international education enthusiasts simply to assume the importance of their mission, ultimately they need to be able to explain what they're about and to persuade others; self-evident truth will not do the job. Besides, exploring the foundations of the global enterprise is interesting, the challenges involved intriguing.

* * *

American higher education has long been linked to a wider world. The uni- versity system itself gained much from contacts with patterns elsewhere: the modern research university, to take the most obvious example, derives directly from contacts with German and other progenitors in the late 19th century. American commitment to educate so-called international students, from countries like China, goes back to the early 20th century. Americans have been eager participants in study abroad programs, again for many decades. And in certain curricular areas the United States has long been considerably less parochial than many other countries. In both high school and college, the nation long taught English-language literature from authors both American and British; from the 1920s onward it often emphasized a requirement in European history, or Western civilization, besides the cherished American history survey—in contrast to many countries that emphasized a purely national list of great books and a purely national historical menu. Global education, in many of its aspects, is hardly a new commitment.

The commitment is changing, however, with new opportunities and new problems attached. And an increasing number of educators and educational administrators are involved in some aspect of global education, some eagerly, some swept along with the tide. This book is dedicated to a discussion of the goals and facets of global education in the early 21st century—to match the crucial changes in the field. And it is dedicated to the growing number and diversity of concerned faculty and administrators, hoping to contribute to training in specific areas and to wider debate about the basic purposes involved.

Addressing Challenges

Challenge is the key word. It would be tempting to invoke the overused "crisis" instead, but that risks crying wolf. Change, however, against a backdrop of some more endemic issues, makes challenge, and the need for both heightened attention and deliberate innovation, appropriate. The word is apt as well because it conveys both invitation and caution, and the opportunity to meet the new issues that complicate the global education endeavor.

Change includes, obviously, the power surge of regions of the world beyond Western Europe, long the center of American curricular outreach beyond national borders and the darling of study abroad programs. The growing need to deal with the rising prominence of China and India, new tensions and diversities within the Middle East, and the complexities of Africa and Latin America shake many established mindsets among international educators in the United States, though the same need creates exciting opportunities as well. International education becomes truly global in this sense, and while there were moves in this direction in American programs in the 1970s, with new federal funding for diverse area studies efforts, the full context has been installed only in the past fifteen years.

Change includes the growing international hostility to American foreign policy—possibly a short-term issue, not necessarily entirely warranted, but a fact of life nevertheless. International opinion polls, drawing from most of the world's regions, make it unmistakably clear that various American policies have fairly steadily lowered the nation's image abroad. Hostility to the invasion of Iraq heads the list of concerns, obviously, but disagreements over environmental policies and other issues figure in as well. In some cases, the gap here goes well beyond the specific directions of the Bush administration, to wider disputes over priorities: though recently closing a bit, for example, the gulf between American recognition of global warming as a key problem, and public opinion in most other industrial countries, has been impressively wide.

All this has several implications for global education. Anti-American sentiment invites exploration. Surely a valid purpose for global education, at least over the short term, involves helping college students understand why we have fallen into disfavor abroad—not to persuade them to agree with the critics, but to see where these critics are coming from. Yet this approach is by definition sensitive, and if clumsily handled can draw a global education program into domestic disrepute. Many Americans understandably resent foreign criticism, and many others are essentially unaware of it: how would many parents react to a course or a study abroad preparation kit that highlighted intense hostilities to the United States and the need, as part of global understanding, to grasp their bases? There are dilemmas here that are not easily resolved.

Questionable American standing abroad inevitably invites efforts to use higher education to compensate in part. To some eyes it provides an additional reason to court international students, trusting that their experience in the United States will modify or complicate their vision of the nation as a whole. Innovative efforts directly to establish educational operations abroad, though motivated by various factors, gain momentum when it becomes clear that American higher education enjoys far greater prestige in many regions than do many other national trappings. As a Middle Eastern leader noted, in discussing his support for an American branch campus, it is important to see the United States exporting something besides troops and guns (and he might have added, some questionable popular culture products). Yet anti-Americanism can challenge these same efforts. Many Americans, even amid academic ranks, become nervous about going abroad or at least about visiting certain regions: how can one develop or maintain contacts in this atmosphere? Many administrators, dealing even with friendly colleagues in foreign countries, must expect periodic harangues over deeply felt policy disputes. Again to the Middle East: a government official, generously supporting a branch campus initiative, feels authorized to deliver a 40-minute diatribe against American support for the Israeli incursion into Lebanon in the summer of 2006. Tensions and anomalies now go with the territory.

Change follows, inevitably, from the reactions to 9/11 and widespread American fear of terrorism. Practical problems and contradictions abound. New visa requirements impede the entry of international students, and discourage some from applying at all. Administrative costs for international student offices soar, forcing explicit decisions about what is worthwhile. One sector in the federal government may try to encourage efforts in international education, as the basis for needed expertise or as a bridge to public opinion in other regions, while another sector sets up new restrictions and barriers. The confusions may be entirely understandable, but they unquestionably interfere with international operations in higher education. There are broader issues as well. While 9/11 and its aftermath did not jeopardize basic commitments to study abroad, it raised new questions and concerns. A problem—the terrorist threat—that invited greater efforts to understand the complexities of the global environment could also complicate these same efforts.

The reshuffling of the power balance in global affairs, with obvious implications for traditional American preferences for Western Europe; the rapid deterioration of the national standing in world opinion; and the chilling impact of anti-terrorist efforts form part of the context in which global education must respond to challenge.

There are other, more subtle challenges as well, though some of them are less novel. Global education is most often associated with the humanities and some of the social sciences, perhaps particularly the "softer" social sciences like anthropology. This means, and has long meant, that the most eager applicants for study abroad programs are self-selected for their interests in literature and culture, history and international relations. But the need to convey global issues applies to more reluctant disciplinary areas as well. Engineers and managers have just as much need, as citizens, for a grasp of global education as do Latin American anthropologists; and their work may provide at least as many opportunities, if sometimes unexpected, for international competence or an appreciation of international impacts. Yet, if only as a practical matter, it is characteristically difficult to pry open some of the curricula in the "harder" fields for much serious global exposure. Add to this the conviction in many quarters, whether justified or not, that foreign technical training is unlikely to measure up to American standards, and the makings of another global education dilemma become very clear.

A not dissimilar tension applies to foreign clients and collaborations. The keenest interest in American education, by potential international students or supporters of branch campuses, has long focused on engineering, agriculture, the sciences and—with increasing zeal—management. Nothing wrong with this, though of course some fields have in the process become dangerously dependent on international recruits given waning national interest and competence. But American higher education normally prides itself on more than professional training; it vaunts the exposure it provides to various disciplinary approaches, through general education programs and beyond, and the contributions it makes to critical thinking. Some of us would contend that the real strength of the higher education system rests strongly on these features, and that this is where we can make the greatest contribution abroad. But this is not what many foreign students or potential international partners look to when they seek access to American or American-style education. The result is not only an abstract confusion about educational principles, but some very practical dilemmas, for example, about what requirements should be imposed on international students at various levels or how "real" American degree programs can be marketed abroad.

This book will not pretend to resolve all the complexities of this sort. It will, certainly, add a few more—for example, the enticing confusion between multicultural educational efforts, often resolutely American despite international derivations, and global exposures. But it will explore the complexities, and it will offer some potential steps toward reducing them, based wherever possible on best-practice examples. The obvious point is that one does not enter the global education arena blithely, whether the subject is curriculum, or study abroad, or foreign collaborations. Good intentions—and they often burn bright in this field, where so many academics and administrators seek to use education to improve international understanding—do not suffice. The following chapters will seek to juxtapose desirable goals with some obdurate realities, with suggestions about how to win through.

The Parochial Challenge

Arguably the biggest challenge—and here we step deliberately into risky territory—involves the tension between global education needs and goals, and a strongly parochial American society. This challenge, to be sure, is not new at all. The United States has long manifested inclinations toward isolation along with a (less unusual) mixture of apprehension and superiority concerning things foreign. But the inclinations become more troubling as the global environment intensifies. And they have some new enhancements. The end of the cold war, in 1991, measurably reduced global coverage in the American news. Media of various sorts cut back the number of international correspondents and the space allotted to developments abroad; news about health and medical developments expanded, as one result, in a society that was becoming more self-preoccupied. And while events forced some restoration of international coverage after 9/11, the expansion remains characteristically narrow, with little sense of what is happening outside the range of American military efforts. Higher education itself was hardly a global leader, overall, in the 1990s; only a minority of institutions gave the subject any recognition in mission statements and many participated in reductions of programs in areas like language training—which means that the more recent surge of interest follows on the heels of a real deficit in institutions themselves, and not just the wider national culture.[2]

Reactions to 9/11 could feed parochialism as well. Some Americans, including educational leaders, saw the terrorist attacks as a reason to circle the wagons around national values and national educational emphases; the wider world, visibly hostile and dangerous, simply did not merit much classroom attention.

The sense of the world as a fearsome place, while understandable, did not grip all Americans, but it generated some new impulses toward ostrichism. Other changes may contribute, if unintentionally, to parochialism: the reduction of attention to the social studies in the primary grades, for example, in favor of skills training in reading and math, means that many students over the past decade are encountering schooling on global topics later and more incompletely than was once the case.

But the basic dilemma, again, is not new. The United States has long been a big country, with less need to think about or depend on relationships with other countries for economic or cultural purposes than, say, most European countries or (since 1853) Japan. The country's New World remove from battle-fields in Asia, Africa or Europe can also feed a withdrawal impulse (here, Latin American countries can join in as well). The fact is that the only major war fought on American soil for over 200 years was a domestic conflict, not imported from abroad—and no major European or Asian power can make that statement. The attack of 9/11 surfaced a widespread claim of violated innocence—we've never before been assailed like this, why does the world hate us—that was I believe somewhat forced and inaccurate—after all, cold war threats and fears had been both real and legitimate for several decades—but whether justified or not the claim revealed a sense of or hope for global immunity that few other societies would advance.

The nation's immigrant past, or its management of immigration, ironically contributes to a sense of remove as well. The United States has been comparatively friendly to immigrants, despite some obvious blots of racism and exclusionism. But its friendliness has typically been predicated on a belief that immigrants could and should be quickly Americanized, stripped of their most blatant foreign qualities. They should shed their language, their socialism (if that was an issue), and their dress, in favor of the national embrace. Sure, after a certain interval immigrants could be indulged references to Italian-ness or Irish-ness, with the kids dressed up for a harmless ethnic dance festival or even a more blatant celebration like St. Patrick's Day. And, a huge point, they could keep their religion. But they should stop being foreign and, with a few exceptions and with allowably nostalgic trips back to the old country, they should largely cut off ties with the wider world as well. Language was an obvious case in point: most immigrant groups were pressed to shed their language of origin and, by second or certainly third generation, most did so, a process that national officials are, in the main, still trying to urge on immigrant groups even today. Immigrants did not, of course, fully comply. Far more simply returned home than national imagery of successful assimilation acknowledges. But most did come to accommodate, because of the benefits of national participation and, often, a real sense of gratitude for the material and political advantages of American life. Some would become fiercer parochialists than the suspicious nativists who pushed the Americanization process in the first place.

Signs of parochialism abound, some charming or harmless, some neutral, some more clearly questionable. The nation participates very incompletely in the world's leading sports interest, soccer football. It clings to non-decimal measurements in a decimal world. Until 2006 it was for several decades one of only two countries that did not sign an agreement not to impose capital punishment on minors. Its widespread hostility to seriously learning foreign languages has become legendary. The joke goes: what's the word for someone who speaks three languages? Trilingual. For someone who speaks two? Bilingual. For someone who speaks one? American. And there's much truth in the linguistic slap, though it's fair to note that when they purported to rule the world the British were accused of similar limitations, suggesting that part of this problem simply involves power position and a sense that other people should learn you, not you them. Parochialism can infect policy. An army general, in the mid-1960s, involved in planning next steps in Vietnam, asks a historian-consultant if he has ever heard of this thing called Buddhism, which he's been told might be a factor in the country he's been asked to worry about. A military shipment of humanitarian supplies to Iraq, in 2004, includes a large batch of pork products. Many Americans, seemingly, and not just men-in-the-street, don't know much about places even when we've become intimately involved with them. And back to the larger point: in an affluent, globally engaged society, less than a quarter of all Americans (until very recently, when they began to be required even for entry to Canada) had even bothered to get passports. Americans can be surprisingly, and deliberately, cut off from the wider world.

Parochialism, again, isn't all bad. Preferences for football over soccer may be entirely benign (I have to say this, because, product of the culture, I share them). And, bad or good, almost every nation or region displays some parochial tendencies, as part of history and identity. It is well known, for example, that geographical knowledge on the part of American students is deplorably bad. Large percentages can't even find Florida on an outline map, much less Russia or Iraq. But students from many other countries, including the highly schooled Koreans who do surpass their American counterparts in math or science, also do rather badly on world geography. Another example: the Dutch have recently been engaging in an intense debate over teaching "Dutch-ness" in the public schools, especially in history courses, in the context of massive Islamic immigration, with an emphasis on taking care of the local with little attention to the global. The debate rivals anything Americans can put up in the category of narrow nationalism. On several fronts, then, it's important not to exaggerate an American national weakness. Further, in the case of the United States, elements of parochialism are completely understandable, and at the same time they have not prevented some very constructive international efforts emanating from American soil or some dedicated and informed internationalists among the nation's citizenry. With all this—hesitations abroad and initiatives at home—it's impossible not to realize how much more college-bound students in other countries know about the wider world, including the United States, than their American counterparts do (any conversation with international students on American campuses drives this point home). And it's impossible not to be struck by the gap between the nation's world position and its dependence on the rest of the world—whether the subject is the international investments that sustain the national economy or the collaboration we seek against the terrorist threat or the markets we expect for American cultural products like Disney films or McDonald's restaurants—and its relative lack of familiarity with what the world is all about.

And, the globalist would add, making a point that is harder to prove, our parochial gap is not only striking, but dangerous, depriving us of the knowledge we should have to operate effectively. Indeed, one of the truly depressing features of involvement in global education efforts over the past few decades is the realization of how small a dent these efforts have made on the larger national knowledge base or consciousness. To take an obvious example, that does not depend on a partisan judgment of whether our recent Iraqi action was right or wrong: we pretty clearly went into Iraq with no more knowledge of local conditions than we had managed in Vietnam four decades before. The ignorance, and the blithe assumption that major action could be undertaken without a solid knowledge base, applied both to relevant policymakers, who scorned caution and the rich historical evidence of Iraqi complexities alike, and the general public. Insouciance at the policy level is particularly scary, but it's important to remember, in a democracy, that despite the current critical public mood toward the Iraqi involvement, enthusiasm was reasonably strong just five years ago, with no concern for regional details. The divide between American power and global involvement, on the one hand, and awareness of international conditions is both great and troubling.

The contrast between widespread parochialism and the realities of a globalizing age drive and complicate discussions of global education in several ways. The contrast helps account for the crusading zeal of many global educators, present author possibly included: there's a sense of mission that is quite understandable in context, but which on occasion may press too hard for wider acceptance.

The contrast sets up a potentially demanding set of goals for the international education efforts that do occur. There's so much to ask apparently ignorant students to learn, to bring them up to global speed, that the sheer factual demands in global education movements may become truly daunting. World history courses, increasingly introduced with the explicit goal of improving student capacity for global understanding, are a case in point, in an admittedly data-filled discipline. The number of facts world historians sometimes assume that properly competent students should have mastered, visible in the typically 1,100–1,200-page textbooks that anchor survey courses, risks counter-productivity. Yet the targets are understandable given characteristically poor student preparation and the realization that, for many collegians, only a course or two stand between their current levels of knowledge and a launch into the obligations of adult citizenship. Any global education program, anywhere, faces decisions about selectivity: it will never be possible to train most students in the knowledge levels globalists themselves aspire to. But selectivity may be a particularly challenging goal in the American context where, given prior parochialism, there seems so much to do, with so little educational time to do it in.

Parochialism, and its strong traditional roots, also makes many global education programs contestable, and this is the final point. The tug between global demands and a sense of America first (and in some quarters, America almost only) can be quite acute. Again, this is not unique: the current Dutch debate, in a country long known for both tolerance and international involvement, highlights the intensity of issues of identity precisely because global influences are accelerating. But debate over global education components—as we will see shortly, tensions even over the use of the word—rides high in the United States, even within college faculty communities themselves. It is striking, for example, that the leading federal effort in the history field in recent years, the massively funded Teaching American History projects that have greatly facilitated college–school contacts in this one branch of the discipline and that explicitly privilege attention to the national past, almost flies in the face of the more obvious needs to use history to facilitate broader global understanding. At the time of growing global pressure, whatever the new opportunities involved, it is tempting to focus education on a simpler values framework, nonglobal and sometimes anti-global in nature. Given proud traditions of isolation, American education can be particularly torn by this tug against reality.

In between the temptation toward excessive zeal and the resistance to anything that smacks of global, but centrally related to parochialism: an odd hesitancy to push very far, in fact, at least in some aspects of global education. Thus: send students for study abroad but in carefully sanitized, American-run institutions where they may not have to run into too many foreigners. Thus: teach modern languages, but make sure students don't get pulled away from English too fully, lest psychic balance be disturbed. These are caricatures, to be sure, but not entirely off the mark. Even some of the most devoted advocates of global reach pull their punches a bit, to make sure that fundamental American-ness is not challenged too abruptly. Here is another element of the national puzzle to be considered in dealing with the outgrowths of parochialism.

Why This Book?

There is a rich, perceptive, and useful literature on global education, both worldwide and in the United States—indeed, this study would have been impossible without this material. So the obvious question, even granting acceptance of the importance of doing more with the field, why another entry? There are three elements to a response.

First, the field changes rapidly. The opportunity to evaluate global education's needs and prospects in the "post" climate—post-9/11, post-Iraqi invasion and the souring of world opinion, and with the prospect of post-Bush—is important to exploit. Even beyond this, the increasing efforts of other countries to globalize their higher educational programs—Japan, South Korea, and China are cases in point—and also the growing competition, particularly from Britain and Australia, but also Germany and elsewhere, for international student clients, adds another important element of change to the mix. The field will not hold still even after 2009, of course, which is one of the reasons global education is such an engaging preoccupation, but a new stake in the ground is truly timely.

Second, most existing efforts focus primarily on a single aspect of the subject, whether it is study abroad or curriculum. Efforts that go beyond this, to talk of global education more generally, often come in the form of pamphlets, great for highlighting goals and suggesting issues but inadequate really to guide the administration of global programs. This book, focusing on synthesis across specific fields and bent on combining manageable brevity with something beyond statements of principle, serves a distinctive need. The opportunity to combine discussions of curriculum and assessment—basic educational goals—with more specialist topics like branch campuses, in a single volume, is particularly engaging. Combination also facilitates critical appraisal, highlighting problems in the field as a whole, as well as in specific sectors. And of course suggestions for further reading will credit the many strong existing studies (and a few others in the works, in areas like study abroad) and allow opportunities for more detailed exploration—a selective bibliography follows the book's conclusion.

Third, while many existing materials are relevant for training purposes, this book is specifically designed to mesh with educational programs in higher education administration. As noted, administrators dealing with global issues are typically highly motivated and, often, thanks to long experience, well versed in relevant issues, whether the subject is student visas or study abroad. But most came into their line of work somewhat fortuitously, not infrequently as a result of their own positive experiences in courses abroad or through prior work in the Peace Corps or some other relevant branch of government. Opportunities for formal training—as in so much of higher education administration—have been limited, and it seems legitimate to assume that, on balance, some explicit exposure, as part of higher education preparation more generally, will produce greater, or at least quicker, quality among administrators themselves. Leadership in global education is a key issue. Much ink has been spilled about the need for inspiration from the top—from university presidents and the like—and there are indeed important examples of this, as we will see. But this kind of impetus needs staff follow-up, not just from global specialists but from other administrative sectors; and there are important opportunities for initiatives directly from the ranks as well. Here is another set of reasons for wider exposure to, and training in, the main facets of higher education's internationalization, along with awareness of characteristic problems and deficiencies. Further, the urgency and complexity of global education issues increasingly impinge on the work of non-specialist administrators as well, even in such far-removed reaches as budget and planning and certainly in areas like student life. (For example, the Society for College and University Planning—SCUP—has included panels on administrative and budget issues in international branch campuses at several recent annual meetings, and we will see that opportunities for wider discussions of budgeting and strategic planning for global education should draw in even more officials in the future.) This book aims explicitly at interacting with training programs, fitting into general courses on current issues in the field and encouraging the additional development of specific higher education courses on international opportunities, where the book can be combined with some of the more detailed specialist literature. There is attention as well to different facets of higher education, including the community colleges where so many American students gain whatever experience in global education they have at the post-secondary level and where so much work with international students takes place. Here too, the book seeks to make a distinctive contribution.

My own credentials for venturing a contribution are several-fold, though of course, in an overall field with so many facets, there are gaps as well. Trained as a historian, I have long been involved in curricular projects seeking greater global understanding, particularly around the expansion of world history programs but more broadly as well. The process has also given me some direct experience in moving from a largely European to a more genuinely global framework. It also taught me a good bit about developing the habits of mind appropriate for global understanding, and not merely a memorized factual arsenal. My curricular work entailed active contacts with secondary school programs, another component utilized in this book as part of the real context for international education at the college level. I have been an academic administrator for 16 years (and before that, a department chair), and have had global education initiatives on my active agenda throughout that time—first as a dean at Carnegie Mellon University, more recently as Provost at George Mason. I have worked on committees bent (not always productively) on internationalizing the campus; on student life projects, including establishing an international day tradition at Carnegie Mellon; on modern languages development and integration with other aspects of the curriculum; on the care, feeding and utilization of international students; and, at George Mason, on a variety of collaborative international programs and the establishment of a branch campus in the Middle East. In the process, I have dealt with some of the issues of relevant professional administrative organization, governance and funding that this book addresses as well. This varied experience does not, I hasten to add, establish me as a card-carrying specialist in the field, though I have participated in some of the relevant gatherings; and it certainly does not serve as sufficient basis for what this book covers overall—where I depend on a much greater variety of best practices and cautionary examples than I have been involved in, and on the varieties of secondary literature referred to as well. But the experience in the field is relevant, and I advance it both as an admission of limitations and as a credential of which I am considerably proud.

One final caveat is obvious, and I hope not evasive. Global education in the United States, in its various facets, has seen a wide variety of initiatives, with clear acceleration in recent years. It would be presumptuous to claim that a single book, and one deliberately kept short in the interests of service to updating broader instructional programs for higher education administrators, encompasses or even hints at all the relevant activities, or the challenges and results they involve. There is an effort to provide specific examples, brief case studies in some instances, in a number of areas, from various kinds of American institutions. But selectivity is extreme. Happily, the existence of several key periodicals in the international education field allows fairly ready and ongoing access to additional illustrations as well as to further initiatives in the future.

Coverage and Sequence

A brief word about the book's organization. Two principles predominate: first, the effort to touch bases, if only briefly, in a comprehensive fashion, so that all the major parts of the global education puzzle are on view, and their mutual relationships established. And second, a consistent interest in relating administrative issues to larger principles, whether the topic is curriculum—where basic goals are often discussed, but not always coherently—or funding, where principles have not always been on view at all.

We begin with goals themselves, to stake out some targets that can then be used in association with the specific topics that follow. The subsequent chapter expands on the contexts for global education, admittedly in brief compass, including relevant government initiatives, but with particular attention to what students bring into college from their prior education, and the opportunities and challenges this preparation presents. Curriculum is next, for without a sense of what kinds of courses and programs make up a global education effort, discussions of global education or branch campuses risk a lack of anchor; to take the obvious point, study abroad makes full sense only if it is explicitly integrated with work taken both before and after the experience, but these connections are not always thought through. The book then turns to more familiar segments of the international education administrator's repertoire: study abroad; international students; partnerships and branch campuses. Here, in addition to a survey of issues and practices, the intent is to cover a variety of settings, from community colleges to research universities, and again to probe interrelationships and the connection with basic goals. Issues of administrative organization and funding pick up vital themes, too often ignored in the excitement of more ambitious ventures: but in fact there are some concerns and options that are fundamental to successful engagement with global education. An ensuing main chapter, only partly in summary, picks up the topic of learning outcomes and assessments. Often evoked, the outcomes issue is rarely explored beyond pious hopes, yet it must be explored if claims of preparation for global citizenship are to have any reality. Two final chapters then return to broader principles, the challenge of integrating component parts, and the need to maintain a commitment to high priority, amid the welter of pressures and opportunities facing higher education in the 21st century.

Global and International

In discussing both goals and methods, this book privileges the term "global" over "international," though diligent readers will have noted some efforts also to interchange the terms in this chapter simply to vary the verbal menu. Though overlapping, the terms have somewhat different advantages and risks, and a final comment here will complete the initial presentation of what this book is about.

Some authorities argue that "global" is most commonly used for programs beyond the national in K-12 efforts, "internationalization" for activities in higher education. A recent American Council on Education brochure (2007) agonized over this very issue and ended with an endorsement of "international" as best serving "the process of integrating an international, intercultural, or global dimension into the purpose, functions, or delivery of post-secondary education"—a completely acceptable definition; but the simpler term global was dismissed only because it was "conventionally" associated with K-12 programs.[3] The discussion might be held to suggest that the terminological choice doesn't matter too much, and on the whole I agree. But I do opt for global even so. On the K-12 front: in fact, the term global carries some adverse freight in the school systems to which higher education may be more immune. Rumor had it, for example, that curricular discussions in one southern state actually banned use of the term global, for its connotations of extra-national governments, the United Nations, and other targets of disdain. International, in this sense, would be safer.

On the other hand, international relations programs, within or without political science departments, have increasingly chafed against the confines of tradition. International relations once meant diplomatic activities above all, the formal interactions among states. But obviously, in contemporary life and indeed well before, actual international contacts involve far more than statecraft, in embracing trade, cultural contacts, disease transmissions, migrations and, now, environmental damage as well. While international may simply be redefined, and many international relations programs pride themselves on this upgrading, the scope of the extra-national world that we want students to know about is arguably better served by the term global—despite the political baggage it carries for some.

International also, by definition, privileges the nation state, while contending that wider relationships must be given their due. In higher education, international has often highlighted emphasis on area studies programs, of the sort that contributed so greatly both to research and to teaching in the later 1960s and 1970s and that continue to burn bright at many prestigious universities. These programs often transcend the nation, focusing on larger regions like Latin America or Southeast Asia, but they focus attention on often detailed features and distinctions in individual regions, without much attention to larger transnational systems. This approach must be part of a program in global education, but not, I would argue, the whole—again a reason to prod attention toward the larger systems in ways that the term global implies. The nation state is not dead, though it is being transcended in many ways; traditional culture areas must figure strongly in any educational effort toward greater understanding; but there is more besides, which is why the more succinct term, despite some contentious connotations, is the more appropriate.

For global education must involve not only a sensitive study of different cultural traditions and institutional frameworks, with the analytical skills attached, but also an appreciation of the kinds of forces that bear on societies around the world—including the United States, and how these forces have emerged. Global training in this sense requires attention to migration patterns, to cultural dissemination, to the role of transnational institutions including not only formal agencies, like the World Health Organization, but private human rights and environmental groups—the international NGOs, and of course to the technological connections that now knit the various global systems. Forces of this sort (not all of them brand new) blend and clash with regional interests (again, including phenomena like American parochialism)—the story involves the local and the global, to introduce the common phrase, not the global alone. But global, as a term, captures this aspect of the educational agenda better than the now slightly dated international—which is the main reason for its preferred use in this survey.

One final point: global does not necessarily mean good, and it very clearly does not mean good to many of the world's participant-observers. There's an upbeat tradition in global or international studies that tends to assume that whatever binds the world community more tightly must be seen as benign, and that what is foreign should be likeable. My own biases probably incline in this direction—I am fascinated by diverse ways of doing things and eager to see greater harmonies across political and cultural borders. But global integrations visibly disadvantage many groups and displease many more, and these downsides are a vital part of global education properly construed. Outright attacks on global patterns, including American attacks, must be given their due, and the global links must not be seen as inevitably triumphant (after all, they measurably retreated less than a century ago). There are data that students should learn, relevant global-analytical skills that they should master, but there must also be room for debate and diversity when the subject matter moves into the area of value judgments. This, of course, leads us directly into the arena of basic goals of the whole global educational enterprise.

2
Goals:
Where We Should Be Heading

Global efforts in American higher education have two basic purposes: first, to improve the knowledge and skills of American students—as wide as possible a swathe of American students—to function adequately in an increasingly intense global environment. Second, to use the prestige of American higher education to improve the nation's standing abroad and to forge relationships, both individual and institutional, that provide mutual benefits in this vein. These purposes are, of course, far easier to express than to implement, and a number of goals and issues follow from them that form the substance of this chapter. The purposes are also unabashedly do-gooder, bound to evoke cynicism from an academic audience schooled to be skeptical; this aspect, too, must be addressed.

But the simplicity and significance of the basic purposes must be emphasized as well, along ultimately with their mutual relationship. Currently, most American students know considerably less about developments in other key regions than their counterparts know about the United States. The contrast surely reflects power differentials in part, but it is nonetheless undesirable, and contrary to the long-term national interest in terms of effective American policy and economic outreach, especially in a time of changing global balances and the intensification of global contacts. Global education, in its most elemental goal, seeks to close the gap. It seeks also to use the strengths of American postsecondary education—its technical strengths, but also its liberal mission—to help, however modestly, counteract some of the more negative features of the nation's presentation to the world. In both its key functions, global education aims at improving the chances for constructive interactions between the United States and the world community. Grand claims, again—but claims that explain why the mission of global education is so critical.

Stipulating basic goals—and I confess that no great sophistication is required to lay out the fundamentals—is important for several reasons. It provides a standard by which particular facets of the global education enterprise can be measured, ultimately indeed a basis for more formally assessing learning outcomes. A study abroad program that conveys students to another country but then largely isolates them with American instructors from their college of origin, spiced by an occasional tourist field trip, is probably not doing much to meet basic goals—even though it will add to the statistics on study abroad efforts. As in any endeavor, there are well-meaning but mindless efforts in global education, and juxtaposing them with the two key purposes is a legitimate corrective. Highlighting the fundamental purposes should guide curricular efforts and must be front and center as well in shaping any international collaborations; they must not be overshadowed by the excitement of getting one's own course into the global list or by the details of global deal-making.

The goals also help identify false gods—goals that are sometimes tempting but which would in fact distract from, or at least seriously complicate, the desirable aims of global education. The most obvious candidate here is profit. It has been tempting at various points, for various kinds of institutions and organizations, to look to global operations as a significant source of funds. Attracting full-paying international students was the most obvious target here, but study abroad groups have also been reaping rewards possibly beyond reasonable measure, and some of the excitement about foreign branch campuses involves dollar signs as well. Global activities may make a bit of money, though costs are considerable as well—we'll turn to the vexed issue of funding later on. But, ideals to the fore, casting any international education effort primarily in terms of the bottom line would be a serious distortion of purpose and, where exploitation of foreigners is involved, truly and reprehensibly counter-productive. Any global program that has profit high up on the priority scale, whether explicitly or implicitly, is deeply suspect.

Confusion, not greed, centers another common distraction about goals: the relationship between global programs and multicultural initiatives. Global education is by definition multicultural, with part of its mission to provide students with the data and skills needed to interpret different cultures and the impacts these have on institutions and behaviors—a goals relationship is undeniable. But merger of the goals is undesirable and distracting for at least two reasons. First, the global component is not just about different cultures, but also about larger global forces and institutions—too much confinement to cultural issues is a disservice, vital as they are. Second, multicultural in practice often means exposure to different subcultures—races, ethnicities, and religions—within the United States. International components are accepted, but mainly as add-ons. American multicultural education is a valid and important project, but however complex, it is an American, not a global endeavor. It involves cultures of origin but invariably modified, often massively modified, by interactions with contexts within the United States. How many "multicultural and international" centers end up being dominated by Americans, however hyphenated, whose numbers but also whose experience in working with American systems tend to displace international students save around very specialized functions like visa assistance? How many "international days" are in fact largely days in which Americans, again however hyphenated, show off a certain degree of nostalgia by bringing out costumes from their parents' homes or from tourist visits; international students, less accustomed to American-type shows and often bent on working as hard as possible in any event, are often far less visible. Again, there is every reason to allow various American subcultures to express themselves and find common cause, and every reason to teach the shared skills that can help students (including, by the way, the hyphenated groups themselves, who don't always know as much even about cultures of origin as they think they do) appreciate both domestic and international diversity. But the global focus must be kept distinct, and its importance must not be subsumed under domestic accommodations.

Finally, the two basic goals—American skills and the national role and standing abroad—not only provide an outline map and a source of performance criteria and distinctions, they also set up a number of subsidiary issues and implementation directions that constitute signposts in their own right.

American Education and the Wider World: Contributing Globally by Export

One of the two fundamental purposes of global education looks outward. American colleges and universities can seek, carefully and modestly, to provide value to people and regions outside the United States, to offer something genuinely American that brings real social and individual benefits and that serves as an antidote to some of the less savory expressions of what the nation currently has to offer. A variety of activities can further this goal, and the main categories will be addressed in later chapters. Recruiting international students and forming branch campuses and international collaborations constitute the most common methods.

Whatever the tactic, the underlying assumptions behind international outreach by colleges and universities involve a conjuncture between the belief that there are some special values attached to higher education à l'américain, that can benefit international students as individuals and (with more ambitious projects) whole regions, and a belief or hope that exposure to these benefits will, on average, additionally improve perceptions of the United States. Obviously, other goals can supplement and, in some instances, complicate the effort. A profit motive has already been discussed, not usually predominant but an undeniable factor in some programs. Sheer dependence on international students in certain disciplines, particularly in science and engineering at the graduate level, feeds recruitment, and while not contradicting more ambitious motivations it may be more immediately self-interested; in certain cases too, the results draw students to the United States for work after graduation, which attenuates any international benefits.

The assumption of special virtues in American higher education is tricky in itself, in a post-colonial world. Unquestionably, many international students and leaders harbor this assumption, even when they are strongly opposed to major aspects of American foreign policy and even culture. It is not unusual to find a potential international partner eager to import American programs while proclaiming, frankly somewhat incongruously, that these programs should not instill American habits or values. By the same token, the acceptance of American educational merits may be ill-informed. Or it may rest on valuations different from those Americans themselves would prefer. Most obviously, international preference for very practical programs, with immediate job outcomes, reflects a belief that American higher education is directly associated with the nation's business and technical success; whereas many internationalist American educators would prefer to emphasize broader and more liberal educational goals, including diversity of disciplinary approaches and a capacity for critical thinking. We will have to return to the resultant dilemma, which is by no means a total clash but which can lead to real disputes about what programs to export, particularly at the undergraduate level. Still, the proliferation of colleges and universities proudly bearing the label "American" in many parts of Africa, Asia and even some European countries—many of them not really American at all, but reflecting the popularity of the brand—bears out the claim that something distinctive may be involved, certainly in perception, possibly in reality as well.

The idea of special merits, whether intrinsic to American-style higher education (as many of us would like to believe) or simply reflective of other admired achievements in American society, is both fragile and dangerous, which produces a refinement of the basic goals statement. It is fragile in that it is subject both to competition and to change over time. The past five years have seen heightened rivalries, both for international students and for the establishment of branch campuses abroad, particularly from British and Australian universities but also from other countries as well. It is still fair to say that an American label preserves special cachet, but there is no telling how long this will last. We can expect, as well, growing confidence in regional and national university systems as these mature and expand. Chinese leaders, to take the most obvious example, are working hard to establish a top tier of universities equal to the MITs and Stanfords, and it would be foolish not to expect them to succeed. Chinese officials are also working with other Asian counterparts to organize international education within the region itself. For the moment, the Chinese are also interested in access to American education, sponsoring a number of undergraduates directly. And it is also true that, again at least for the moment, educational capacity in places like China and India, in terms of the sheer number of seats available, rides well below demand from qualified students, which is another source of opportunity; but with further gains in prosperity, and system expansion, this opportunity may also erode. American institutions can still benefit from a desire to expose students to international issues; "study abroad" programs are gaining popularity in places like Korea and Japan, and American semesters can be part of the mix along with programs in many other places. But this development, though desirable and significant, is not the same thing as a real American advantage, and it may not generate the same numbers. There is no way to predict how long the enthusiasm for an American label will last, but it would be unwise to assume permanence.

The more basic danger to efforts based on assumptions of educational superiority derives neither from competition nor impermanence, but rather from potential arrogance and ignorance. Many American administrators, during the past two decades if not before, have been involved with faculty who so assume the virtues of their research and teaching that they see internationalization only as an opportunity to export American programs unaltered, to bring civilization to the natives. Admittedly, in some circumstances the hunger for the American label and for access to management or technical expertise is so great that the arrogance succeeds at least in the short term: some internationals accept the claims or swallow hard and collaborate despite private skepticism. But, again if and as economic success spreads more widely, and particularly if American political success is also challenged, the approach, questionable in principle in any event, is likely to become increasingly counter-productive.

None of these issues vitiates the basic goal: it is desirable to use some of the qualities of American higher education, and the prestige it has at least for the moment, to spread educational benefits more widely and to promote a more favorable image and better understanding of the United States.

Joined to this goal, however, must be a sense of mutuality and collaboration. Benefits, in the first place, must be genuinely bilateral or multilateral. A venture abroad that just helps the American institution does not further the real goal and may actually be counterproductive. More specifically: efforts themselves must be framed in terms of active interaction with visions and strengths derived from the host region itself. Unthinking export of American programs without elements that reflect local strengths and contributions are needlessly narrow and, if not immediately, politically vulnerable. Ventures that do not seek local advice about how to improve, for example, the exposure of American students to that culture, in favor of simply trotting out a standard management curriculum for the benefit of the natives, forgo a valuable global opportunity and, again, court local displeasure as well, at least after an initial excitement fades. Mutual learning, as well as mutual benefit, are the keys to constructive engagement while offering best promise of long-term success. It follows, finally, that not only attitudes, on the part of American educational exporters, but institutional arrangements must wherever possible reflect a collaborative spirit. Solo international branch campuses may have a place, and this will be discussed in a later chapter. But generally, however, and I think increasingly over time, active interchange with local higher education programs, again toward mutual learning and mutual benefit, will provide the most durable approach.

Mutualism and collaboration raise of course the question about how American-ness and American standards will be preserved, and the issues here are part of the branch campus/collaboratives discussion as well. It is easier, not only for United States accreditors but for many faculty nervous about international qualities, to insist on down-the-line mimicry. But educational maximization, bent on combining American and regional cultural resources, and simple political horse sense, in a century that will become increasingly skeptical of blatant statements of Western superiority, argues for greater complexity.

American higher education, at its best, does have some desirable qualities that can be touted with validity and that do provide benefits, as well as image repair, internationally. But the basic goal must be shaped by concomitant reliance on openness to the educational assets that can be conjoined with the American effort. Not surprisingly, the result will be more durably global than a made-in-America approach alone can provide. In this sense the global outreach goal connects directly with the domestic goal of enhancing global citizenship and professionalism within the United States.

Global Knowledge and Global Skills: Importing the Wider World

The need to train American college students in the data and analytical capacities that enable them to comprehend leading global issues, now and in the future, reflects requirements of responsible contemporary citizenship. Even though elections hinge still disproportionately on domestic issues, the importance of global problems and their periodically inescapable intrusion into general consciousness make the connection directly. Global education does not guarantee sensible judgments about foreign policy concerns broadly construed, but at least it provides some alternative to sheer emotion and stereotyping, and to the persistent overuse of misleading analogies in which every conflict, to take one obvious example, becomes an extension of Munich/World War II or the battle against communism. Providing a new, global level in critical thinking is the best that we in higher education have to offer.

A subset of this broad citizenship goal—and for many, in jobs that have or will have global connections, it's a matter of professional enhancement as well—involves training a larger number of genuine global specialists, who can provide the leaders and technicians American business, government, NGOs, and even academic institutions desperately require, with among other things the cultural and linguistic experience to surpass the contemporary leadership generation in numbers and acumen alike. The cadre is in desperately short supply at the present time.

Several subsidiary goals and issues plug into the main training thrusts. The most obvious, again to be pursued in further detail, involves the inherent interdisciplinarity of the charge. In seeking to have students familiar with key global issues, some of them enthused enough to pursue relevant degrees and careers, we are inevitably talking about a package that involves economics (balance of payments patterns loom large, for example)—but also culture (the nature and impact of global consumerism on belief structures), as well as international relations in the more familiar sense. The temptation to park a conventional course that deals with things foreign but within the framework of a single discipline really does not work. The interdisciplinary challenge can be met in a variety of ways, to be sure, but it must be acknowledged or the larger goal will be incompletely addressed.

Interdisciplinarity, but of a somewhat less familiar sort, also applies to the package already suggested in the previous chapter: the need both to deal with comparative issues, in which regional specializations can loom large, but also with larger global institutions and processes. The latter, less familiar in most introductory courses aside perhaps from economics, need special emphasis; they form a crucial part of the world we live in and the students will live in.

There's a special charge to the history portion of the global agenda. Many historians, myself included, would eagerly contend that historical understanding, both of the emergences of comparative relationships among major societies and of the development of global contacts and components, form a vital part of any global education agenda. Certainly this figures strongly in the kind of curricular discussion that anchors Chapter 4. But historians have divided in several ways around their involvement. First, of course, a large number remain resolutely parochial or, more kindly put, purely nation-focused, with U.S. history heading the list. Recent federal support for American history and none other, in the (relatively) huge Teaching American History grants, has exacerbated the isolation. There is an interesting compensatory movement afoot to "internationalize" the American history course, but its prospects are uncertain. Other historians, quite international, also invoke constraints: the area studies focus, which has produced so much useful new knowledge (and some attendant teaching) can be quite hostile to broader global agendas. Most strikingly, world history, which has gained great ground precisely because of the need to adjust history surveys to current international needs, often has its own blinders. Many partisans of world history focus strongly on a relatively remote past, and falter when they move toward the present. Add to that the hoary tradition in history surveys of getting bogged down in early material and never getting past World War II and we have a problem. In fact, the history contribution to global education must be global, not merely based in area studies, and it must spend a good bit of time explicitly tying past to present. This means breaking some deep habits—just as global goals require adjustments in other disciplines—but there's no avoiding the challenge.

The most pressing need of all, the clear sub-goal underneath the fundamental charge to prepare students for a global world, involves identifying and emphasizing core analytical skills, or habits of mind, and privileging them over masses of factual data and memorization tasks. Every major discipline involved in global education—whether contributing to a general education program or participating in a relevant college concentration—has a host of must-know facts, based of course on the growing volume of expert research in the field.

History may be a particular sinner—show a historian a world history course (or any survey course, for that matter, in what is at base a highly empirical discipline), and the list of what every educated person should know quickly builds. A 1994 guide for secondary school world history, for example, offered 17 separate data points on post-classical Islam alone, in a 300-page compendium that had several hundred factual standards overall—and this was just for high schools.[1] The 1,100–1,200-page world history texts generated for college use (and I have helped author some) reflect the challenge, for educators and students alike. Other globally involved disciplines may be a little more forgiving; geographers, more practical, responded to the same call for secondary school criteria with an impressively compact 70-page pamphlet. But details about political and economic systems and institutions quickly pile up, and some of the social sciences, along with cultural studies in the humanities, require knowledge of various theoretical postures as well, like post-colonialism, subaltern studies and the like. The point is obvious: it's a big world, and we know a lot about it, and we understandably want our students to know a lot too. But there's real risk of overdoing it, of drowning durable learning results in an unmanageable mass of data and requirements of memorization.

One of the first bits of advice I encountered, as I entered world history, from a seasoned practitioner was: "dare to omit." Easy to say, of course, but harder to accomplish. Clearly, however, any global curriculum has to strive for feasibility, and must develop principles of selection of the factual points that students must master.

And at the goals level, the need for selectivity is both enhanced and guided by the primacy of relevant habits of mind—a point easily neglected in the daily struggle with masses of material. Of course the analytical skills must be based on data—about different regions of the world and about major global institutions and processes. But memorized materials are not the main point, particularly since we know they tend to slip from the mind as the college class becomes a more distant recollection and particularly because relevant sources of refresher data are increasingly ready to hand. (Indeed, teaching students how to find, interpret and verify global data sources should be one of our key curricular aims.) Whatever factual requirements we impose, as part of more detailed curricular discussions, they have to pass the analysis test: how do they contribute to student abilities to handle global issues—many of which, in their own future lives, we can glimpse only dimly if at all. The aim, always, is the development of capacities to think globally, to foster (and assess) skills that will transfer beyond the single class, beyond indeed the college career.

The key habits of mind, in turn, are not really numerous, though again they are far easier to cite than to translate into successful learning outcomes. Three targets stand out. Gaining experience in accessing and, especially, evaluating global data, and disputed data claims, is a key point. Familiarity with comparative techniques, with sufficient practice that comparative analysis can be undertaken on issues arising in the future, is the second guideline. And experience in assessing the balance and interaction between local and global factors rounds out the set.

The comparative thrust is central. Of course we want knowledge of particular major regions. Beyond this, however, we want students to be able to figure out how and why other significant societies differ from each other and from the United States, though also (since in the global arena students in fact pick up differences more readily than similarities) the ways in which they resemble each other. Comparison does not come easily, partly of course because it requires handling data from two or more cases rather than just one. But a concerted focus on comparison does improve student capacities, weaning them from the impulse to juxtapose separate sections of commentary (here's one society, here's another, why don't you, the teacher-reader, do the actual comparative work) to an understanding that systematic, point-by-point comparison is the way to go. What we want, of course, are students who think comparatively in the future, who realize that claims about special qualities, whether concerning American distinctiveness or the difficulties of the Middle East, have to be run through a comparative filter—and who know how to take the necessary steps.

The global–local skill is, frankly, less well defined but equally fundamental. Globalization theorists and popularizers bravely frame a commitment to understand how regional and global patterns interact, even as they posit the increasing power of the larger influences. Several curricular programs have identified local–global relationship as well. The goal is to gain experience in seeing how regional–national factors, on the one hand, and global factors on the other combine to shape individual and social behaviors. A sense of change over time—a historical sense, to put it bluntly—will help here. Seeing how the balance between regional and global influences has shifted at several key junctures, but perhaps most crucially in the late 19th century and again more recently, provides particularly appropriate opportunities to assess how the local–global balance operates in fact, and to determine how much the global has gained ground. But we need additional contemporary case studies in areas as diverse as disease transmission and control, the nature and role of consumer culture, and the impact of balance of trade, with opportunities to assess not only student mastery of the specific case but their capacity to identify types of analysis that can be applied to other cases as well. Comparison may also come into play, as different regional reactions to a similar global pressure focus the assessment. The need is obvious: no reasonable prospect suggests that global factors will ever eliminate the significance of regional response. The educational challenge involves further identifying and honing the habits of mind that respond to the need.

Assessment of data and sources of data; comparison; and analysis of local–global interactions set the framework for a globally–educated student body. They provide a litmus test for more specific curricula, particularly at the level of general education but to some extent with more extensive programs as well. They move, or should move, the discussion of what global education is all about away from a primarily descriptive plane, toward the more fundamentally analytical level. They also, like the desirable curriculum itself, transcend specific disciplines: the goals can be pursued in a variety of disciplinary combinations; economics and cultural studies, political science, global health, environmental policy, as well as history can contribute to the basics. The idea is the promotion of people who know how to think globally—not in terms of uniformity of conclusions, certainly not in the sense of uniform support for globalization, but through the shared availability of key interpretive skills.

Americans have been treated to a variety of lists of facts, often with supporting evidence that college students do not do very well with the lists. Most commonly, of course, the lists have focused on producing shock at the ignorance about American history and institutions, or occasionally concerning Western civilization. Comparable lists can easily apply to the global arena. And we must be concerned when we uncover complete factual gaps or misinformation about something as fundamental as Islam or the World Bank. But concerns here must not distract from the more important goal, less easy to measure but far more significant. We should learn to ask if students have had adequate opportunity to develop, identify, and transfer the three skills that allow constructive use of global data. We should consider how best to inculcate these skills, how to define learning outcomes in their terms, how to infuse them into the curricular discussions aimed at meeting the goal of creating global citizens.

Cynicism and the Basic Goals

Most global studies professionals are enthusiastic about foreign cultures, eager to use education to promote greater understanding, hopeful even that higher education can contribute to a more peaceful world. Their zeal and intentions almost invite critical comment, and no statement of goals would be complete without acknowledging this. The do-good quality inherent in both basic goals is very real, but it may be unpersuasive.

The ability of higher education to improve the nation's international standing can be challenged to a point. Studies suggest that most international students take back a favorable opinion of the United States, but this is not uniformly the case, and there are certainly instances where misfortune directly contradicts the basic claim. Instances of overt prejudice or violence against foreign students create understandably bad press back home, to take an obvious example, and there is no way of knowing how many quietly constructive experiences counterbalance the bad news. More ambitious international undertakings, including branch campuses, can fail, again with resultant hard feelings. And there are plenty of cases in which potential international partners, collective or individual, are simply not interested in American wares.

On balance, I think it's the complexity, not the outright downsides, of the first global goal that commands attention. A vigorous international effort may not heal the wounds which current American foreign policy or the increasingly demeaning visa procedures create. The tension between appropriate local accommodations and insistence on pure American standards, and the rift between expectations of specialized technical programs, from students and students' families bent on job relevance, and an American interest in wider educational goals, raise important issues in their own right. And, as noted, it is unclear how long the willingness to treat American higher education separately from other things American will last. Not every educational thrust will actually improve perceptions of the United States—again, some caveats are quite legitimate. But this is less of a problem than are the challenges of defining and implementing successful programs in the first place.

On educating global citizens, in contrast, cynicism can range more freely. The goal can seem menacing, or pompous, or both. To some conservatives, long worried about international plots to unseat American sovereignty, the threat looms large. We can assure that global values do not displace national loyalties, that the injunction to compare American society with others does not mean that distinctive American strengths cannot be identified, but the goal will still antagonize some. Of greater concern, though this relates to partisan opposition, is the sense that references to global citizenship or global under-standing imply some kind of ideological strait-jacket, in which students who do not end up loving other cultures or sending donations to UNICEF are somehow disqualified.

Here, despite the do-goodism of the goal, it is possible to be very explicit: global understanding is not a singular term. Students can be introduced to other cultures or institutions and decide, hopefully after some thought and comparative analysis, that they really don't like them (this will be true, of course, for some foreign students encountering American culture as well). They can really dislike the United Nations. Global education does not dictate a single point of view or even a commitment to internationalism. Many global educators may hope that their programs on balance encourage new levels of openness to foreign contributions and a new appreciation for international efforts to control environmental damage or limit war—but compulsion would be out of place. The goal is to provide appropriate levels of information and, above all, the appropriate skills. There can be no assumption that students will all use these in the same ways. Debate, indeed, should be part of the program.

Indeed, and here we reach more familiar ground, it should be obvious that a key reason to study global processes lies in the fact that many of these processes are hard to control and that many have questionable impacts. Here is a key aspect of the local and the global, and a comparative challenge as well: to figure out what aspects of current global forces yield particularly troubling concerns in different regions—including the United States. Global understanding in this sense can open better opportunities for challenge, more informed efforts at control; it does not require a uniform global embrace. The analytical skills that define the most important outcomes are in this sense neutral; the hope is that they will be available for use, not that they will produce a standardized result.

There is of course a lingering expectation of active tolerance. True comparison, where other regional cultures are involved, requires a temporary suspension of belief, in order to make a best effort to understand the "other." After the effort, of course, one can return not only to one's own values but also to disapproval of the other. It remains possible to hope that the effort will on balance produce some willingness to appreciate other values, that in this sense an analytical effort does enhance the likelihood of a personal stance conducive to greater international understanding. But even tolerance cannot be assured or required.

The bottom line: it is legitimate, even essential, to ask that successful students learn certain data and habits of mind that allow a more informed approach to key global issues. That this will not in fact uniformly produce students who like the global world they live in goes without saying—no learning result assures a broader unitary outcome of this sort. The more subtle point is that global citizenship itself cannot legitimately be confined to any particular set of values. One can hope for some reorientation in addition to mastery of data and skills, but there is no requirement.

Even with the caveats, however, the ambition of the two basic goals of global education shines through. The goals ask that American higher education reach out, as appropriate, rather than retreat to domestic isolation in the face of new challenges and tensions abroad. They ask that American higher education add a fundamental criterion to what it seeks from its own students, partially redefining the nature of liberal education in the process.

At best, finally, higher education faculty and administrators can work to connect the two goals themselves, toward mutual benefit and reinforcement. The recruitment of international students, essential for the outreach goal, can be made to help the domestic educational process as well—though we need some experiments to accomplish this effectively. International branch campuses and collaborations, again intended most obviously for outreach, can provide learning opportunities for American students, faculty and administrators as well. In turn, programs in modern language training or global education produce both students and professionals who can be part of outreach efforts, creating, for example, genuine student exchanges instead of the foreign imbalance that currently plagues most efforts. All global education must be measured in terms of the basic goals, but imaginative combinations deserve particular encouragement. The result is nothing more or less than an adjustment of the higher education system to contemporary realities.

3
Contexts for Global Education

Appeals for greater attention to global education, or at least more internationally oriented programs among American colleges and universities, dot the landscape of contemporary history, from the 1960s onward.[1] A few have had impact in the past; many have led to only passing response. The pleas for new commitment followed from passages in the cold war but more obviously from advancing globalization. The fact of incomplete response forms part of the context in which the current round of college and university initiatives takes shape.

For global education not only wins differential interest among various groups of Americans—including many faculty. It can be an explicit source of contest and conflict. Moves toward a more global curriculum during the 1990s were unquestionably part of the bitter national culture wars, and while passions may have eased a bit a concern about partisan dispute forms a second, and related, aspect of the global education context.

Finally, and most directly, anyone looking at the big picture of global education for undergraduates must consider, even if briefly, what high school students bring with them to college. This is an understudied aspect of higher education—dealing not only with formal preparation or lack thereof, but also with assumptions and stereotypes—but it has to factor into what is planned for college.

This is a short chapter, opening topics that are undeniably complex but whose evocation, at least, must form part of higher education planning. It's a chapter that can make some encouraging noises, but one which also marks a number of pitfalls and warnings. Among global enthusiasts in college ranks, the sense of vital and worthy prospects sometimes overrides awareness of constraints. But the constraints are there, an inescapable part of the national context.

Government

Many initiatives, by individual colleges and universities and higher education collaboratives, involve contact with government agencies and leaders abroad. For better or worse, there is no clearly responsible agency in the federal government to move global education projects forward. Some funding sources exist, most recently, for example, in efforts to encourage the teaching of strategically important languages. Visa regulations are critically important.

Individual ambassadors and consular officials are often quite helpful in supporting international initiatives by university officials. In no sense, however, on the American side, is government systematically involved.

The federal sector has, however, sporadically tried to push some version of global education forward. The Fulbright program, initiated more than 50 years ago, has sponsored a large number of scholars and students, from the United States going abroad and internationally to these shores. The results have benefited not only individuals, but many institutions. But the program is small and has been cut in recent decades. The Soviet launching of its Sputnik, in 1958, generated a cold war competitive flurry in the United States, in which higher education played a critical role. The National Defense Education Act brought considerable investments in the development of area studies programs (with lively support for graduate students) and language experts.[2] There is no question that the encouragement was effective, and the growing richness of American knowledge of many key regions, represented by area studies sectors in most leading universities, is the ongoing beneficiary. Actual funding, however, dwindled steadily, to under $100 million per year. A few federal initiatives in the international field were added in 1991, in the National Security Education Program, supporting some study abroad by undergraduates, some international and language study by graduate students. But annual awards in this program never topped $7.5 million, and by 2000 they had dropped to under $5 million. Overall, by 2002, federal spending on international education, from departments of State, Education and Defense, was at most $280 million, less than 1% of all discretionary expenditures for higher education overall. Welcome, of course, but not a lot of help.[3]

Periodically, federal agencies tried to incentivize the field by appeals, more than funds. In 1979 a President's Commission visited the sorry state of language training in the United States. Its report was helpful in providing data on levels of activity, but quite obviously it failed miserably to spur remedies.[4] In 1999 Bill Clinton issued a "Memorandum on International Education," committing the government to supporting and encouraging more efforts in study abroad, faculty exchange, and international partnerships—again with attention to training people who know foreign languages and foreign cultures. But the sweet words were not accompanied by significant funding, and the ensuing Bush administration turned its attention away from higher education and a global educational agenda alike. The federal government has yet to establish itself as a significant, positive player in the global education field. Most recently, visa policies aside,* it has invoked higher education in discussions about

---

* I leave apart, in this book, the expansion of research areas for which security clearance is required, and which therefore excludes foreign faculty and students. This is an important issue, but not one significantly impacting global education beyond the viability of international students in some graduate study categories, where concern is mounting.

international free trade, as education becomes increasingly regarded as a negotiable service; it has offered some modest support for training in critical languages at K-12 and college levels; but, more important, its touted K-12 education initiatives, in No Child Left Behind, have discouraged attention to global issues in the primary grades, in shifting attention from the social studies to reading and mathematics. Neither strategic vision nor systematic impact can be expected, in this area, from federal ranks.

There is one significant exception to an overall pattern of constraint and inconsistency where federal programs are concerned, yet while it would be unfair to argue that it almost "proves the rule" about inattention to the contemporary demands of global education, it has significant limitations of its own.

For nearly the past half century, the Department of Education has funded university-based "National Research Centers" (NRCs), selecting seven or eight universities, on a regular basis, for each of the major world areas. The centers channel support for graduate students, programming and infrastructure (including library holdings). Overall, more than a fifth of all major universities are involved, and NRC capacities have considerable impact on all levels of teaching, through the range of faculty enlisted, and on outreach to the respective areas of the world. They also support language training, in some cases almost uniquely as with major African language groups. Centers also sponsor summer study programs for immersion in non-Western languages (like Hausa, in northern Nigeria).

There is no question about the strength of these programs, but they have two crucial limitations that constrain their impact on American global education overall. First, they tend to go to essentially the same small number of leading research universities—great for them, but despite a mandate for cooperation with other educational institutions, of limited utility for the vast majority of American institutions. A tension between some of the more innovative aspirants in global education, and the established institutions with a sometimes rather traditional tenured faculty is obvious, but there is no resolution in sight. Further, and this is limitation number two, the NRCs focus so strongly on the regional approach that the cross-regional linkages, which are the core of contemporary globalization, are insufficiently examined. Here, of course, is precisely the opportunity for the newer, possibly nimbler entrants to the big-time global education game, but the disparities of federal funding pose obvious problems—even for the expansion of relevant foreign language training outside the familiar Western staples. One may hope that a more internationally minded presidential administration will reconsider—will expand but also reorient—this vital effort, but that is a prospect for the future at best.

Research funding, the NRCs, and student loans aside, of course, the federal role in higher education generally is slight at best. But whereas in other aspects of higher education states step in massively through their regulation and support of public universities, the state role in global education is also trivial, save in the criteria developed for the primary and secondary schools to which we turn later in the chapter. States rarely push universities to do more than they currently are attempting in the global arena (New Jersey put forward an unfunded mandate in the early 1990s; Georgia is an interesting recent exception, as discussed in Chapter 9); nor, save in understandably seeking to make sure that public monies are not spent abroad, do they significantly constrain. State efforts to impose learning outcomes assessments on public colleges do not normally include a global component, as they tend instead to writing, science, mathematics and IT.

The scant involvement of government may of course be a good thing, though other governmental initiatives can distract from the global mission and the lack of state involvement certainly deprives colleges and universities of a potential funding source. The lack certainly contrasts with greater government encouragement abroad. Countries like Germany and China pour significant amounts of money into universities' global outreach, including international student recruitment and educational collaborations. But the main point is that American institutions are effectively on their own in this field, aside from the assistance of various collaboratives and consortia. They need to define their own goals, and to the extent they serve the national interest, even the national economy as a source of foreign earnings, they are again acting individually.

Public Opinion and Educational Leadership

No more than government does wider American opinion play into global higher education, in most respects and in most times. Programs like study abroad, which are almost always optional in any event, have not triggered public concern. While many Americans doubtless feel that foreign language training is a waste of time, since everyone speaks English, they have not actively interfered with remaining programs—it is lack of support and encouragement, not outright hostility, that matters here. Polling data, in fact, suggest considerable public interest in key elements of a global educational approach, at least within the current decade; the interest may not be particularly intense or effective, but it exists. Thus polls taken right before 9/11 suggested wide beliefs that learning a second language was important (85%, as against 65% of the public surveyed in 1965), with considerable support for its requirement. Adult belief that knowledge of international issues is relevant to individual careers has also increased. It is probably fair to say that most global education efforts operate either in a neutral or mildly favorable public climate, at least by the early 21st century.[5]

There are however revealing exceptions that suggest some potential constraints. Problem one is not new, and it is difficult to resolve. Global engagement can involve higher education institutions in some speaker programs that seem (from the academic standpoint) highly desirable, in terms of providing insights and perspectives to the college or university community. Elements of the public, however, may view these same efforts as offensive or subversive, and their concern has filtered into some legislative proposals for greater regulation. Foreign affairs are hardly the only domain in which publics misunderstand what most university officials see as their function, in encouraging a free exchange of ideas in ways that do not involve any institutional endorsement and do not require immediate, tit-for-tat provision of opposition speakers. But pressures can be considerable. Universities that have invited the European Muslim intellectual, Tariq Ramadan, to speak (by long distance, because the State Department has refused a visa despite efforts by Notre Dame actually to hire him on the faculty) have drawn harsh comment, with claims that the programs encourage terrorism. Columbia University did manage to arrange for the President of Iran to speak, but had to surround the appearance with a scathing, arguably rude criticism by university officials that probably defeated the purpose of the whole exercise. Global efforts, in other words, can import some of the tensions of world politics, and public understanding may at times break down.

More serious, and more novel, was the ensnarement of curricular issues aimed at global education in the culture wars of the past decade. An unexpected bombshell exploded in 1994. A large group of historians and history teachers had been working for some time to develop standards for history learning in the schools (other disciplines had been similarly engaged), establishing separate headings on U.S. and on world history. World history in turn constituted a clear effort to recast conventional survey history offerings away from the traditional Western civilization approach, toward a more globally relevant take on the past; we will turn more explicitly to world history's relationship to a global curriculum in the next chapter.[6] The *National History Standards* issued the results of the long deliberations late in the year, in a masterpiece of tactical mistiming shortly after the victory of Newt Gingrich and his revitalized conservative Republicanism in the congressional elections. Led by conservative spokespeople, including Lynne Cheney, erstwhile head of the National Endowment for the Humanities, the *Standards* drew immediate fire. Greatest was scorn heaped on the U.S. standards, but world history came in for its share. Soon, in fact, the United States Senate voted to disapprove both sets of standards by a 99–1 vote, Democrats rivaling Republicans in their zeal to make it clear that conventional history should not be tampered with, however much globalization was changing the larger environment (or, one is tempted to suggest, precisely *because* globalization constituted major change, against which historical familiars would offer a comforting remnant of older identity). The Senate resolution blasted the world history effort, among other things, because it failed to show appropriate respect for the special qualities of Western civilization. This came on the heels of mounting conservative criticism of efforts to introduce non-Western coverage into any required curriculum, with charges of "globaloney" or worse. William Bennett, for example, as Secretary of Education, had earlier excoriated a Stanford decision to replace a freshman core course in Western civilization with a mixture of options that would allow more attention to other regions as a left-wing faculty plot to "drop the West": "an unfortunate capitulation to a campaign of pressure politics and intimidation" from a left-wing cabal of Marxists and feminists. Indignant charges of political correctness, undermining "our Judeo-Christian values," had mounted from the late 1980s onward.[7] The unprecedented Senate vote showed how sharp, and public, the rift had become.

There were politics on both sides, of course. World historians, eager to move beyond the narrowness of a purely Western framework, sometimes can't resist taking implicit or explicit potshots at the West. The *Standards* document quite appropriately noted some large warts on the Western history profile, such as leadership in the Atlantic slave trade, but tended to ignore potential downsides in the past experience of other civilizations (such as, for example, human sacrifice in some though not all of the Amerindian civilizations). So there was room to debate appropriate balance and editorializing.

But the tendency of many conservative educators to cling to a less-than-global model of education, or at least history education, and to express hostility to global curricula as potentially subversive, was deeply troubling. It was not uniform: many conservatives recognized that the world required increasing study. But battles over innovation in teaching matter, particularly in the social studies where so many identity issues nestled, raised some warning flags about the core educational aspects of global studies. The debate of course was not simply national: similar attacks on educational globalization occurred at the state and local level (indeed, discussions occurred in many societies besides the United States). Clearly, fears provoked by globalization, including anxieties about the integration of growing immigrant populations, made educational issues into opportunities for contest. While globalists welcomed the increasing diversity of American student bodies as a chance for mutual learning, many conservative leaders took the opposite tack, arguing that the need for focus on a common set of Western values was actually increasing. Not surprisingly, "what every student must know" lists, even when they had a world history label, were filled with largely Western, and largely familiar, factual content. New pressures to mandate Western civilization actually increased in some settings, on individual college campuses, as the new century dawned. World history leaders continued to press for change, but they swam against the political tide.

The tension may have eased a bit in the United States since the 1990s confrontation, though amid some compromises that potentially dilute the global agenda. The Senate's resounding slap at world history criteria did not prevent planning agencies in most individual states, bent on establishing assessment criteria for K-12 students, from developing world rather than Western history programs as part of the social studies core. Conservative states like Texas actually took a lead in insisting on world history. Clearly, the need to respond to a global environment reduced the constraints of national-identity politics where it counted, at the actual school or classroom level, even as national educational leaders continued to posture about the special virtues of Western civilization. (A favorite: a leader who argued that only Western civilization should be studied because only the West featured tolerance for other cultural values. A statement not only contradictory on its face, but factually inaccurate about many tolerant traditions elsewhere.) On the other hand, most state-mandated world history programs continued to have a disproportionate amount of Western content—about 67%, in most assessment criteria and in standard high school textbooks. California, for instance, with a brilliant world-focused history curriculum through the 15th century, then succumbed to the lure of Western staples from 1500 onward, with the rest of the world hovering around Western achievements from the Renaissance through the Industrial Revolution, dependent on Western contacts and initiatives for whatever coverage they might merit. Outright partisan attacks on world history dwindled, in other words, but transitions to a more global framework were incomplete in fact— retarded by habit and political caution alike. And all of this was compounded by the reality that many social studies teachers, whatever the state standards, had little or no training about the rest of the world.[8]

A similar muddy compromise described federal initiatives after 9/11. While a few doughty conservatives argued that terrorism must not be the occasion for a more global curriculum, that the need to emphasize Western values was greater than ever before, world history actually continued to gain ground, though often around the West-centered approach that many globalists dismissed as inadequate and misleading. The need for more attention to critical languages, including Arabic, prompted calls for new educational emphases. On the other hand, there was no governmental appeal for an enhanced global approach more generally. Individual institutions and higher education consortia stepped into the breach, and their efforts were not systematically attacked, but no public move at either state or federal level really supported a more global set of educational priorities. Federal attention, indeed, shifted elsewhere, expressing indifference though not explicit hostility. As we have seen, the major new initiative, No Child Left Behind, drew attention away from social studies, particularly in the primary grades, in favor of skills training in reading and mathematics. If any time was left over, science clearly became teacher's pet. Coverage of social studies issues, whether traditional or global, receded in the grade schools. The decline of frontal assaults on topics like world history was welcome, but in many educational quarters it seemed to yield to apathy rather than to relevant innovation. And the culture wars of the 1990s may have left a larger residue of caution, in some educational sectors. State mandates to emphasize Western subject matter even under world history headings thus did not generate a particularly coherent response, as many global advocates accepted compromises as better than nothing or turned away from the schools in favor of more responsive college curricula.

Clearly, the gap between periodic alarums over the level of international education in the United States, and coherent action particularly in the public schools is not an accident. General support for global educational goals rarely rises to the level of high priority, and at times the goals themselves are mired in political controversy—which makes it easier to focus on other, less contestable items. The climate has not prevented the obvious surge of global interest in colleges and universities; but it creates some tensions, and it certainly impacts the global exposures available to the students entering college—the human clay that globalists must work with.

What Students Know

Not surprisingly, in this larger public context, there were no striking gains in the overall global preparation of students prior to college entrance in the decades around the turn of the century. New divisions emerged, with a sector of students unquestionably more highly engaged and better-versed; but the larger statistical indicators languished.

Modern language preparation was the most obvious villain. Large numbers of college-bound students had little or no foreign language work in high school, and increasingly their experience in college itself did not compensate. By the early 21st century, only 8% of higher education enrollments were in languages, down from 16% in the 1960s. While 68% of all colleges still have some language requirements for graduation, this too was down from 89% in 1965. And the change was not due to superior school preparation. Few American students systematically encountered a foreign language before high school, though there were scatterings of grade school programs in wealthy school districts. Most students who did language work, in other words, began at a later age than is desirable for linguistic fluency, particularly in speaking (age 12 is the standard cutoff where accents are concerned, and many experts emphasize the age 7–9 window). Once in high school, many students took only a year or two of language, at best, and colleges, for their part, increasingly downplayed language recommendations as part of admissions criteria. By the early 21st century only 23% of all colleges had a language requirement for entrance, a reflection both of a low priority in higher education itself and a recognition that, given high school patterns, too much insistence would defeat the larger goal of finding enough students to enroll.[9]

Even more disturbing was the extent to which the high school language work that was available was itself lackadaisical at best: very few students emerged with anything like fluency or a real language capacity—and by the time they got to college, often with a year or two gap from desultory high school work, their memories had dimmed even further. For while requirements were an issue, so was the way many language courses were taught, as if students had to be protected from encountering too much strangeness too suddenly. American elementary language books, lavishly illustrated and with many distracting stories (in English), cushioned students from too much drill or, arguably, too much seriousness of any sort. Classes filled as well with group exercises about the region involved and, often, many songs—all well-intentioned, capable of generating some international learning, but diversionary in terms of language mastery itself. Not a few innovative school programs launched with claims of immersion, only to find that there were not enough qualified teachers to handle other subject matter in languages other than English and that there were far too many parents who really worried about strain on their offspring if forced to sit through more than 45 minutes a day listening to a foreign tongue. American students were, quite simply, far less likely than their college-bound counterparts in almost any other country to have much acquaintance with a foreign language (unless they came from immigrant households). Most of them would come to college with no sense of language competence or any capacity or interest in using a language other than English in non-language coursework. The fact that colleges had to place so much emphasis on elementary language availability was itself a testimony to the distinctive qualities of this vital aspect of the American context.

Many students who had taken languages in high school opted for beginner courses in college, often not even bothering to submit to placement tests because of lack of confidence or linguistic laziness—if of course they continued at all. The result was not only a low level of achievement but a degree of variety in the college classroom that was instructionally challenging.

Less surprising was the unavailability of non-European languages before college, the fruit of routine-mindedness and a lack of adequate teacher supply. Interest did develop, particularly in recent years, with large numbers of high schools, for example, claiming hopes of adding Chinese and a few school districts actually introducing pioneering programs (some beginning even at grade school level). And certainly there were college entrants who, because of special aptitude, family background, or travel experience had real foreign language ability and interest—though their superiority could add to the hesitancy of other American students. Overall, however, the lack of widespread linguistic competence constituted a serious constraint on global education at the college level—from coursework to capacities for study abroad to overall outlook on the achievement of significant global learning outcomes.

Positive change could be reported, beyond the modest pre-college expansion of available languages. Some public school systems from the late 1970s onward set up Language and International Studies high schools, usually magnet schools, with language competence a graduate requirement. (Some diluted this requirement after a few years, with the common concern about the stress of too much immersion.) In language training generally, emphasis on oral skills expanded, a global education asset, and with this not only a communication emphasis but explicit attention to cultural sensitivity. (Not a few colleges, bent on traditional grammar-and-memorization, were challenged as a result to keep up with their better students.) But some innovations involved more playful enrichment than language learning, while leading some students to be disappointed with college work that pointed more single-mindedly to language mastery itself. Sequencing in language learning was probably improving a bit—it was certainly widely discussed—but new misunderstandings among leaders at different levels add to older problems. And still the bulges in college courses were at beginner levels, with only handfuls of students ready to take on work, in language sequences or otherwise, demanding real competence.[10] Many experienced language faculty, even in relatively accessible cases like Spanish, reported no change in the basic pattern over several decades: students with one to three years of high school language study placed into a beginner course, or more commonly a course that started with basics but accelerated slightly more rapidly than the outright beginner level; a happy few (with four or more previous years, or family heritage) moved into advanced courses. Almost no one was ready for college intermediate.

Language was not the only issue. We have already touched on the limited availability of social studies coursework that offered significant global perspective. Surveys in the 1990s revealed that American students had a surprisingly limited grasp of basic geography (even of their own country: over a quarter of all high school students, working with an outline map, could not find protrusions like Florida); here, to be sure, the ubiquitous comparative tests demonstrated that students from other places, like Korea, were also weak on global geography, but there was a gap nevertheless.[11] We have already noted that standard curricula in the schools, while increasingly emphasizing the term world history, actually often only modestly supplement a conventional European history course. Many teachers themselves lack much experience with "non-Western" history and retreat to their comfort zone as much as requirements allow. As a result, while college freshmen by the 21st century increasingly reported that they had already taken a course in world history, what they actually knew about Islam or China or any systematic patterns of global development was typically quite limited. While hardly erudite, they were much more confident about conventional Western staples. High school economics, not widely required in any event, did less with global issues than with domestic patterns. The fact was that, with the slight exception of the world history modifications of a typically 10th-grade course, sometimes prepared by a bit of 9th-grade attention to geography, college-bound high school students had faced little required material, whether in social studies or literature, that did not come either from Europe or the United States. And delivery in practice frequently fell short even of on-paper standards. A characteristic, if understandable, deficiency of the typical survey history course was the frequent failure to have much time left for developments after World War II. Many actual high school textbooks, after having lingered lovingly on the glories of Western civilization from the Renaissance through the age of imperialism, actually do open up again in their coverage of the past half century, with chapters on decolonization in Africa, the rise of Asia and so on. But beleaguered teachers too often run out of gas, so that the period most relevant to student understanding of global diversity and global issues is actually the least examined in the schools.

Lack of significant school background helped feed common simplifications or misinterpretations from the wider culture. Islam suffered particularly in the perceptions students brought to college, but older notions of Chinese isolation and inscrutability surfaced as well, along with the wider tendency to measure the world in terms of Western achievements. On the whole, student interest in cosmopolitan tolerance ran fairly high—as polls of younger Americans also suggested—but this could coexist with serious knowledge gaps and misleading stereotypes.

Here too, as with languages, there are bright spots, including of course a substantial number of eager and well-informed high school and middle school teachers, and a few imaginative grade school programs as well. Geography has been gaining new emphasis in the social studies, with the backing among other things of well-funded programs from National Geographic. A new Advanced Placement course in world history, introduced in 2002 with the largest number of test-takers (at over 20,000) of any first-time AP subject ever, rapidly rising to over 100,000 participants, reflects wide interest in more systematic global coverage—the course resolutely specifies that no more than a third of its content will be Western, and works hard on global patterns and comparative topics—while providing new standards for coverage and analysis in turn.

Developments of this sort (and the growth of International Baccalaureate programs as well), as with some of the newer language efforts, actually pose challenges for colleges, to provide stimulating sequences for students that do not needlessly go over familiar global ground but rather build toward more sophisticated materials. While numbers are small still, some students reach college capable of levels of Japanese or Arabic that few schools offer. Some are eager and capable of an advanced world history course, only to find that while their AP work gets them out of a requirement there is actually not much available that directly utilizes and builds on their experience. Several of the newer initiatives in the schools, in other words, invite more careful attention and more imaginative response from higher education than they yet systematically receive.

The more general challenge, however, remains compensation, more than the provision of new levels of coursework. Particularly in the languages, but to a real extent with regard to global knowledge more widely, colleges must expect uneven and often inadequate preparation from their new students. In the 1990s, lack of school emphasis helped explain the fact that very few collegians spontaneously opted for courses or programs with global content—only 14% taking as much as four credits of internationally focused coursework, according to one estimate. This situation changed by the early 21st century, both because of new levels of student awareness and more imaginative curricular efforts in higher education. But these developments often dramatized, though in a different way, the results of unsystematic backgrounds in the schools, as many collegiate programs, in languages or beyond, found that they could assume relatively little prior knowledge. Here was a part of the American context for global education that hit home quite directly.

* * *

Gaps in high school preparation are not the whole story, of course. Many students bring deep international interests and experiences with them when they come to college, regardless of the average school curriculum. Growing numbers of students travel abroad before college, and while some of this is largely tourism there is a widening array of opportunities for study visits (including language training) and internships. One 2001 study, polling 500 college-bound high school seniors, found that 62% had traveled abroad—an interesting result qualified by the obvious fact that this was a skewed sample.[12] The expansion of Advanced Placement World History and International Baccalaureate programs provide even curricular reminders that colleges need to be ready to deal with varied student backgrounds, and not assume some uniform lack of preparation. There are some troubling reports, in fact, that some colleges are not responding adequately, particularly in taking the trouble to acknowledge IB backgrounds. Overall, despite or perhaps because of deficiencies in many high schools, a large percentage of high school graduates talk about the importance of international learning and experience, including foreign language study, with a substantial majority claiming that global education opportunities were a significant factor in their choice of college. Systematic knowledge may be less than desired, but apparently there is a level of interest that higher education can build upon directly.

Still, the overall high school situation completes a somewhat challenging picture of the context for higher education's global initiatives. American students do know less about the rest of the world, and about global systems, than do their counterparts in many other regions. Along with concerns about public response to too much global innovation, and the obvious lack of systematic government assistance, this makes the need for extra effort and independent initiative, on the part of colleges and universities, inescapable. Happily, as we will see, many schools are facing up to the needs, beginning with important innovations in their own curricula (which as a result are changing much more rapidly, overall, than those of the high schools).

There is a final implication as well, again being acted upon by a number of institutions particularly in the public sector. Need and opportunity suggest responsibilities for reaching out to schools and even pre-college students, to provide at least a partial remedy for the sluggishness of K-12 training in the global area. Many faculty members, sometimes with official institutional encouragement, are seizing the chance to participate in the training of existing teachers on international subjects, particularly in the Advanced Placement world history program. Many centers operate each summer, helping the hundreds of teachers assigned to world history without formal background or training—and the results, though scattered, can be encouraging. When Indiana University made a new commitment to global education, with the active leadership of its president, provision of summer institutes for high school teachers was a key component of its program. Centers of history education, like Long Beach State University, provide wide leadership in preparing both future and existing teachers in world history, through regular course requirements and special summer work. George Mason University is one of several schools now offering education courses to foreign teachers of Chinese and Arabic so that they can qualify for teaching stints in the literally thousands of American high schools eager to set up relevant language programs but struggling to find suitable instructors. Kennesaw State University, in Georgia, has taken a particular lead in bringing Chinese teachers from China into its education program, with similar goals in mind—as part of a significant planning commitment to global citizenship. The fact is that many social science majors and education programs, at the college level, have lagged shamefully in their global preparation of teachers—failing, for example, regularly to offer the kind of world history that would give future instructors any sense of comfort with this increasingly taught subject—so it is past time that a number of institutions are making a special effort to reach out.

Opportunities to interact directly with students before college can also develop. Princeton University has announced an ambitious program to encourage up to a tenth of its entering freshmen to take a year off before actual matriculation, to engage in social service work in areas of need around the world. The program, being organized for inauguration in fall 2009, hopes to recruit as many as a hundred students, possibly providing some financial aid for travel and living expenses. The University believes that a pause year might be good in and of itself, in improving student motivation, but it is particularly interested in the additional perspective students would bring to their own education and to the freshman class as a whole. The Institute of International Education, hailing the program as the first of its kind, noted also that "the rest of the world will get to see our future leaders doing really significant and socially important things."

Princeton, of course, has its own distinctive opportunities, not available to most institutions. But the invitation to think of new ways to reach out, both to students and to schools, is both real and general. Programs for existing teachers must be combined with innovations in social studies preparation for teachers-to-be, a task for schools of education that has yet to be widely taken on. Some institutions could also press for the provision of governors' schools or their equivalent in international education, making direct contact with high school students in ways relevant to their orientation for college. Obviously, there is much to do to meet the needs for global education in higher education itself. But the deficiencies in pre-college schooling need attention as well, as colleges and universities rethink this aspect of their regional outreach.

4
Curriculum:
The Foundations for Global Education

The basic structure for any program in global education involves courses and programs available to, in some cases required of, undergraduates. Curriculum is not, of course, the primary province of higher education administrators. Nevertheless, curricular innovations are an administrative as well as a faculty issue, even as primacy properly lies with the faculty. Furthermore, knowledge of curricular options and the exciting developments in global coursework is a precondition for sensible treatment of the more specialized features of global education, such as study abroad. Inevitably, discussion of curricular options involves a host of elements, and could easily generate a larger study. Still, some of the main lines are emerging clearly, at least for the moment.

Four areas focus attention: adaptation of general education to include more explicit global components—and the role of world history figures into this mix as a particular topic; recasting foreign language instruction, an old subject with some important new twists; figuring out how to move global content and competency into a wide variety of subject matter areas, building of course on general education but extending into an "across the curriculum" approach; and developing interdisciplinary connections through offerings in global affairs. These are undergraduate topics primarily, but they may also imply some adjustments at the graduate level (important among other things for training future teachers). Curriculum is of course the primary academic issue, but in the global arena co-curricular embellishments deserve some distinct commentary as well.[1]

Finally, even as we focus on major components, the primacy of interconnections must be emphasized: no single curricular approach works, no magic solo course will suffice. It is the totality of courses and connections among various levels that require the greatest need for attention once the first, preliminary curricular steps have been launched.

Gen Ed: World History

Most general education programs have long had an international component—but, typically, neither a contemporary nor a global one. American education has traditionally been distinguished by a willingness to engage seriously with societies besides the United States, as part of a commitment to broad educational components that is in itself unusual—left, in many societies, to the schools, with college a triumphant movement into specialized study alone. American educators long felt uncomfortable, in a society with a short history of its own, and a literary tradition that similarly might by itself be found wanting, if they did not require students to do some work outside a purely national canon. The result was a truly good start, in the sense of some breadth of view, but also a set of commitments that can prove difficult to undo for the sake of global education as now defined—even granting, as is vital, the need to recognize various pathways to the global goals.

In the 19th century, the counterweight to educational provincialism in college was a set of classical requirements, including Latin and, often, Greek. By the early 20th century this began to seem less relevant, and what was increasingly called general education began to focus instead on European history and literature (sometimes, still, with a classical component). By the 1920s a strong movement toward a standard, European-history-dominated, Western Civilization course was developing in the United States, spearheaded by leaders like James Harvey Robinson at Columbia University. The purpose was twofold. European history should give Americans a firmer sense of identity, as they saw how crucial American characteristics, particularly in political systems, originated from European roots. This was a time of educational adjustments to the massive immigration that had occurred from Southern and Eastern Europe, so the issue of establishing a somewhat larger historical presence than American history alone allowed seemed extremely important: Americanization and Westernization could go hand in hand. As a Kansas State catalogue put it, early in the 20th century: "in order really to understand American history you must know European history"—and indeed, around 1910, more European than American history was being offered on college campuses. But there was a second urgency as well by the 1920s, when the full Western Civ curriculum pattern was actually constructed: a fear that, in the wake of World War I, the European system itself was in disarray, such that an American defense of the principles of Western Civilization was needed to help hold a valued but beleaguered tradition together.[2]

These motivations helped create a really important element in American general education, one that produced many courses that could be deeply meaningful to at least some segments of a student audience (required courses never, of course, have quite as much persuasive power as their proponents hope). They help explain why many educators persist in clinging to a Western-focused view of the past, and the resultant culture-wars challenge to any new departure. Indeed, the factors that generated Western Civ offerings may still seem compelling today: many educational conservatives undoubtedly see in the ethnically mixed student bodies of the present, after an even larger wave of immigration than that of the 1900s, another invitation to a strong dose of Westernism. While Europe itself is in better shape than in the 1920s, a concern about the fate of Western values amid contemporary global demographic and economic patterns, which obviously reduce the relative importance of the West, can still surface strongly. And an appropriate place for a Western Civ course may still be found—globalism requires a serious modification of the West-centered curriculum, but not a frontal attack. Yet it is important to note that the key spurs to the Western Civ curricular tradition emphasized past far more than explicit past–present connections. It was far more important to dwell on hallowed origins (though in practice some courses went back implausibly to Egypt and Mesopotamia, others lingered lovingly in Greece and Rome, while still others found key originating values in the Middle Ages) than to talk about the messy world of the present. This is why historians were able to capture most Western Civ courses and why so many history teachers did not worry too much if their schedule prevented much discussion of recent decades. One terrific Western Civ program for years actually deliberately omitted discussion of the 20th century altogether, on grounds that its awfulness would distract students from the Civilizational beauties they should contemplate. And of course there was no intention at all of dealing with the whole world. Everything was slanted toward the emergence of the West (which is why ancient Egypt might be force-fed into a primary role as a Western origin, while Middle-Eastern contributions to Europe during the Middle Ages would be largely ignored save insofar as they seemed to transmit Greek or Roman learning) and then, later on, the Western mission in the wider world, only partially modified from the white man's burden concept. (Africa, for example, would come in for mention only after Europeans got there.)[3]

Needless to say, these parameters, however understandable in terms of our educational past, fail to capture the kind of history course now needed as a general education component of a global educational agenda. The parameters do, however, help explain why world history continues to generate controversy.

But the fact is that global education strongly implies, if it does not compel, a world history component, and certainly the displacement of the centrality of Western Civ. The rise of world history has been pushed by several factors, including the changing composition of the American student body that periodically produces agitation for identities in addition to the Western, but primarily by the simple fact of the global rather than European context in which the United States now operates. World history has also responded to new research findings, though in the main these have emerged as part of the field's response to changing global conditions, not as part of the origination. The desire to use history as part of the exploration of global relationships, and the contention that a meaningful world history course can be constructed for this purpose, really explains the growing momentum for this key change in the content of general education.[4]

To be sure, world historians have their own hobby horses (or at least so it can be argued). They have sometimes paid more effusive attention to the origins of other, non-Western Civilization traditions than to contemporary issues, in response to the need to contest excessive claims in the Western Civ camp. This aside, world history programs as they have emerged at a variety of colleges and universities over the past two decades emphasize some combination of three approaches, all of which (and certainly in combination) are directly relevant to a larger global education effort. First, world history at the college level inevitably requires active comparisons among various major societies, as these societies have emerged over time and as they interact with key factors such as technological change or missionary religion. Comparison sharpens student understanding of shared features and distinctions across the human landscape—it even facilitates a deeper grasp of Western characteristics both good and bad—and it contributes actively to the relationship of world present to world past. Second, world historians increasingly delight in dealing with the effects of contacts among various societies. They take joy in early forms of contact—for example, along the Silk Roads—but, even more important, they develop a framework within which more recent contacts, and the acceleration of contacts, can be assessed. Interactions among societies generate mutual change, accommodation and resistance, and current patterns gain perspective when viewed as part of a process over time. Syncretism becomes a great term for students to understand and use. Finally, world historians deal with the emergence and evolution of cross-cutting forces, ultimately of the kind that became global in nature—such as technology diffusion, migrations, epidemic disease, or intercontinental trading patterns. In showing how these forces have a history of their own, as well as how they elicited varied reactions from specific regions, world historians directly treat how the contemporary global context was shaped. World history, in sum, provides not only selective factual coverage (and selective is the operative word, so that the program does not become an overwhelming data list) but analytical skills that arguably provide crucial support to a global studies agenda—for ultimate specialists and non-specialists alike. The progress of some serious version of world history in college curricula is one of the encouraging curricular markers in American higher education over recent years.

World history goals can be achieved in various specific course frameworks, but there is little question that some approach of this sort offers the most appropriate historical foundation for the global components of general education (whatever the history courses, including Western Civilization, that could be included for later sequencing). It is also true that a world history program offers vital preparation to potential social studies teachers, addressing one aspect of the outreach issue discussed in Chapter 3. It is also possible, of course, that a global agenda might be achieved without a formal history course—though as a historian I think that a good bit would be lost, not only in perspective but in serious analytical engagement. It is unquestionably true, however, that even with world history a general education program needs additional global facets. World history seems a logical anchor, and builds on the wide though not universal commitment to some history survey work as part of liberal training. But more is needed, even with the world history base.

Indeed, given the existing if still-contested movement toward world history, provision of an additional phase in the general education program, where even more innovation is required, commands even more attention. Ideally, this further phase could be sequenced with the world history offering—so that not only factual perspective, but skills such as comparison and assessment of change and continuity in global forces could be actively called up; but the complexities of student scheduling risk making too much insistence on logical order an exercise in fatuity. Still, a relationship should be envisaged, and the global category needs the same kind of care for basic principles that a good world history program will establish.

The Global Category

Many general education programs, beyond world history or even where a world history requirement does not exist, have experimented with a more explicitly global and less purely disciplinary category, as part of the requirements of liberal training. General education rosters have long permitted some global exposure—an economics course might take up international topics, while constituting one of the options available to fulfill a social science requirement—but they have not normally compelled or defined it. Global coverage has been one of the many victims of what is most commonly a smorgasbord approach to liberal education, with a host of courses fulfilling very general categories into which subsidiary elements might or might not crop up.

The most common effort to build something more global into general education, beyond a Western Civ course and possibly a language requirement, has involved a requisite non-Western Civ course. It's a great gesture, pushing students reasonably deeply into a different culture and historical experience. The gesture is improved when some explicit comparison emerges, developing this vital global analytical skill as well as enhancing understanding of similarity as well as difference. Nevertheless, the risk of a rather nonanlytical experience, however engaging, is real as the requirement is frequently stated—descriptive coverage may readily win out. So is the lack of linkage to global factors and, in some cases, the failure to bring the case into a clearly contemporary setting. The requirement is important, in other words, but it can fall short of full global service without some further stipulations.

More recently still, some gen ed programs have added a more explicit global affairs category, quite different in purpose and to an extent in content from the non-Western Civ approach. George Mason, introducing a required global understanding component six years ago, specified courses that examine some of the principal global issues and concerns "that shape our world today." Analytical targets included identifying the causes and consequences of change in significant global issues and helping students see how global issues are perceived and dealt with in different cultural traditions; comparison of several different cultures was also recommended though not required. Courses in this category "stress the interconnectedness, difference, and diversity that are central to understanding and operating in a global society." The requirement was new, against a longstanding earlier general education system that evaded these kinds of specifications in favor of much more sweeping social science, science and humanities catchalls. Obviously it compelled some choices, about what previous staples could be left out (the victim was a compulsory philosophy course, though this survived in some subsidiary programs in individual units). It also turned out to invite an amazing array of entries, as departments sought to demonstrate their relevance to global issues and competed for enrollments. A tourism class, various religion courses, some music and dance offerings, an administration of justice introduction, 10 anthropology courses, 18 largely region-specific history courses—in all, over 80 courses were soon available for fulfillment. The richness and ambition were impressive, but the result impelled concern over undue specificity and internal disciplinary focus, along with inadequate attention to the core analytical goals. The challenge—and in the best cases it was met, but monitoring was difficult—was to remind instructors that they had a responsibility not only for detailed subject matter, but also for some perspectives, learning styles and habits of mind that students could carry into other courses and beyond college itself, even when the specifics tended to fade from memory. The category survived well, amid good overall student reactions, but it commanded more pedagogical concern and more efforts at coordination than did any other gen ed component—a sign of a possibly healthy lack of conventional comfort with what was being aimed at. The alternative—the same basic category, but with a smaller number of explicitly crafted courses—promised greater coherence, more genuine interdisciplinarity and easier measurement, but it also required more initial administrative input and less certain faculty motivation. The choices were not easy, though the idea of the category itself won growing approval as one of the leading adjustments of general education to the global environment for which students must be prepared.

Other schools move diversely in the same basic direction. Eastern Michigan requires Perspectives on a Diverse World, one course focusing on domestic issues, the other on global awareness. This latter talks about diverse nations and cultures, American culture in this context, and interrelationships in the global community; it uses "diverse sources" to "make informed decisions regarding global issues," while exploring intolerance in the world. California State—Long Beach attempts a similar combination, requiring a course on human diversity, in the United States, and a course on "global issues" focusing on systematic comparisons or global systems. Eighty-seven courses are available within the global designation. The University of Wisconsin-Stout insists that students either take four university credits of a foreign language (unless they have had two years of the same language in high school) or take six credits in courses that directly address global issues or "focus on other subject matter while emphasizing understanding and appreciation of global issues" or teach professional skills that include a "global perspective component." American University moves farther, in requiring that about 10% of the gen ed program be taken in a two-course sequence in "global and multicultural perspectives." UNC-Chapel Hill in 2003 replaced Western Civ with world history, hoped for a foreign language enhancement that had to be deferred for lack of funds, and added to a course on the North Atlantic World a new requirement of "Beyond the North Atlantic World." Wyoming more directly added a global awareness category, focusing on comparison and interconnectedness plus exploring the aesthetic traditions of one non-U.S. culture; there were more courses in this category than in any other general education segment, with 72 in 2008, and the hope (perhaps ill-advised if the goal was a definable commitment to global habits of mind) was that more would come on line. The University was proud of how many different departments were contributing.[5]

These, and many other recent gen ed innovations in the global direction, were significant. They obviously tended to do more with culture and diversity than with global systems, they varied greatly in rigor, and they tended to stimulate abundance at (possibly) the expense of rigorous criteria. This was change in mid-stream, at best, with more work to be done to translate global goals into more systematic course content. And all of this of course was on top of the fact that many schools had no global category at all. Global in gen ed was gaining, but the pattern was clearly transitional.

Modern Languages

In contrast to some of the other categories in global education, many of the key issues in the foreign language field are not new. Most obviously novel, over the past two decades, has been the need to adjust the languages offered. German has declined precipitously, to the sorrow of some senior faculty, and French has faded a bit. But language departments face the need to compensate by adding strengths in some mixture of Chinese, Arabic, Japanese, Farsi, Hindi, Korean, Portuguese—and the list can expand—while keeping up with growing student interest in Spanish. The challenge here is real, from finding budget in advance of enrollment growth to recruiting qualified faculty. But student response makes the effort worthwhile, as a combination of global interest, career calculation, and heritage nostalgia boosts enrollments to at least satisfactory levels, usually in a short span of time. Follow-up issues inevitably involve building third- and fourth-year experiences for the smaller numbers of students interested in developing real competence and able to do so.

A second update is obvious: higher education language training must include greater attention to speaking and listening than was once the case. The availability of language labs and, now, of programs that can operate on student laptops facilitates addressing these larger needs. In some cases, having international students serve as class visitors or the provision of language tables and clubs provide support as well. Here too, budget concerns may intrude. And language programs must increasingly address the question of optimal class scheduling, with more frequent and intensive meetings desirable but not always easily blended with other aspects of a student program. Another issue can be more difficult, particularly in older language programs. Most tenured faculty achieve their rank by work in literature. Yet much of the language teaching now emphasizes other qualities, and certainly for budgetary reasons if nothing else relies heavily on term appointments (sometimes multi-year), adjuncts and graduate students. Adjusting expectations and evaluation criteria to the evolving needs of language teaching, particularly in schools reluctant to tenure on the basis of teaching primarily, is an obvious concern. In departments divided by appointment types and orientations, winning agreement on pedagogical reforms is often extremely difficult, and this in turn complicates the goal not only of widening student interest but enhancing effective learning in the field.[6]

As against these challenges in updating the language roster, and building in greater oral and aural facility, where issues are not easily resolved but are certainly clear-cut, the question of what to do about foreign languages of any sort in the curriculum overall has a more classic, but less tractable quality. The key issues involve what kind of requirement to impose on students—and whether this should be general or confined to certain kinds of majors—and how to build up real competence and willingness to use a language as opposed to fairly useless time served. Given the inadequacy of pre-college training, dealing with these issues in higher education remains difficult, and responses understandably vary greatly.

Many institutions still require a year of language, unless students place out by testing. Some confine the requirement to bachelor of arts students, assuming that science, technology and management students face such hurdles on the quantitative side that they can be excused from this nicety. Always, however, there is the quandary about what purposes a single year serves—even on top of a bit of half-remembered high school training. Many students contribute the *Sitzfleisch* because they have to, learning very little however—certainly not enough for further use—and forgetting what they did learn as quickly as possible, with parochialism often increased in the process. Some, to be sure, may gain some useful cultural exposure, and a smaller number, though not to be sneezed at, may be drawn into further study. But the requirement game, though defendable as better than nothing (without it, after all, even the minority might be lost), produces mixed results at best.

The alternative, of course, for global education enthusiasts who in no sense seek to abandon the language need, is to work on inducements for real competence, even amid a smaller student pool. This can be combined with a language requirement, or built in its place. The goal is not simply to provide more advanced language courses, though that is part of the need. Additionally, students must be encouraged to find ways to extend and use language capacity actively, and then they must be served. A whole variety of systems operate here. More demanding language requirements, up to testable competence, can be built into some attractive programs—a feature of the new global affairs majors discussed below. They can be added to special options in fields like engineering (Rhode Island University has a successful program here), often combined with a study abroad segment or a foreign internship. Another approach—and obviously several variants can be combined—involves adding language use components to other courses, or offering key courses in a foreign language (an area where international faculty can be actively utilized). George Mason is introducing a number of geography courses taught in Spanish, Arabic and the like. A new consortium including Iowa and North Carolina is breathing new life into a languages-across-the-curriculum project. There is some potential cumbersomeness in this endeavor. A one-credit add-on with reading and writing in a foreign language can make great sense in a history or politics or even social work or management course, but who is going to make sure that the language component has real vigor, and how are faculty to be rewarded for extra effort? Obviously, study abroad itself (though linguistic limitations are increasingly evident here as well, as we will see in the next chapter) can be a vital complement to language training.

The problems—promoting language competence in a difficult terrain—can be readily defined. A number of institutions have been working on them for some time. Still further experimentation and wider discussion remain desirable. Language experience is a vital component of global education, if not for all students at least for a greater number than now encounter it in any meaningful way. The gap, between desirable goals and current achievement, remains too great.

To be sure, there is some modestly good news in this category, resulting from new student interest and responsive colleges and universities: language enrollments have gone up 13% since 2002, with huge surges in Chinese and Arabic leading the way, abetted by a 37% rise in Korean language study. Shortage of teachers remains a constraint in the newly popular languages. This is part of the problem in low levels of student persistence: upper level language study draws only 10% of the enrollment of beginner courses in Arabic, only 40% even in Spanish. Community college language resources remain rather weak on average, outside of Spanish (American Sign Language was the second most commonly taught language in community colleges overall). Even with the welcome gains, only 8% of all college students are now enrolled in a foreign language class in any given year compared to 16% in the mid-1960s. While language experts expect enrollments to continue to gain in the foreseeable future, the area was still at best a glass half full, with serious impact on other aspects of global education.[7]

Global Across the Curriculum

The idea of disseminating global components across the curriculum, to build on general education segments and maintain the thrust even into more specialized majors, is a natural in the current higher education context. After all, if global starts with general education, there is a foundation to connect with many undergraduate majors and to make sure that relevant habits of mind do not atrophy. The project mirrors "across the curriculum" efforts in other areas, seeking to maintain and embellish a competency area once confined to the underclass years (if available even there), now too important to allow a loss of momentum. Few institutions really pretend that a global component will be achievable everywhere. Dickinson College, for example, with an early effort in this direction, mandates "internationally focused" courses in all the social science and humanities majors, with departments responsible for monitoring their inventories; but it has not pretended the same breadth in the science fields. "Across the curriculum" efforts also risk mutually damaging competition: many institutions are running writing, IT, and critical thinking threads across the curriculum already, with pressure also for multicultural diversity and possibly more besides; the skein might easily tangle, with so many fibers, or the whole project dismissed as mere rhetoric.

Still, a number of projects have developed in the global vein that merit further attention. Many English departments are adding world literature courses and specialists, with particular attention to works in English written outside the conventional Western world—in Africa, to take an obvious and important example. These efforts are mirrored in French programs that build attention to francophone literature in Africa and the Caribbean. Comparative literature, including works in translation, an older field usually focused on seeming classics, maintains some interest, but attention to particular literary disseminations strikes a somewhat different chord, opening avenues to additional societies and cultures while remaining accessible to many students.

A buzz concept in history programs these days involves "internationalizing" the American history course, to relate it more closely to work that students do in world history and other Civilization areas. American history has traditionally been rather parochial, its textbooks filled more with domestic issues than with foreign influences and engagements. The "American exceptionalist" approach to the field, explicitly or more often implicitly, has defined American history as quite distinct even from its maternal West European ancestor, and certainly from more troubled regions like Latin America. Internationalizing American history involves introducing careful comparison into the survey course, rather than blithe and sometimes rather arrogant assumptions of American distinctiveness, while also doing more with similarities in patterns, shared influences, and the complexity of American involvements in the world at large. The result is a considerable transformation of a conventional staple, though not an impossible one, and a significant contribution to linking this aspect of a history program to a broader global sequence. Similar efforts have been introduced to do more with global influences and mutual impacts in European history. How widely these challenging redefinitions will catch on is unclear, in a field constrained by convention and identity politics, but the discussion can be compelling.[8]

Planning and implementation range more widely. Portland State University sets internationalization as a goal for all disciplines and departments, so that the subject is not treated as someone else's responsibility or the province of international relations programs or modern languages alone. An associate dean and member of the school's Internationalization Committee put the key point well: "There's always a tendency to assume it's [global education] going to be taken care of elsewhere. And it isn't." Nursing and health programs increasingly add components on global health issues, while intercultural communication courses assist nurses in dealing with patients from diverse international origins. The latter is a recent requirement at Bellevue Community College, near Seattle. A number of programs deal with engineering. The University of Michigan has developed a global engineering program. Not required, the program introduces students to global engineering, environmental and policy issues, while encouraging work in a foreign language. Several other engineering programs, some signing up as much as 20% of the entire enrollment, emphasize a study abroad segment and a minor in a foreign language. Not the norm, the options nevertheless demonstrate that the combination of global and technical-professional is also quite possible.[9]

A growing number of management schools are introducing programs in international business, but also individual courses that can combine with other specializations, including even accounting. Education programs often develop options dealing with global issues in this field, training teachers for work in international schools, for example. The University of Wisconsin-Milwaukee uses its BA/BS program in Global Studies to partner with professional schools to provide concentrations in global management, global classrooms, or global communications, among other areas. Science programs innovate less aggressively, but obviously environmental science programs, a clear exception, move into international issues out of real necessity.

Community colleges get into the act. The president of Butte College, in California, noticed that global activities were pulled back every time there was a budget crisis. She brought in a new staff to firm up a more durable international commitment. Today, the president contends that the curriculum committee won't approve any new course, in any unit, without a global component. An official from another college, noting the growth in global activities at the two-year college level, revealingly added: "One of the challenges, though, is how you fit them into whatever else you need to do." Commitment and staffing are issues at various levels.[10]

The larger point is clear: international components can become integral parts of an impressive range of disciplines, sometimes displacing older, more parochial foci (as in the humanities), sometimes, as in engineering, building quite new connections. The goal can reach ambitiously into a hope that global interests will become part of lifelong learning, with skills and habits developed in college a true source of inspiration for years afterward (indeed, into an active retirement)—in ways directly germane to citizenship, effective careers, and quality of life.

Global Studies Majors

New majors in global affairs have been a crucial expression of the growing interest in issues of global education and the need for innovation. Programs have developed at a variety of institutions, and the list continues to expand. The University of California at Santa Barbara introduced a global affairs option several years ago and quickly had over 700 majors. Its director recently noted the program's relatively hoary status, having begun "in the last century." George Mason's entry, only a bit more recent, now hosts over 500 undergraduates, constituting one of the largest concentrations in the school within a mere five years of operation. The University of Wisconsin-Milwaukee has a vibrant program. The University of Texas plans an option to begin in 2009. And the surge continues. Entries at the community college level are less clear as yet, and there are opportunities for greater articulation than has yet been realized. There are important holdouts still among four-year institutions as well, where faculty see no need for additional efforts given majors in international relations and area studies. Indeed, any campus seeking to install a global program must anticipate serious concerns from faculty with stakes in existing efforts and must find ways to give at least some of them a real share in any new endeavor.[11]

Arguably, however, the innovation is worth undertaking—and student response certainly suggests this is so at least for the medium run of things. Some programs, indeed, have been constructed initially in response to student concerns, as individual undergraduates tried to build combinations that were difficult without some organizational umbrella. The University of Texas, for example, was initially responding to international relations students who wanted more than the political science department could offer. The major need not and should not replace current activities (portions of which can also be built into global affairs in any event). Most global affairs majors, furthermore, are kept deliberately brief, in terms of credit hours, so that students can combine this training either with more traditional international sectors or with other interests such as management or environmental science.

The characteristic major—and there are hosts of specific variants, that however build in some standard basic features—involves several emphases that do distinguish it from curricular business as usual. First, it is massively interdisciplinary, contrasting, for example, with international relations majors usually housed in or near a political science department. Programs offer requirements or at least tracks in trade, cultural globalization, environmental issues, human rights efforts, conflict analysis as well as international relations. Most have some core courses that combine disciplines and topics directly, around multifaceted themes like globalization. Faculty are drawn in from cultural studies, economics, political science, sociology/anthropology, and sometimes beyond—programs that cut across not only disciplines but also collegiate units are not uncommon. Options are usually available for work in international management, health and sometimes other areas as well.

Second, the new major is global, dealing with global patterns and issues, and not an amalgam of some mix of area studies offerings. Many curricula offer an area studies track within the program, where students can take a subset of related courses on Africa or Latin America after the more general core program; and of course some students themselves will build a double major to extend the relationship. But this is not a "Civilizations" approach, as opposed to an effort to talk about linkages and comparisons.

Third, the global affairs majors normally build in a serious foreign language component, requiring enough coursework (or tested ability) to demonstrate competence and, often, an opportunity to use this competence in a research paper or internship. Many students actually welcome this aspect of the requirements as a means of forcing them to a level they might otherwise not aspire to. The University of Texas will insist on six hours of upper-division language coursework, and many other programs have similar stipulations, perhaps bending a bit when a student seeks time to launch preparation in a non-Western language.

Fourth, while the new majors build on a great deal of international enthusiasm on the part of faculty and students alike, they must not be cast in a simplistic pro-global mode. Core courses deal with drawbacks, new inequalities and diverse resistances, as well as the plus sides of globalization. Regional tracks help students explore further how aspects of globalization harm particular areas and groups, and comparison of diversity—in impacts and reactions alike—must be built into the program's analytical core.

The field remains new, which means that further developments and new concerns must be anticipated. Tensions around the departures from more conventional International Relations provoke afterthoughts as well. A recent global affairs conference drew a number of half-in, half-out remarks like "I would urge us to think of global studies as much more than warmed-over IR and much more than renamed international studies. But what does that mean? Where does that leave us?" Yet, even as faculty members continue to harbor doubts, an impressive number of students, for the moment at least, vote with their feet. There has been no coherent surge of this sort in the United States, in the international education arena, for at least a generation, and possibly since the advent of training in modern languages toward the end of the 19th century.[12]

The Co-curricular: Certificate Programs

While global affairs majors command legitimate attention, they directly draw only a minority of undergraduates. Attention must continue to apply to global components of the whole curriculum, and to efforts to go beyond the curriculum itself to additional platforms.

One of the most interesting aspects of the push toward more global education has been the efforts formally to combine curricular elements with extra-curricular involvements. The thrust has a positive and negative side. On the positive, it involves recognition that students can develop relevant global experiences by interacting with foreign students, collaborating in activities from international festivals to mock United Nations efforts, as well as participating in study abroad or international internships. Global competence embraces but is not confined to classroom activities. Business leaders, for example, often want students who can demonstrate experiential success in translating classroom concepts about globalization or other cultures to actual work or community settings. On the minus side, some of the enthusiasm for activity-filled global competencies certificates may substitute optimism and good intentions for much real learning and may implicitly signal a lack of focus on the more conventional academic side. It is sometimes easier to engage student affairs offices, already preoccupied with international students, than entrenched academic departments, and again the results, like the motivations, may be mixed. The innovation involved is real, but it falls short of the rethinking needed, for example, to generate a full global affairs major. At times also, the global element itself recedes into more general goals of civic action and student participation.

There's no question, however, about the momentum involved. Well over 25 institutions established some kind of global proficiency or citizenship or leadership program between the mid-1990s and the present, sometimes under an international center, sometimes through an academic department (like the University of Rhode Island's well-established international engineering activity or Virginia Commonwealth's global scholar in business), sometimes through an administrative-academic amalgam. A typical arrangement, on the more purely academic side, is Binghamton University's International Studies Certificate Program, that requires two global or multicultural courses plus work at the intermediate level in one foreign language; a study abroad experience or an internationally focused internship rounds out the program, which is capped by a one-credit capstone project where the student writes a short essay about his or her experience and global perspective. The Boston College certificate, in contrast, emphasizes four multicultural co-curricular activities with some coursework, to be worked out with an advisor, and a capstone reflection. The purpose is to unite student activities in study abroad with other aspects of the college experience, to produce "interculturally competent" students relevant to an increasingly global workforce. Other efforts combine a bit of coursework—anything global may count, from non-Western Civ or art on to international management—with a vague injunction to attend "events, social and cultural activities which enhance international understanding and provide valuable contacts with experienced professionals and international students." Service learning may be emphasized, with groups active in the international field (the pathway at Drake University). Here the approach may merge with a more general Civic Engagement movement, and in some cases may be rather buried amid its larger goals. Service learning is great, but it is often less easy to organize in the international arena, absent explicit travel abroad, than for domestic social action projects. Some programs organize topical lunches on particular countries, to embellish coursework in what is in effect a minor. (Drury University requires this effort for graduation.) Lehigh simply offers a set of courses from a mix of language, global literature, and introductory social science electives (some of them not necessarily very international in orientation), to generate a certificate, asking that students also join the World Affairs Club, Students for Sustainable Development, or some other organization; the program serves most obviously to prepare for a study abroad experience. Rochester Institute of Technology encourages engagement with grassroots organizations on topics related to globalization with efforts to have faculty develop global modules in an array of existing courses. Rutgers focuses on study abroad (required for its certificate) plus working with a group of international students (at least six of them) on some common project.

Many schools, of course, seek to take advantage of locally available resources. Fairleigh Dickinson thus sponsors discussions with United Nations representatives, or Internet conversations with international faculty, recording the talks for use in courses. Portland State sponsors short trips to Mexico, to focus on migration issues in ways that can then be sustained by coursework and community service activity back home.

Variations are numerous, but the global certificate programs in the main try to encourage a mixture of academic training and practice. They seek to stimulate students who might not have time for a full academic program (or in some cases might not be able to find an adequate offering; global certificates often try to cash in on rather diffuse academic coursework) to stretch their interests globally, with the inducement of a formal certificate to enhance other motivations. They attempt to encourage faculty themselves to add global components to courses, while motivating a larger audience for symposia or outside lecturers. In some instances the programs involved build on well-developed curricula, simply making elements available to students whose majors preclude full involvement or who are drawn by the mixture of hands-on practice with modest coursework. The popularity of the programs suggests that they tap into an interesting mixture of student motivation and staff/faculty leadership, and there is every indication that the certificate movement continues to gain momentum alongside more conventional curricular engagement. It unquestionably adds to purely faculty interests by involving a wider array of administrative leadership, from the student affairs side of the house and of course from study abroad offices.

Certificate activities do not capture all the co-curricular possibilities, of course. East Carolina University, which does have a global certificate program, also embellishes the global component of its general education humanities course with electronic links with universities on four continents. Several joint projects have emerged from these connections. The State Department initially supported the enhancement, which interested some other American institutions, but the larger project faltered amid technology gaps with countries like Pakistan plus fears by American faculty about traveling to some of the sites to facilitate the links. At East Carolina itself, however, the collaborations proved very meaningful. One female student reported that her encounters with a Pakistani student, a second wife sent to school by her husband to advance the family, gave her insights about polygamy that she had never expected to experience—exactly the kind of cultural extension that ordinary coursework might not be able to convey. Less dramatically, George Mason has organized electronically shared sociology classes with the Higher School of Economics in Moscow, allowing not only mutual conversation about common topics and reading but some collaborative projects. Global education benefits, obviously, by this kind of thinking beyond orthodox classroom walls.

The Terra Incognita of Graduate Studies

The push for global education has only tentatively reached out to the graduate level. Obviously, a host of older graduate programs are relevant to the initiative, including the important area studies opportunities that emerged in the 1960s and 1970s, as well as the many, often well-established opportunities in International Relations. Many institutions will doubtless decide that the existing roster is adequate to meet advanced training needs. It is true that burgeoning opportunities in government (where imminent retirements in the State Department and other agencies create growing needs, at least for the short term), business and the NGOs should stimulate at least an enrollment expansion, but they do not necessarily dictate curricular innovation.

Change is occurring however, in some areas. A growing number of MBA programs are adding opportunities in international management, a course or two on relevant global management issues, and in a few cases a required brief study trip abroad. These changes will almost surely develop further in the coming years. A number of sociology programs, even at the PhD level, are developing a more explicit global track—this is true, for example, of the new doctoral sequence at George Mason. New or expanded Masters opportunities in global health or global environmental science and policy (including earth observation and climate change) add significantly to the global education roster at the graduate level, and sometimes spill over into PhD programs or more general Masters programs as well.

A few schools, translating to the graduate level some of the innovations occurring in undergraduate global affairs programs, are also introducing new, global Masters programs. The move is still tentative. The Fletcher School at Tufts has led the way, with participation also by Rutgers, New York University and George Mason. These new programs offer generalist opportunities relevant for a number of career tracks, both for beginners and mid-career professionals. They emphasize the same kind of interdisciplinarity that the undergraduate offerings feature, with work on trade, diplomatic relations, education and the environment, management, cultural exchange, and health, usually with some combination of specifically designed core courses and a minor or track in one of the more specific fields. Some programs also spin off a certificate opportunity that can be relevant for other graduate students in business, environmental science, global health and other areas.

Some discussion has also emerged about a global affairs PhD effort, but skepticism so far predominates. A North Carolina official, enthusiastic about the value of an undergraduate global degree, pours cold water on the doctoral idea: "I daresay that not anytime soon will any of our history or politics departments hire a global studies Ph.D."[13] On the other hand, it is relevant to note that some new journals are cropping up, such as *New Global Studies* and *Globalizations*, suggesting the birth of a research dimension that could relate to further graduate training. The University of Illinois has even defined a global studies librarian position.

Certainly, the graduate field overall is ripe for additional discussion. Many moves are still limited or tentative. The thought that has gone into the undergraduate level has yet to reach graduate ranks. Again, perhaps innovation needs will prove to be less acute. It is also true that the graduate field may be more resistant to challenges to routine, less well organized to pick up new kinds of global signals. The jury is out.[14]

Habits of Mind

A survey of the various curricular facets of global education risks a sense of fragmentation, and indeed this may develop in fact, as different faculty and different groups of students engage in separate activities. There is a larger linkage, however, that must be emphasized, related to the ways in which student learning and the global endeavor must ultimately be assessed (see Chapter 9). The goal centers on the definable habits of mind, inculcated often enough and explicitly enough that some students—hopefully, many students—will emerge with some globally relevant thinking patterns that will easily outlast college and even graduate study. There is no getting around the great variety that a global educational experience embraces, with a host of courses, extracurricular experiences, relationships to varied majors. College, and life itself, are too short to embrace fully the world we should perhaps strive to know. But there are the core analytical perspectives that must inform the variety itself, bringing some shared qualities of mind that faculty as well as students need to refer to explicitly. We come back to the basic goals discussed in Chapter 2, but with more curricular specificity.

The list here is not long, though of course details can be debated, with the first two deriving from the basic goals:

- The components of a global curriculum should teach students how to compare, and the value of comparison in looking at one's own society through a global lens, as well as examining others.
- It should provide experience in relating global factors to local developments, and vice versa. The local–global interrelationship is more often evoked than clearly defined as a curricular component, but it is fundamental.
- The global curriculum should of course generate general cultural awareness, a sense of how some cultures differ from our own and some capacity to comprehend and utilize these differences (and attendant similarities).
- It should help students identify magnitudes of change in global frameworks, and to assess changes and continuities in major global factors and the causes of both.
- It should encourage students to see connections, not only among different parts of the world but among different components of contemporary global systems—the ways that environment relates to trade which relates to culture or to migration. The interdisciplinarity of global understanding is a fundamental feature.

Emphasis on the habits of mind is particularly important, of course, at the more elementary college level—as part of keeping world history honest, and not just a litany of memorizations; as a fundamental element in any other global general education category; as a theme in co-curricular activities along with the excitement of specific experiences. But the habits of mind should crop up explicitly as well in global across the curriculum, where courses should directly refer to and build on previous analytical gains. And they need not be forgotten even in the richer opportunities of a global affairs major—where the same basic habits can be further advanced—nor lost in the professional apparatus of a Masters degree program.[15] Global education means having certain kinds of information and knowing where to get more, and it means having real and ongoing familiarity with essential modes of thinking and analyzing.[16] Above all it means that students use and retain these habits—a learning responsibility academic leaders must take very seriously.

Faculty

Any discussion of extending a global education curriculum must, quite obviously, talk about faculty preparation and engagement. Faculty have indeed driven all of the developments covered in this chapter, sometimes with initial administrative encouragement, often on their own. At the same time, a number of internationally comparative studies have indicated that American faculty are collectively less interested in global education and research than their counterparts abroad. Hiring faculty with global competence, or a willingness to move in that direction, remains a vital component of a global education program.[17] The development of new language areas and coverage of global economic and cultural forces alike often requires additional staffing. At the same time, existing faculty must be brought into the picture, not only to take advantage of the real strengths harbored in language, social science and other departments, but to extend strengths further.

A number of schools have developed methods that improve faculty motivation and preparation simultaneously. Subsidizing faculty travel abroad, particularly for people with little prior international experience, rouses enthusiasm and expands expertise—and often very limited resources can do a lot. Having such faculty participate in study abroad trips is a variant on this same theme. Faculty can also be encouraged to join in special language-immersion programs to prepare for a trip, a facility developed, for example, at Dickinson College. A small grant for global research, but also for preparation of global materials in coursework is a very desirable component of an expanding educational program. Quite ambitiously, the University of Pittsburgh offers grants of up to $25,000 for faculty engaged in collaborative research with two or more foreign colleagues. Bronx Community College set up a $50,000 fund to support international activities by faculty, which quickly showed that a new president was serious about global goals. Faculty in several institutions, reporting on how demanding (though ultimately rewarding) preparation of a global component in an existing course can be, refer back to a (more modest) summer grant as a vital source of support and motivation.[18]

A crucial challenge involves faculty in disciplines not conventionally associated with global issues—in technology and science, for example, or in management. Ironically, faculty members in some of these disciplines are particularly likely to have foreign origins, and sometimes there are ways to utilize these backgrounds, without distortion or condescension, in a globalization effort. Here is where some special educational grant funds and encouragement to join in study abroad trips can have particular salience, though the competition with standard research demands in some of these fields makes the process difficult and uneven.[19]

Overall, soliciting faculty input but also encouraging their competence form essential parts of the global educational effort. Many institutions (SUNY,

Binghamton, is one example) are beginning at least to talk about including global effort in the criteria formally considered for promotion or salary enhancement—not requiring it, amid the many other demands, but giving serious credit where it is due. Attention to the faculty base remains a critical element in the whole global education process.[20]

Conclusion: The Challenge of Innovation

Current movements in the global education curriculum are both promising and demanding. They require new thinking from a variety of faculty—about what languages now deserve emphasis, about how to fold international relations into a broader interdisciplinary umbrella, about how to involve a wider variety of majors and professional programs in serious engagement with global issues. The changes called for must be interconnected. It's great to expand general education by including a new category and highlighting world history, but these developments will be far more meaningful when students encounter the global at a later stage of the curriculum. Co-curricular activities are fine but they risk superficiality if not directly connected to a full and updated pattern of coursework.

Change can also be threatening. Some language faculty, most obviously, have experienced the pain of seeing their lifetime commitment downgraded because of changes in global usage and the need to put resources into non-European tongues. But even other faculty need to be pulled out of routine, to think, for example, about the analytical habits of mind a global gen ed course must foster, beyond the conventions of a standard introductory course in West European or even African history or political science.

To date, curricular changes, though exciting, are uneven within many institutions. As a report on global education at the community college level indicates, coursework and co-curricular efforts that highlight cultural diversity plus comparison and communications issues are much more advanced than programs that encourage understanding of global systems. Global affairs majors capture these latter elements deliberately, but general education and across-the-curriculum efforts thus far lag behind.[21]

Some institutions, inevitably, are much farther along the process of innovation than others. Leadership and motivation have varied, and so has the tug of older curricular habits. The bellwether schools provide models, and this chapter hopefully can be used to encourage further probes into the possibilities that already exist. But even the leading innovators will agree that the task has yet to be completed. We have not yet fully figured out how to define what we mean by global competence on the part of every undergraduate, and we certainly have not figured out how to deliver on that definition. We reach too many students inadequately or incompletely. We still do best with the students, whose number happily grows steadily, with a deep interest in global issues, and we need to find ways to serve them even more fully but also to reach beyond.

Some of the most exciting global programs are quite new, and time will bring unanticipated tests.

Finally, as curricular and co-curricular developments themselves suggest, standard coursework is only part of the story. Global education must embrace other facets, including study abroad and appropriate interaction with international students. The next chapters take up these facets directly. But even as we move on, it must be obvious that the curricular foundation is essential to any global education program. The specialist care and passion that have long gone into study abroad is wasted if the preparation and ensuing coursework are not appropriately designed, and we need similar nurturing passion for the curriculum components themselves. It is fair to say that a promising start can be registered, but a challenging distance remains at the heart of the global effort in higher education.

5
Education Abroad:
Redefining a Staple

Study abroad programs have expressed an extraordinary level of commitment by many American institutions of higher education, and by countless American students, over many decades. By the 21st century virtually every college and university had some kind of study abroad office, often with a wide array of programs in terms of location, specialization, and duration. A major group of professionals had developed in the field, replete with significant journals like *Frontiers*—and with the United States clearly in the lead in its level of organization and its commitment to study abroad aimed substantially at global awareness. During much of the 20th century, study abroad was the major gesture American higher education made to responsibilities for providing exposure to international issues. By 2008, with a somewhat more abundant curricular repertoire, study abroad programs stood out a bit less strongly. On the other hand, many educators and educational policymakers continued to think of study abroad as the most obvious (and easiest) response to the importance of widening American student perspectives. It was deeply reassuring that, in the wake of the many fears provoked by the 9/11 terrorist attacks, study abroad did not significantly slacken—a real tribute to intelligent student interest and to the vigor of response by the higher educational establishment in the United States. The federal government, indeed, began debating increased levels of support as a means of recognizing growing needs for global awareness and expertise. Other countries were beginning to identify similar responsibilities. Japanese and Korean institutions, for example, began to plan study abroad semesters, frequently with American destinations, for the same reasons that American universities pushed their programs. Korea University, for example, is now requiring a semester experience for several categories of undergraduates, and has even built some dormitories in North America to underwrite opportunities. And, amid all this general fanfare, it is vital to remember how life-changing study abroad experiences have been for many individual American students, deeply affecting careers and outlooks for decades after the visits ended.

The rapid increase in study abroad programs is also incontestable: in 2000, 65% of American campuses had programs, but by 2006 the figure had soared to 91%. Clearly, study abroad was seen as meeting pressing needs in the global education field, though there had to be some concern that a gesture here might substitute for more systematic thinking about larger global needs for which study abroad was, properly, only a partial response.[1]

Despite both history and current popularity, or perhaps as a result, study abroad programs have long raised a host of questions, and the urgency has hardly diminished as requirements for global perspectives have increased. Issues come under a variety of headings. Most obviously, study abroad covers a multitude of engagements, from the most cursory week or two to deeply involved semesters or even full years of academic work. They range from operations conducted exclusively by American faculty, which differ from the home institution only in location and a field trip or two, to real immersion in an international setting. They include student interests in partying, often to take advantage of laxer drinking laws, as well as deep student interests in acquiring new knowledge. Too often, study abroad assumptions have tended to gloss over highly variable degrees of adequacy, on grounds that anything that gets students away from the narrowly American must be a good thing—even though study abroad realities are at times considerably less reassuring. At an extreme, but not an unusual one, the national parochialism that study abroad seems to counter actually may define the experience, from dependence on instruction in English or the need for elaborate chaperonage to an insistence on being assured that all basic American amenities will be available. There's no question, also, that many institutions—in the past and still, despite some growing awareness— have dumped too many responsibilities on study abroad programs, using them as excuses not to think through broader curricular issues and, even more commonly, assuming that study abroad could be a self-contained experience requiring neither preparation nor follow-up to be educationally successful. And, in this vein, heaven forbid that anything so crude as a formal assessment be attached to something so obviously beneficial.

There are other issues too, including the exploitative costs of some programs that take advantage of admirable student zeal and, sometimes, a certain amount of laziness on the part of the universities involved. Questions about the relationship between most study abroad destinations, still Europe-focused despite a changing world, and the regions American students should increasingly become acquainted with, have become increasingly pressing. The obvious question of self-selection looms as well. The Americans who study abroad are hardly broadly representative, and not surprisingly many of the students who may "need" the experience most, in terms of ingrained parochialism (whether on the students' part or on that of professors who discourage any departure from American standards), are least likely to acquire it. At the very least, study abroad programs must be part of a carefully considered, intentional commitment to global education, not a self-contained one-shot bow to the highly motivated.

A final cautionary note emerges from a recent survey: only 44% of all faculty seem to feel that study abroad is particularly important. There is clearly a more than small gap between the high confidence many globalists place on study abroad, and what a (however slight) majority of faculty think—and that gap complicates efforts to fit study abroad into many curricula. Faculty are noticeably more interested, for example, in undergraduate research experiences than in foreign study, which in turn constrains study abroad opportunities directly when not only faculty lack of interest and passive advising but outright curricular barriers intrude.

This chapter considers study abroad from two primary vantage points. First, we take a look at current patterns (with a brief bow toward historical origins), including both strengths and measurable deficiencies and the kinds of assessment efforts that help pinpoint both qualities. Then we move to more directly administrative issues, though more briefly, around the organization of study abroad operations. Policy concerns emerge here too. But the real question is how the two segments interrelate: how structure helps explain recent gains, but also the extent to which structure can help address some undeniable concerns.

We know quite a bit about how study abroad works, though rather less about how to address some increasingly recognized limitations and deficiencies. Assessing study abroad, its obvious strengths and the impressive student motives on which it can build, but also maintaining awareness of problems and desirable additional steps, is obviously a central feature of any overall administrative commitment in the global education field.

* * *

There's no question about soaring goals and hopes for study abroad. In February, 2007 a variety of organizations, including the National Association of Manufacturers, the National Association of State Universities and Land Grant Colleges, and the Brookings Institution, sponsored a forum on study abroad and economic competitiveness. Speakers from several vantage points were unanimous in their endorsement of study abroad as a cornerstone for the "global competency" of American citizens. Study abroad fosters better knowledge of geography, it directly forces students to encounter people who "don't necessarily think the way we do" and (currently at least) who often don't like Americans or American policy very much. There was recognition that too many Americans are unduly ignorant about the world around them and that even businesses often lag in acknowledging the importance of global awareness and specific international skills. But the fix, clearly, was more study abroad, amid some claims that employers themselves are becoming increasingly aware of the desirability of hiring graduates who have study abroad experience.[2]

Commentary also recognized, of course, that not all study abroad was equally useful. Short stints involving little change from normal routines and associations clearly might not advance the basic goals. While global citizenship requires some experience abroad, it must be in-depth. There also must be greater recognition that study abroad is vitally important for students in all fields, and not simply people aiming for specialized careers in government service. Emphasis focused strongly on study abroad as a lesson in cultural differences, promoting awareness, adaptability, and an ability to operate amid ambiguity—qualities deemed essential for the contemporary global economy. Interest in enhanced foreign language abilities surfaced as a subordinate theme, and there was also generalized praise for how study abroad promoted personal creativity and innovations in problem solving among students. Study abroad experts admitted that research on the results of study abroad was not as comprehensive as one might like, and that in the business field there were better data on the consequences of global ignorance than on the positive effects of foreign exposure. But they insisted on the central claim, that most students, whatever their particular country of choice (and whether or not it was English-speaking) or precise length of stay, found their study abroad experience to be "life-changing." In the contemporary world, study abroad was fundamental to competitiveness in the global marketplace and to national security alike.

Not surprisingly, the Forum concluded with resounding endorsements:

Study abroad is a key tool for students to obtain global competency, which broadly consists of tolerance for ambiguity, intellectual flexibility, and an ease of conducting affairs in multicultural contexts, among other traits: and

Studies show that business has a growing expectation of new employees having global competency, and that there is a growing appreciation by employers of the strong correlation between study abroad and global competency.[3]

And, of course, the nation requires far more study abroad than now occurs, and (though this was not clarified in any detail) with greater depth than some current exposures involve. The head of the American Institute for Foreign Study, a for-profit organization promoting study abroad since 1964, announced at the meeting the goal of expanding the experience to one million American students annually by 2016–7, with legislation to be introduced to provide unprecedented federal support.

* * *

The belief that there was special virtue in study abroad affected many individual American students during the 19th century. Initially, a key impulse was to acquire knowledge unavailable in the United States itself—the fact that it would be sought internationally was a subordinate theme. Thus many medical researchers, scientists, budding psychologists, and of course artists sought, almost exclusively in Europe, access to advanced achievements that they could bring back home to further their careers and to further American professional competence in a variety of fields. The idea of the research university itself was the fruit of this kind of exchange, particularly on the part of American scholars and academic entrepreneurs who gained experience in Germany.

Intriguingly—and this is a crucial point—this early motivation increasingly evaporated because of the rapid success of the research university itself within the United States. In contrast to foreign students explicitly seeking the highest levels of specialized knowledge in the United States (or Europe or Japan), most current American students do not see study abroad as an opportunity for access to greater professional expertise—though of course there are exceptions for individual students with particular scholarly interests. This contrasts not only with students from Africa, Latin America or South Asia who see their study abroad as part of an exposure to the scientific and technical strengths of advanced industrial societies, but even to students from places like Australia or New Zealand, who unlike their American counterparts do see specialized knowledge and not just cultural exposure as an international education goal. In fact, as we will see, many American students worry that study abroad actually disrupts their professional training, exposing them to inferior levels of expertise that may, or may not, find compensation in the wider opportunities for cultural awareness. The very eminence of the American research university in the 20th century, allowing a growing sense of international leadership in specialized scholarship, shifted the context for foreign activities by American students just as study abroad, as an organized movement, saw the light of day.

The modern American study abroad experience, involving organized groups of students and not individual knowledge-seekers, began in the 1920s, with a definite vision of the desirability of cultural breadth as the key target. The context, obviously, was post-World War I, with many American leaders concerned that the war, and the subsequent turn to isolationism, had revealed a dangerous parochialism among their fellow nationals that explicit encouragement to stays in foreign countries might cure. Promotion of foreign language skills ran alongside this more general goal.[4]

The Junior Year Abroad program was launched in 1923 from the University of Delaware, under the auspices of a professor of French who had served in World War I and had stayed for further education in France. The arguments put forward to draw other institutions to sponsor students for the program had a decidedly contemporary ring: "We shall always be at a disadvantage in our foreign relations of every kind ... until there is a much larger number of Americans who know the language and in some measure the customs and methods of the peoples with whom we have to deal." Two years later Smith College formed its own program in imitation, also with a primary focus on France and French majors, with less specific emphasis than in the Delaware operation on careers in international affairs and business and with more general goals of humanistic cultivation. By 1939 the two programs had sent over 1200 undergraduates abroad for a full year of French study.[5]

As this precedent developed, building on the basic motivation of allowing foreign exposure to challenge American parochialism, and with a stronger language emphasis than would survive the spread of English after World War II, two other motives for study abroad emerged strongly as well—again, with obvious continuities running to the present day. First, of course, was the desire to use the change of venue as a means of personal challenge and growth—including, back then at least, desirable refinement for young women. Sometimes this was framed in terms of a liberal, humanistic education on the part of students who, as one put it in the 1920s, "had no special plans for the future but who wish to broaden themselves by this rich cultural experience." On other occasions—and this tended to increase over time—it was phrased more explicitly through the idea of breaking out of routine and proving to oneself that one could operate in an unfamiliar environment. The idea of personal growth was not, quite obviously, incompatible with the more socially or professionally oriented goal of exposure to another culture. But it could, in the minds of participants or college administrators, make study abroad seem little different from an unusual internship or volunteer experience back home—like tutoring prisoners or working in the political office of a congressman whose views you opposed. "Life-changing" served as the focus here, with operating in a foreign culture only one among many possible vehicles.[6]

Then, of course, there was simply having fun. One of the reasons France was such a popular target for early organized study abroad activities, besides the World War I alliance and the wide currency of French language instruction given the war-induced decline in the viability of German, was the nation's notoriety for good food and, particularly, lax regulations concerning alcohol consumption (this was, after all, the decade of Prohibition back home). Some students were amazed at accompanying faculty members, notorious for enforcing the rules on the American campus, who began inviting them to join them for a drink even on board the ship carrying them to France—much less the easy availability of wine and more in France itself. Of course a few purists might dissent—even as most of her colleagues enjoyed their first access to champagne, one student in the Delaware program noted that she and a few others could "have a good time—by ourselves—*not drinking any cocktails.*"[7]

Having fun, of course, was also compatible with other goals, from personal growth to cultural acclimation—indeed, it could be part and parcel of both. But the interest in seeking study abroad as a means of busting loose—and specifically, in many European settings, to drink a great deal—could compete as a priority and, unfortunately, as a daily focus with the more serious purposes of the whole endeavor.

Obviously, a full history of American study abroad reveals far more detail and a more intricate set of progressions, but for our purposes the carry-forward is fairly clear-cut. American college students, and academic leaders, developed a sense of the importance of a foreign experience fairly early, chronologically, as they moved to replace largely individual initiative with more organized structures and inducements, notably through the junior year programs. While a few schools pioneered the collective initiatives, students from many colleges were able to associate with one of the larger operations. The movement reflected a desire to counter national narrowness in the interest of providing culturally sensitive graduates who could fill necessary diplomatic and business slots—while the broader ideas of global competence and related citizenship needs were not yet available, the notion of the transforming effects of simply operating in a foreign context was well developed. The effort to use this curricular addition to counter perceived inadequacies in contemporary national policy—in this case, outright isolationism—also launched a process still visible today. All of this occurred as the national sense of academic and scholarly inferiority, which had previously prompted so much individual foreign study in the interests of disciplinary advancement, was yielding to perceived leadership in higher education, such that study abroad had to be justified on the more generalized grounds of international awareness (combined of course with specific opportunities to sharpen language skills). There was little focused interest in what courses of study were involved (though art and culture courses were common targets de facto), languages aside, so much as a sense that the fact of being abroad and interacting with foreign cultures would somehow work a liberalizing effect through osmosis. The sense that students in the main had little to gain in specific disciplines could actually complicate interests in studying abroad, by implying that international programs might actually disrupt superior American curricula outside the language arena, whatever their other merits.

The existence of additional impetus, again from the early phases of the organized movement to study abroad, was unsurprising, but this introduced undeniable complexities that also survive in programs today. The personal enrichment goal followed from deep interest in European cultural legacy—which could actually overshadow learning goals about contemporary settings; it would long bias, indeed continues to bias, study abroad programs toward a European rather than global focus. The idea of study abroad as part of a challenging course of personal development might, as already suggested, lead students and administrators to see the programs as one of several options, with the actual international learning focus downplayed in favor of personal challenge.

Most obviously of all, the early interest in study abroad as a chance to party outside normal American campus rules—again, entirely understandable in context—could seriously complicate study abroad's more somber aims. The student who saw an international opportunity in terms of food, drink and possibly sex might in the process pick up some unintended learning, but amid obvious tensions. More than one program would turn out to suffer from students who spent the bulk of their time in lifestyle experiments, gaining little else and sometimes harming themselves in the process. Personal misfortunes aside, a key result could be compensatory efforts by American administrators to provide campus-like supervision and largely American companionship, which might inhibit excess but which simultaneously and dramatically restricted exposure to anything really foreign. Goals and realities could easily conflict. Over time, some improvements in screening might permit greater compatibility with some latitudes for students, but the gaps between some academic expectations and foreign permissiveness were not easily closed—at least without also reducing the foreignness.

* * *

Since the inception decades, when key assumptions were formed and some characteristic complexities developed, study abroad programs have developed growing strength in American higher education. As noted, whereas until the 1960s most institutions sent students to international programs either on their own, individual initiative or by having them sign onto Junior Year programs like Smith's or, later, Sweetbriar's, by the end of the century it was essential for large numbers of colleges and universities to each have its own office and, usually, some signature programs of its own. It was in the 1970s and 1980s that individual operations began to form widely, both a testimony and a spur to broader participation and to new commitment, on the part of quite varied American institutions, to gain a direct stake in this experience. By the 1990s and certainly after 9/11, student applicants to all sorts of colleges and universities routinely checked on the existence of institutional study abroad offices, as part of their sorting through admissions options and defining what institutions made the respectability cut, even though most would not in fact follow up. Large numbers of schools sent student groups, under one or more professors, for programs of study in a host of countries. Commercial study abroad operations developed apace, extending options still further.

The process of change, amid considerable continuities, involved two currents beyond sheer expansion. First, as with higher education itself in the United States, there was a commitment to greater democratization: no longer, at least in principle, should study abroad aim simply at a private school elite. Second, the language learning emphasis in much of the original thrust was diluted in favor of an awareness of the growing pervasiveness of English (and the deterioration of language exposure among many American undergraduates) and the broader goal of global awareness. The two shifts intertwined to some degree, though for better or worse there was more movement in the language area than in widespread democratization.

All of this occurred against a backdrop of frequent diplomatic uncertainties, fostered by the cold war and then the rise of terrorism. It occurred—as in the 1920s—amid many signs of pervasive American parochialism and, sometimes, outright xenophobia. It occurred amid student generations that were often rated as increasingly self-absorbed, apolitical or (by the time of Gen-X after 2000) parent-dominated and exceptionally risk averse.[8] Study abroad bucked trends, or it appealed to students slightly out of the American and generational mainstream, or a bit of both. It was a logical response to the new uncertainties of a global environment—a recognition that it was more important than ever to gain international exposure—but it was a response that might require no small amount of gumption precisely because of these same uncertainties. Study abroad was an important educational answer to the nation's complicated involvement in world affairs.

Yet a look at who went, and who didn't, reveals another glass half empty—or perhaps half full. In 2005–6, over 220,000 American collegians studied abroad for credit. This was a doubling of the figure just eight years before—an impressive achievement in the post-9/11 years of real fear and confusion internationally. Growth from the previous year also stood at 8%. Percentages rose as well—the 2005–6 figure, as a portion of the total student population, had essentially doubled from the levels of the 1980s, and numbers had risen more than fivefold—startlingly, only 40,000 students had participated in formal programs abroad in the mid-1980s.[9] Between that point and the early 21st century, with overall student numbers increasing only 25%, the explosion of study abroad testified to dramatic gains in student awareness of the relevance of global issues and of foreign study as a means of addressing them, and to an equally dramatic spread of organizational networks available to promote and facilitate the activity on most campuses. A *New York Times* article in 2007 noted, with some justification, that study abroad had become a "prized credential of the undergraduate experience." All of this occurred, it might be added, despite not only new kinds of international threats but also a rapidly deteriorating dollar that made particularly the most popular targets for study abroad increasingly expensive.[10]

A number of individual institutions and types of institutions stood out on the American study abroad landscape. Participation in study abroad was not random: some schools obviously put more effort into advertising the option than others; commitment of key disciplines to encouraging foreign study and facilitating its integration into the major was crucial. Thus an interesting mixture of private and public institutions headed the list in terms of sheer numbers. New York University, in general emerging as a global leader among American universities, topped the charts with 2,611 students doing credit-bearing work in 2005–6; most of the other standard-bearers, however, were prestigious public universities, including Texas, Penn State, Michigan State, Florida, Illinois and Virginia; the University of Pennsylvania was the only other large private institution in the top numerical ranks. Other prestigious privates were simply a bit smaller than their public competitors, but also in some cases slightly more reluctant to forgo valuable tuition by promoting the option with full energy. In terms of percentages of students sharing the experience, it is crucial to note that the leaders were not big schools of any sort, but rather a set of private liberal arts institutions whose study abroad commitment reflected

Table 5.1 Report on International Educational Exchange.

INTERNATIONAL STUDENTS IN THE U.S. (CONTINUED)

F. PRIMARY SOURCE OF FUNDING of International Students, 2006/07

Primary Source of Funds	Int'l Students	% of Total
Personal & Family	358,281	61.5
U.S. College or University	152,017	26.1
Current Employment	29,262	5.0
Home Government/University	18,704	3.2
U.S. Private Sponsor	8,003	1.4
Foreign Private Sponsor	6,682	1.1
U.S. Government	3,450	0.6
International Organization	1,685	0.3
Other Sources	4,901	0.8
TOTAL	**582,984**	**100.0**

G. TOP FIELDS OF STUDY of International Students, 2005/06 & 2006/07

Rank	Field of Study	2005/06 Int'l Students	2006/07 Int'l Students	2006/07 % of Total	% Change
1	Business & Management	100,881	103,641	17.8	2.7
2	Engineering	88,460	89,137	15.3	0.8
3	Physical & Life Sciences	50,168	51,863	8.9	3.4
4	Social Sciences	46,132	48,978	8.4	6.2
5	Math & Computer Science	45,518	46,019	7.9	1.1
6	Fine & Applied Arts	29,509	29,588	5.1	0.3
7	Health Professions	27,124	28,294	4.9	4.3
8	Intensive English Language	17,239	22,417	3.8	30.0
9	Education	16,546	16,825	2.9	1.7
10	Humanities	16,480	16,189	2.8	-1.8

U.S. STUDENTS & STUDY ABROAD

H. U.S. STUDY ABROAD TRENDS

223,534 U.S. students studied abroad for academic credit in 2005/06. U.S. student participation in study abroad has grown 150% over the past decade.

Based on estimated figures for 2006/07 from over 800 institutions, the number of U.S. students studying abroad for credit is projected to continue its steady increase in 2006/07.

I. LEADING DESTINATIONS 2004/05 & 2005/06

Rank	Destination	2004/05	2005/06	2005/06 % of Total	% Change
	TOTAL	205,983	223,534	100.0	8.5
1	United Kingdom	32,071	32,109	14.4	0.1
2	Italy	24,858	26,078	11.7	4.9
3	Spain	20,806	21,881	9.8	5.2
4	France	15,374	15,602	7.0	1.5
5	Australia	10,813	10,980	4.9	1.5
6	Mexico	9,244	10,022	4.5	8.4
7	China	6,389	8,830	4.0	38.2
8	Germany	6,557	6,858	3.1	4.6
9	Costa Rica	4,887	5,518	2.5	12.9
10	Ireland	5,083	5,499	2.5	8.2
11	Japan	4,100	4,411	2.0	7.6
12	Greece	2,445	3,227	1.4	32.0
13	Argentina	2,013	2,865	1.3	42.3
14	Czech Republic	2,494	2,846	1.3	14.1
15	Austria	2,757	2,792	1.2	1.3
16	Chile	2,393	2,578	1.2	7.7
17	New Zealand	2,657	2,542	1.1	-4.3
18	South Africa	2,304	2,512	1.1	9.0
19	Brazil	1,994	2,328	1.0	16.8
20	Ecuador	1,711	2,171	1.0	26.9

J. HOST REGIONS of U.S. Study Abroad Students, 2004/05 & 2005/06

Host Region	2004/05 Total	2004/05 %	2005/06 Total	2005/06 %
Africa	7,100	3.5	8,459	3.8
Asia	16,571	8.0	20,811	9.3
Europe*	124,292	60.3	130,274	58.3
Latin America	29,655	14.4	33,902	15.2
Middle East	1,977	1.0	2,585	1.2
North America**	1,121	0.5	1,151	0.5
Oceania	13,787	6.7	14,033	6.3
Multiple Regions	11,480	5.6	12,319	5.5
Total	205,983	100.0	223,534	100.0

*Cyprus and Turkey were re-classified into the Europe region in 2004/05.
** Includes Antarctica.

K. FIELDS OF STUDY of U.S. Study Abroad Students, 2004/05 & 2005/06

Field of Study	2004/05 Total	2004/05 %	2005/06 Total	2005/06 %	% Change
Social Sciences	46,552	22.6	48,537	21.7	4.3
Business & Mgmt.	36,047	17.5	39,478	17.7	9.5
Humanities	27,396	13.3	31,810	14.2	16.1
Foreign Languages	15,449	7.5	17,547	7.8	13.6
Fine or Applied Arts	15,655	7.6	16,829	7.5	7.5
Physical/Life Sci.	14,625	7.1	15,457	6.9	5.7
Education	8,445	4.1	9,056	4.1	7.2
Health Sciences	7,003	3.4	8,540	3.8	21.9
Engineering	5,974	2.9	6,556	2.9	9.7
Math or Comp. Sci.	3,502	1.7	3,318	1.5	-5.3
Agriculture	2,472	1.2	2,818	1.3	14.0
Undeclared	7,003	3.4	7,583	3.4	8.3
Other	16,067	7.7	16,005	7.2	-0.4
Total	**205,983**	**100.0**	**223,534**	**100.0**	**8.5**

L. DURATION of Study Abroad, 2004/05 & 2005/06

Duration	2004/05 % of total	2005/06 % of total
Short-term (summer, January term, or fewer than 8 weeks)	51.4	52.8
Mid-length (one or two quarters, or one semester)	42.3	41.7
Long-term (academic or calendar year)	6.3	5.5

Source: Bhandari, R., and Chow, P. (2007). *Open Doors 2007: Report on International Educational Exchange* (New York: Institute of International Education), p. 34.

traditional connections to the intellectual breadth aspect of foreign study now updated with the recognition that study abroad could be an advantage in the fierce admissions competition for students willing and able to support pricey tuition. The top ten campuses sending over 40% of their students abroad, in 2005–6, included Austin College, Colby, Elon, Dickinson, Depauw, and Lewis and Clark. These fine schools, not at the top of the small college heap and sometimes seeking to compensate for a certain degree of geographic isolation, clearly found study abroad a particularly useful element in the overall commitment to liberal education. A few individual institutions, within this general category, proved particularly imaginative and successful. Goucher College claimed to insist on some kind of study abroad from all students, though data suggested that some exceptions had to be made. Goucher boasted of being the first institution in the United States to couple study abroad requirements with a $1200 travel grant to each student. Kalamazoo College, in Michigan, featured study abroad as part of a deep commitment to international education; the College's K-plan, dating back to the late 1970s and involving a mix of special experiences including domestic internships, by 2007 featured 50 study abroad programs on six continents, with 80% of all students opting to participate.

The disproportion in the types of schools sending large numbers or percentages abroad also harbored a clear cautionary note. The glass was also at least half empty. In 2005–6 only 1.4% of all American students were doing any academic work abroad, which suggests that over a normal college career only 1/20 would have any exposure to what so many educators regard as the core experience in creating global competence. Really successful programs at big state schools like George Mason or Michigan State, with a lot of effort and imagination, could manage to send upwards of 15%–20% of their undergraduates on at least a short course at some point during their college career, but given the overall national percentages, this meant that many other large institutions roused scant student interest of any sort. Large numbers of sprawling state universities and many private religious colleges had very little activity.[11] A few community college systems had vigorous programs—the Northern Virginia Community College recurrently sponsored trips to places like China, Cuba and Brazil, with a special venture every two or three years—but many systems had no organized programs at all.

Equally interesting, and troubling to many observers, were disproportions within student ranks. Well over half of current participants in study abroad come from the social sciences (22%), management (18%), and the humanities (at 22% with foreign language students included as constituting 8% of the overall total). This means that huge fields, such as education, the sciences, and engineering, had only modest participation in the totals, despite their importance in the American higher educational scene and, even more, the role many of their graduates will play in American and global life in the future.*

---

* Student athletes are another important category largely excluded from study abroad. International educators have talked about various ways to bring them in while maintaining their other campus obligations, but the discussion has not aroused much interest in athletic departments. More generally, Duke students load up on study abroad in the fall, for example, so they'll be home for the heart of basketball season.

Engineering students produced only 3% of study abroad participants, education (a potentially crucial field in terms of later generational impact) only 4%, agriculture only 1%. Numbers in these areas have for the most part increased during the past several years, but generally only at the overall rate; there have been no significant percentage leaps forward with the possible exception of the health sciences. It has also remained difficult for student-athletes to find time for study abroad.

Disproportions also apply, though hardly surprisingly, to social and ethnic categories. African American collegians, for example, were less than half as likely as white students to engage in foreign study. The percentage of Caucasian participants, at 83% in 2006–7, had slipped only a percentage point over the preceding decade, mainly thanks to increased Asian-American involvement (now at over 6%). Essentially, the same disparities applied to Hispanic students and more widely to low income students of all races. Study abroad appealed disproportionately to students whose parents had relatively high levels of education.[12]

It is also relevant to note that, with the exception of some MBA programs, study abroad attention has focused on undergraduate populations. Individuals in graduate study may of course move actively into the international arena as part of research projects, and some science students participate through their mentors in international research networks, but study abroad per se is not normally considered an issue or option for post-baccalaureate students. As the range and importance of Masters education expand, this may be an issue to consider for the future.

Then, intriguingly, there is gender. We must become accustomed to situations in which a higher percentage of women than men seek higher education—the pattern is emerging in many parts of the world—but the female advantage in American study abroad programs goes well beyond this. Women consistently count for 65% of all participants, with only minor fluctuations over the past decade. This gender disparity relates, of course, to disciplines, with women populating language and humanities classes particularly, while playing a lesser role in low-participant areas like engineering. Besides mutually reinforcing variables, one wonders about other factors in play: are women still more open, as they seemed to be back in the 1920s, to the idea of additional polish or enhancement not directly tied to career goals? Do they still see opportunities for fun abroad that they cannot pursue as readily back home, whereas men can indulge more freely without leaving campus? Are they simply more globally aware, and if so why? Certainly the American enthusiasm about sending women into foreign study reflects a gender confidence and latitude that have not yet reached all societies around the world. But the reasons and the implications for the consequences of study abroad itself are not entirely clear.

Gender aside, a number of barriers, some rooted deeply in American society, others potentially more tractable, kept the glass half empty despite the impressive gains. Money mattered. We will turn shortly to specific funding issues in study abroad, but the bottom line was challenging to many students, often adding the cost of travel to standard tuition fees. Commuting students would have to count on new housing expenses as well. Some students who did venture abroad found themselves in unexpectedly deep financial trouble, and far more did not try. Some standardized programs soared well beyond tuition rates at public institutions. It was not strange, in this context, that many private institutions excelled in study abroad, with students already accustomed and able to pay substantial sums. Money also factored into work commitments. Many students, again particularly at public institutions, could not consider study abroad because they needed to retain a job. Add to this, again for many, family obligations—caring for an ailing parent or sibling—and practical obstacles could loom large.

These barriers do not, of course, largely explain disciplinary variation, though they might play some role. Unusual participation in study abroad by a disproportionate number of foreign language students is a no-brainer; one would hardly expect uniform interests across all disciplines. Low participation by scientists and, even more, technology students, and to some extent males more generally, remains troubling, however, particularly given the roles many of these people may be called upon to fill in American or global society later on. Two factors intertwine. First, the interests that draw students into these disciplines do not connect as readily to global issues as do those in the humanities and social sciences, so clear self-selection is involved in participation rates. But second, resistance by many faculty and departmental advisors, convinced that a set American curriculum simply *must* be pursued and that courses offered overseas cannot begin to measure up, creates a discouraging attitude and a host of very real difficulties for students who have to be able to count study abroad credits for the experience to make any sense academically but are impeded if not barred outright in doing so. Increasing sophistication in the science and technology offerings not only at European but also many Asian institutions may gradually dissipate American arrogance, but the breakthrough has not yet occurred. Global enrichment may make just as much sense to an engineer as to a history student, and may be at least as relevant to future professional goals and service. But the sense that only American programs really qualify in terms of disciplinary level, and the array of practical impediments to adjusting curricula and obtaining assurance that foreign credits will count, trumps the global imperative in the majority of cases by far.

* * *

Study abroad experts are obviously aware of the downsides to their recent success. Several national organizations have launched funding programs designed to compensate for the disparities in student interest or capacity. The Institute of International Education, for example, took over the Boren Fellowship program (originally launched in 1996) and also created the Central Europe Summer Research Institute, funded by the National Science Foundation; while both programs had special topics targets (the Boren aimed at critical languages), IIE administered both with great care for student diversity. Other programs, like the Gilman scholarships, could be even more explicitly directed toward minority students, with clients from historically black institutions like Spelman College. The Gilman program, established in 2000 and funded by the Department of State and administered by IIE, awarded 777 scholarships in 2006 to financially needy and academically accomplished American undergraduates from 323 institutions in the United States and Puerto Rico. IIE understandably trumpeted the program in terms of the promise of the students involved who, "unlike traditional study abroad students," reflect "the full diversity of our society."[13] A corporate grant allowed compensation in another direction: the Global Engineering Exchange enabled hundreds of engineering students from the United States and several other countries to study and work abroad at one of 70 participant universities; a Whitaker Foundation grant focused on graduate and postdoctoral students in biomedical engineering. Specific institutions developed other programs. Carnegie Mellon University, for example, had a longstanding arrangement with a leading technical university in Lausanne, Switzerland, allowing engineering and architecture students to spend a semester or a year taking courses that fit into the domestic major; there was strain involved, for students had to find time to pick up some French, and in many years local applicants fell short of target (compared to exchange participation from Lausanne), but at least there was an explicit attempt to meet the common curricular constraint.

Funding and curricular efforts were important, and there was some sign of increased attention. They obviously did not manage significantly to change the percentage mix of participant students. White, relatively affluent, social sciences and humanities majors dominated the participant pool, with only the growing number of students from management significantly changing the mix during the past decade. The good news, of course, was that the same categories at least kept up with overall growth; the less good news was that vast numbers of students were still effectively shut out by background, financial means, and the sometimes debatable constraints of lockstep domestic majors.

＊ ＊ ＊

Two other disparities also qualify enthusiasm for the undeniably impressive national stake in study abroad. The first involves target locations. Well before 2001 it became obvious that the traditional focus on Western Europe sold foreign study dramatically short in terms of its capacity to prepare individual American students, and through them a broader campus and national community, for the real forces of global existence in the 21st century. Yet, in 2006, slightly under 50% of all study abroad trips headed to one of five countries:

(in order) Britain (with over 14%), Italy, Spain, France, and Australia. Mexico was the leading country that might be labeled non-Western, with 4.5%, China, a rapid gainer with a 38% participant growth rate simply between 2005 and 2006 (though this partly occurred because of residual effects from the earlier ending of the SARS scare, not through a dramatic global awakening otherwise), headed the definitively non-Western list with 4%. Trailing at less than 1%, and not even in the top 20, was India, bafflingly, given the lower linguistic barriers and long Western links Indian society could offer.[14]

A host of factors entered into the sluggish relationship between study abroad and full global diversity. Fear of strangeness, and in some instances discomfort with perceived standard of living and dormitory amenities, surely played a role. Despite the importance of improving cultural and linguistic familiarity with the Middle East in terms of United States diplomatic and (arguably) business interests, no Middle Eastern country came close to the top 20. Even in India, where American students had less reason to feel themselves particular targets of hostility, study abroad activity lagged well behind European and Australian levels—probably because of less adaptability (or less perceived adaptability in the eyes of study abroad coordinators) to different kinds of hygiene and food arrangements. Curricular preparation played a role as well, along with different levels of recruitment effort from the countries involved. China's modest surge as a study abroad target reflected some explicit government initiatives (India was more laissez-faire in this regard) but above all the existence of area studies and, increasingly, language programs in many American colleges and universities. South Asian offerings were simply fewer and farther between, which left all but the most venturesome American students, and many whole study abroad offices, without the necessary orientation or inducement.

Language itself was an obvious barrier (despite the Indian anomaly): there were simply few American students capable of envisaging serious study in non-Western languages, and few enough interested even in tackling French (down to 7% of the study abroad total) or German (at 3.1% slightly behind China). Britain, Australia, New Zealand, Ireland and South Africa accounted for essentially 25% of foreign study participants, for obvious reasons.

Dominating all other factors, however, though consistent with several of them, was a continued interest in using study abroad to achieve some combination of humanistic, culturally nostalgic, and entertainment goals. Australia surged as a target (though with a noticeable drop-off by 2006) because it was safe, English speaking, and also by reputation academically not too demanding and a great place to party. The West European countries that ranked as top four destinations benefited from decades of study abroad experience, the sense that they would offer clear cultural enrichment (Italy's strength, at 12% in 2006, was particularly striking) and (to whatever extent) an expectation that they might provide some diverting latitudes in lifestyles. Several of the small college programs noted above, legitimately proud of their successful emphasis on study abroad, also however harbored a particular nostalgia for Western Europe as the core of humanistic study, not preventing but not very aggressively encouraging options elsewhere.

All of this was quite understandable, in terms of historical continuity in selection and motivation, and hardly an indictment of the gains accruing from study abroad. And changes were occurring, leading to a slightly expanding trickle of students heading to Asia and Latin America, and to a much lesser extent Africa. In 2006–7, Middle Eastern destinations gained 31% over the prior year, Asian destinations 26%, and over time these trends may reduce currently troubling disparities, but the encouraging trends cannot conceal the fact that less than 1% of all students in international programs now target the Middle East, only 4% Africa, and only 9% Asia. A tension persisted between what global proponents of programs urged in theory, and what actual targeting might yield in practice in terms of Americans with any experience in dealing with some of the regions almost certain to be of greatest significance in the nation's 21st century existence. It was difficult to adequately accelerate changes in venue, despite some encouraging signs.

Here too, national and international agencies, like the IIE, along with the more foresightful study abroad programs on individual campuses, tried to increase momentum with special arrangements and some monetary inducements (the recent surge in support for study in critical languages was a particularly important response). Another promising response, also gaining ground, involved coalitions among schools to boost enrollment in otherwise unsustainably small programs. Ironically, the surge of individual study abroad offices, as against the earlier amalgamations in some of the classic junior year abroad initiatives, has tended to balkanize many efforts—no problem, usually, when the target is Paris or Rome, where a single campus can generate adequate numbers. But more specialized programs, and particularly programs in some of the developing areas or situations with less common language requirements, can be another matter. Stanford University's Japanese program, drawing students from many American institutions, and several of the efforts of Kalamazoo College appeal well beyond single school confines, and there are other current examples. Princeton, as well as several universities in the Washington, D.C. area, have adopted an Israel-Palestine program, mounted by George Mason essentially as their own. Groupings of allied schools can help a lot here as well. The Colonial Academic Alliance (an offshoot of a 12-school athletic conference) has been working hard to pool resources, particularly urging each member school to identify a flagship opportunity that the other alliance members could not duplicate on their own. Other consortia efforts are developing as well, to deal with a real but potentially manageable problem. Even with imaginative organizational responses however, tastes and capacities continued to shift only slowly. Study abroad, viewed collectively, was hardly global.

The most interesting recent trend, a microcosm of the larger half-full or half-empty image, involved the proliferation of shorter programs, taking advantage of a few weeks during the summer or winter break. A large portion of the otherwise impressive increase in study abroad participants has come from the growing series of two- to three-week programs organized by eager study abroad offices: well over half of all study abroad students were involved in these programs in 2006–7, and the percentage was increasing steadily. Offerings of this sort loom particularly large for management students (including participants in MBA programs), many of whom have jobs or other commitments that would preclude longer stints; but a wide variety of students can be involved. Short durations raise questions automatically—one cynic, the international education officer in a national association, when asked about results, suggested that "at least they have to get a passport"—which already distinguishes short-termers from the average American student, but in obviously minimalist fashion. Short duration normally precludes significant language exposure—indeed, one of the attractions of the short trip is that presentations by foreigners, about local cultural or business conditions or even simple sightseeing, will be tailored for the group in question and presented in English. Brief trips also emphasize association with one's American colleagues, a feature heightened, in many programs, by tight scheduling and security concerns which minimize opportunities to wander off on one's own. The experience is international, but the degree of foreignness is, often, carefully doled out.[15]

A final growing interest, focused primarily though not exclusively on summer study but with longer durations than the two- to three-week visit, involves internship and service learning opportunities, which may or may not be directly associated with academic programs abroad. Individual American students are often inventive in exploring internships with foreign governments, businesses and NGOs, and there are some organized programs. Numbers are characteristically small, but the experiences can be invaluable.

* * *

The hopes attached to study abroad, and the urgent pleas for expansion, obviously assume measurable educational benefits, particularly in terms of increased global skills and sensitivities. Even concerns about inadequacies in current patterns—laments over the kinds of students who cannot usually participate, or pleas for a global distribution more in keeping with 21st century regional strengths and priorities—typically assume that if we could just do it better, just compensate for current deficiencies, even more notable expansions in global learning would occur. What, in fact, is the evidence?

Evaluation is complicated, of course, as experts immediately note, by the fact that study abroad efforts differ so widely. Even aside from highly varied durations—and we have relatively little assessment of program results from the short stints—it matters a great deal whether an experience involves a language other than English, whether it encourages participation in classes taught by foreign universities or features professors from one's school back home doing essentially what they usually do but in a different place. It would be folly to pretend that one can generalize about study abroad results.[16]

Though somewhat less commonly highlighted, the issue of individual idiosyncrasy also complicates outcomes. Personal quirks, diverse backgrounds, and variations in sheer luck inevitably generate some students who end up disliking their host society and renouncing internationalism in favor of real or imagined back-home values. The rejecters may be part of an otherwise successful program, but simply were inadequately prepared for strangeness or had the misfortune of encountering an unsympathetic host family (a not uncommon experience in the many programs, even some of those with short durations, which proudly house students with willing local families, whose motivations inevitably vary from international hospitality to service-for-a-fee).

On the plus side, in terms of appreciating international experiences on the average, study abroad has benefited from massive efforts at assessment over the past ten years, mostly applying to American students but with an increasingly international literature as well. Not all aspects of contemporary patterns have been checked out as thoroughly as one might like, but we have a wealth of apparently reliable, often repeatedly confirmed, information.[17]

Evaluation has been directed particularly at foreign language acquisition results—an important feature but, obviously, not something that involves the majority of students abroad at this point, who head either to English-speaking destinations or take short courses in more exotic destinations. But where foreign language is involved, more than optimistic speculation can now support the conclusion that, with only a few surprises, study abroad really contributes to learning.

The most important news is that most serious exposure to foreign languages on a trip abroad has positive results. It is important to know that detailed evaluation literature exists—indeed, it is growing steadily—but not all educational administrators will care to get bogged down in details. The largely positive outcome may, for many, be the main point. Most interesting, if unsurprising, is the conclusion that significant foreign language experience, over some duration and hopefully with some immersion periods in which students do not normally operate in English at all, deepens the ability to handle nuance and context far better than standard classroom study allows. In assessment-ese, "students who have been abroad may be expected to acquire a range of native-like sociolinguistic variables" and "meta-cognitive awareness of sociolinguistic differences and potentially conflicting pragmatic demands." They gain a better sense, than do classroom learners, about what language choices fit particular settings, attuned among other things to nuances such as gender variables among interlocutors.[18]

There are some downsides. Some students become overconfident, again compared to classroom learners, thinking they know more about appropriate choices than they do. Some actually acquire stubborn errors, for example, through deviant grammar use or over generalizing certain forms, of which they are unaware. And of course there is a high degree of individual variation, according to some studies more than occurs as a result of conventional classroom settings, with some students forging ahead with striking rapidity but others, not necessarily consciously, digging in their heels against the sheer amount of strain involved particularly in an immersion experience. Another downside from a recent study, extremely important given the spate of short-term programs now current: language learning may be impeded by well-intentioned efforts to have American students speak to each other in the local language.[19]

Assessments also reveal some disagreements in results, along with the standard scholarly pleas for ever more research, particularly about the more subtle gains of more advanced students. Noticeably important, for the study abroad enterprise as a whole, are varied findings about the importance of prior preparation. Some recent studies conclude that benefits from study abroad are greatly enhanced when students have considerable language experience already. These studies point particularly to grammar, which may not improve greatly with international experience if students do not have solid structures in advance. But other studies urge that international exposure may be particularly beneficial for students with initially lower language proficiency (though some preparation, it is uniformly agreed, is essential). Some differences here may reflect the language in question: assessments are most sanguine about relative novices in languages like French or German, whereas the insistence on considerable prior preparation rings loudest in cases like Russian.[20]

Still, the overall finding of substantial benefit remains the key point, however unsurprising. "When compared to students who have not had the opportunity to live and study abroad, these students appear to speak with greater ease and confidence, realized by a greater abundance of speech, spoken at a faster rate, and characterized, correspondingly, by fewer dysfluent-sounding silent and/or filled pauses."[21] The students can handle more complex thoughts, can repair ineptness as they speak—more like what native-speakers manage routinely, and they have a wider range of communication strategies which enable them better to adapt to varied situations. Study abroad helps.

But what about non-linguistic aspects?, a vital point for that majority of students for whom study abroad is either not intended to have much linguistic result or where periods of study are simply too short to have much anticipatable impact, save perhaps in whetting appetites for more experience in the future or, in some cases, generating a frustration that several years of high school and college study have had such meager results. Specifics for a wider assessment reflect the hopes now vested in foreign study programs, seeking to identify increases in cultural awareness and flexibility, including cross-cultural tolerance, and improvements in personal confidence and autonomy.

And, not surprisingly, most program assessments find the broader goals advanced, even by relatively short periods of study in not particularly demanding cultural settings. A Southern Mississippi British Studies course for business students, for example, generated a 12% gain in flexibility and openness, and a 17% improvement in capacity to perceive cultural differences. More personal qualities, like independence and self-confidence, also moved upward but (probably predictably, perhaps even desirably) at somewhat lower rates.[22]

Broader evaluations generated similar results, in finding that participants in study abroad programs acquire "global mindedness"—awareness, as one student put it, that the world is a big place and that purely American assumptions do not capture its reality. There are some cautions, however. A few surveys reveal no change, for example, in a group of Ohio State agricultural and environmental students who participated in study abroad. Examination of some Kent State students after a semester in Switzerland found only a slight increase in interest in international affairs. Even the Southern Mississippi study, arguably, revealed surprisingly modest changes from what is, after all, a considerable investment of time and resources. One ambitious survey, dealing not only with study abroad participants but a control group back home, yielded slightly more optimistic results: gains in specific knowledge about relevant geography and social and economic conditions in the foreign setting improved strikingly; overall orientations—where the key goals rest—were more sluggish, but there were small shifts, for example, in interest in foreign newspapers, and in issues being debated at the United Nations, and a willingness to consider foreign travel in future. Of course students varied, with a minority reporting no resultant change; overall, however, the evaluators were confident that their findings were strongly positive in terms both of knowledge and of global outlook.[23]

There is a possibility, even amid this optimism, that study abroad impact has diminished somewhat over time. Comparing diverse research protocols is risky, and many studies involve very small sample size in any event. It is nevertheless interesting that a 1990 assessment, dealing with American students from a variety of institutions studying in Western Europe, showed much sharper increases in attention to international affairs than more recent surveys reveal. The proliferation of short courses might account for different impacts, along perhaps with deteriorations in prior preparation as the clientele broadens somewhat.[24]

It has also been suggested that American students are finding study abroad a somewhat more jolting experience than they expected, even as the popularity of the opportunity continues to gain. Evidence here is slender but intriguing. A recent comparison of American students in Australia, and their Australian counterparts studying abroad in the United States and elsewhere, reveals a fascinating difference. Australian students, with a rather amorphously defined sense of national identity in terms of prior upbringing and socialization, rather readily adapt to differences in foreign settings and enjoy the experience of broadening horizons. Americans, in contrast, with a much more intense understanding of and commitment to national identity, more easily feel lost outside the home environment. Compounding this general disorientation is specific shock—and here recent conditions definitely enter in—at the hostility they encounter to things American and particularly toward American foreign policy. "I had no idea that people had this view of Americans, that we thought that we were just so great and we just dominate and are in charge. We're very snotty and rude and get our way. And that was kind of a shock to me. So the whole time I was there, I tried not to portray that image as much as I could because I think that's sort of terrible." The result, a defensive posture, not only enhanced a sense of disconnect, but discouraged movement toward a more global understanding—again, in marked contrast to what Australian students gained. Add a final component, the fact that Australians frequently knew more about the United States than the American visitors did, and the sense of constraint was complete. Americans reached Australia, in other words, with a limited global imagination, and then spent so much time negotiating their beleaguered national identity that they learned less than might have been expected—about Australia or the world in general. To be sure, some American students who select Australia, seeking good times and comforting English, may not be pick of the litter in terms of study abroad overall; and there was no denial that the Australian experience generated some gains. Again, however, the cautionary note sounds strongly.[25]

The claim that study abroad can be a life-changing experience remains valid for enough individual students, arguably, to make the whole effort worthwhile. The finding that, on average, study abroad does broaden horizons, and where relevant improve linguistic capacity, is also important. A recent survey adds to the mix: the 2007 report from the National Survey of Student Engagement (NSSE) emphasizes how study abroad correlates, though moderately, with higher order thinking and reflective learning and with self-reported gains both in general education and personal-social development. Students who studied overseas engaged more often in educationally relevant activities once back home, and felt they gained more from college than their peers. (There is of course a chicken-egg issue here: are reflective students more likely to choose study abroad in the first place, or is their distinctiveness really a consequence of the experience? Perhaps a bit of both.) While the finding that students who lived with foreign nationals, in homes or dormitories, reported the greatest gains in integrative and reflective learning was predictable enough, length of time spent abroad did not affect the frequency with which students used deep learning approaches once back on the American campus. This most recent data point provides some unexpected support for the otherwise under-assessed short programs that are becoming increasingly widespread.[26]

We do know, of course, what makes some programs more effective than others by most criteria. Programs with at least a semester duration, programs that immerse students in interactions with locals, housing them individually with families and prompting them to study in a real foreign institution—these have real impact, though the recent NSSE outcomes resulted in the good word even for short stints overseas. Other programs may indeed help, may certainly be better than nothing as the experience (hopefully) continues to democratize among American students. But there is a distance, often, between goals and realities, and a tendency, on the part of very well-meaning leaders, to overclaim. Overall assessments require balance, helping to place study abroad in global efforts more generally and not obfuscating, through excessive promotional praise, the need to seek best practices rather than accepting any effort as satisfactory.

* * *

Study abroad offices define many of the same problems and opportunities that the overall data on the contemporary American experience suggest. They also, however, have their own specific issues—amid great institutional variety—and in one key area they typically face tensions that easily put many of them at odds with student needs.

Administrators in study abroad programs come from a variety of backgrounds. Historically, early staffing focused on faculty from languages programs, but as the language emphasis has declined in favor of recruiting wider student pools and emphasizing broader global awareness goals, this source has declined in relevance. Many program officers had a vivid study abroad experience of their own, and certainly their level of commitment to the general goals of internationalization, and toward increasing the range and success of study abroad itself, is very high. Many, of course, do have foreign language capacity and most are widely traveled. Beneath directorship levels, staffing inevitably focuses on younger personnel, some of them from international backgrounds, who can directly help students figure out what programs make most sense and what they will encounter; but pay levels are not high and there is considerable turnover. It is also true, for better or worse, that there is little systematic training for program officers; most learn from their own background and on the job, though a few higher education programs are at least moving into this gap. Some staffing also emanates from general administrative pools, not necessarily bringing any particular international expertise to bear, at least initially. Nevertheless, it is fair to conclude that levels of dedication are considerable, but ranges of competence and experience vary widely.

National associations provide opportunities for exchange of information and heighten the nascent professionalism in the field. Particularly important is NAFSA, the National Association of International Educators. This group addresses a variety of topics concerning international education, but study abroad issues are high on its list. NAFSA holds regular conferences and also seeks to provide data on some of the most pressing problems such as identifying financial aid for minority students interested in foreign study. The Forum on Education Abroad and the Association of International Education Administrators are two other vigorous organizations in this field. Supplementing national groups are statewide linkages of study abroad offices, particularly of course among public universities, and also some regional linkage. Virginia and New Jersey, for example, have relatively active networks, again exchanging information and, in the New Jersey case, helping to pool study abroad opportunities among participant institutions.

Study abroad offices are variously organized, in relation to the college or university as a whole. Not surprisingly, the important handful of committed liberal arts colleges do the best job of integrating study abroad into central administrative and curricular planning. Faculty discuss study abroad requirements and options as part of the overall structure of study, and directors of study abroad offices work closely with other administration officials, sometimes as part of a broader international education office. Among larger institutions, the University of Minnesota stands out for its integration efforts.

More typical, however, at the larger private universities and certainly in public institutions, is a considerable degree of decentralization. This may have some advantages, in allowing particularly entrepreneurial directors to do their own thing without too much worried oversight, and also to respond to initiatives by imaginative individual faculty, but there are clear drawbacks as well. Decentralization complicates the relationship of programs emanating from the study abroad office, with faculty in the major programs. Many global offices have to negotiate for each program with relevant departments, seeking some academic credit without which many students cannot be expected to sign on. This is fine with well-established offerings, but for new or less common endeavors it imposes a considerable burden on the administrator and places him or her entirely at the pleasure of individual academic units. Some units, in this situation, will simply hold out, uninterested in encouraging their students and eager to husband precious credits for the home team. Occasionally, seeking some special advantage, individual units may even mount separate or rival programs. Degree of centralization, and the extent of shared curricular purpose in the institution as a whole, are key issues. Obviously, entrepreneurial offices have prospered despite the barriers, but there are disconnects that may warrant further attention. Obviously also, even amid decentralization, indeed perhaps particularly in decentralized conditions, the study abroad director must maintain close relationships with the academic administration of the college or university as a whole, making sure, through regular reports, that the key officials (including deans regardless of specialty) understand recent achievements and problems in this vital program area.

* * *

Even more pressing is the issue of funding. While many individual programs handle funding issues openly and carefully, there are many divisions over funding issues that reflect a surprising amount of disagreement over study abroad standards, and in some instances arguably a lack of real commitment to appropriate goals. The obvious tension, between the fact that study abroad operations are not inexpensive and the need to reduce financial barriers to the experience as much as possible, particularly given the pronounced disparities of access depending on students' socioeconomic backgrounds, is not the only problem in the field. Recent trends in exchange rate, with an ever-weakening dollar, further complicate the challenge.

Study abroad programs do cost money. Considerable staffing is needed to monitor wide-ranging programs, deal with participant faculty, and of course address student inquiries and applications. George Mason University, sending about 1100 students abroad annually in recent years, employs eleven people in its operation, and while staff salaries in this field tend to be low the resultant outlay is not modest. Ample travel budgets are essential as well, so that the director can explore new options and check existing programs and so that staffers can, as needed, troubleshoot or simply visit various sites. Program costs must, as well, cover the salaries and travel of faculty mentors. On the other hand, actual academic costs almost everywhere are lower than those in the United States, which creates a useful margin that can be devoted to some of the extra expenses (though with student travel, of course, added on top).

Only a few American institutions cover many of the expenses of the study abroad operation from the regular operating budget; most depend heavily, and some entirely, on program earnings, though there seems to be some variation in how rigorously annual income and expense statements are scrutinized. A few liberal arts colleges, where study abroad looms so large as an expected educational component, do seek to reduce extra burdens on students, building in the resultant costs of course into overall (and usually rather high) tuition charges. Public universities do not venture this luxury, at most trying to find some scholarship money for particular students based on need or on a desire to encourage more innovative programs or destinations. This means, usually, some reliance on a per-student fee beyond regular tuition.

At some private colleges and universities, at the opposite extreme, there has been an implicit attempt to make money from study abroad operations or at least to sustain tuition revenues despite the gap between normal domestic levels and what many foreign programs actually charge. (A similar disparity may apply in public institutions where out-of-state students are concerned, with their own higher tuition rates, though the problem is less acute.) A variety of decisions are involved. Some universities display great concern about loss of tuition revenues, and so charge students the full rate regardless of the actual cost of a specific foreign program. Some try to privilege their own programs, granting scholarship continuation, for example, only for these offerings, and some allow no scholarship aid at all regardless of need. A 2007 study showed 74% of the 100 institutions surveyed maintain need-based aid for their own programs, 61% to approved programs operated by others. Only 35% of all colleges let students pay a program provider directly, the rest insisting on payment of regular tuition and fees.[27]

The result of these various policies can be some absolutely whopping fees, based mainly on home institution tuition: thus a regular international student enrolling at the University of Bologna pays that institution only $1740 per year in tuition and fees, but students attending on a non-exchange basis for Indiana University pay $20,200. Boston College charges $35,250 for a year's tuition at Peking University in Beijing, up from a (Chinese) published rate for international students of $3,420.

Not surprisingly, in these circumstances, a number of students make individual arrangements and simply take off on their own. The results may be less than satisfactory, however, when the home institution refuses to give credit (some simply will not give any credit for programs that compete with their own; others simply balk at credit requests that come in ex post facto.) And of course financial aid is usually out of the question for the self-selected option, though not infrequently the savings in tuition more than compensate.

Financial issues are sometimes compounded by for-profit organizations that offer their own programs, substituting for college operations while kicking back money and honorific appointments for institutions and their officials who subscribe. Thus according to one report the American Institute for Foreign Study offers college administrators some free travel for every 15 students who sign on, along with a 5% rebate on the fees that students pay. Many colleges appreciate the service (even aside from the perks) because it takes care of burdensome arrangements in areas such as security and housing; in some cases, recruitment is left to the outside agencies as well, another saving in time and money. At their best, the private organizations can offer an unusual variety of sites and special features, because of the possibility of pooling students from many different institutions. Critics attack not only the high fees but the extent to which exclusivity reduces student options, in terms of the range and variety of programs available. It is not clear how widely the various outside organizations are used—there may be as many as a hundred of them—but major programs, such as the University of California system, are involved in special arrangements. On the other hand, a number of study abroad offices resolutely shun the private contractors because of the concern about fees and in some cases dubious ethical practices. The recent glare of publicity may force additional decisions in this area.[28]

Short courses, now proliferating so hugely, raise fewer problems of financial gouging—assuming they are worthwhile. They normally involve a fee for transportation, food, and housing, plus enough to cover a faculty mentor and a fee to the study abroad organization—and some rates involve bargain negotiations that make the trip little more costly than an individually arranged vacation. Some institutions then charge a bit extra where credit is sought, but the result—for example, under $3000 for eight days in Western Europe with academic instruction as well as tours—does not conceal any massive markup.

Financial concerns can also be modified, of course, through direct student exchanges. Most exchange programs, where students at an American and a foreign institution essentially trade places, tend to reduce costs, because the American university does not lose a tuition-paying customer. American students simply pay their standard rate, or in some cases a bit less (though at public universities still with the out-of-state coverage maintained—there are limits to generosity), allowing them to go abroad while someone from their host institution takes the domestic slot instead. Costs still range higher than what international students pay on their own, even though there are no special cultural outings as in more conventional study abroad programs, but of course credit arrangements and recruitment costs are assured. On a broader scale, the International Student Exchange Program, grouping 275 colleges in 39 countries, arranges similar switches; but only about 2,400 students used the service in 2006–7. Indeed, the big problem with exchange programs is the disparity between American seekers and their foreign counterparts. This is a huge issue in international education today, significantly denting mutuality—as many foreign officials note. Far more overseas institutions are eager to arrange exchanges than there are American students interested in the slots, particularly of course when courses will be offered in languages other than English. Usually, only handfuls of students a year, from any one American college or university, can be recruited for exchange programs in Asia or Africa. This limits the potential of such arrangements, including their role in keeping costs down, while imposing real cautions on American institutions lest they overcommit on promising exchanges with interesting and worthy international counterparts, only to find themselves coming up embarrassingly short. This is where reciprocity agreements may need to be something other than one-to-one student exchange. More creative options can be negotiated such as student exchange in return for researchers/technical assistance.

Specific circumstances raised new funding concerns in 2008, as domestic economic downturn combined with the weakening status of the dollar vis-à-vis euro, pound, and other foreign currencies. Student capacity measurably flagged, at least for some programs, and it was unclear how long this challenge would persist. Some institutions, admittedly in toughening budget times of their own, needed to consider some additional financial aid or other incentives to keep any sort of momentum going.

Overall, study abroad finances clearly warrant a more careful and sympathetic assessment by many American schools. Arrangements are too often ill-considered, too often counterproductive in terms of dealing with the real issues in the field—particularly in terms of accessibility. Study abroad officials, not surprisingly, would love to see problems reduced by increased investment, either from home institutions or the federal government or private donors. Even without this recourse, even while assuming break-even requirements, some of the more egregious costs could be reduced without undue risk. Priorities need to be established with greater intentionality.

* * *

Funding and curricular negotiations hardly exhaust the tasks of study abroad administrators, and this is really the reason that formal organization, rather than ad hoc arrangements by individual faculty or programs is normally essential.

Marketing obviously requires imagination and energy, and foreign study offices are typically very active in preparing materials and soliciting student interest. Security concerns loom large, as do related issues of university legal liability; this is an area demanding attention *before* trips occur. Security oversight involves awareness of changing political conditions; not too long ago, for example, India raised some anxieties because of religious conflicts. Any office, particularly since 9/11, has to balance appropriate attention to political climate with awareness that some official sources of advice, particularly from the ever-nervous State Department, measurably err on the side of excessive caution in warning Americans away from certain areas. Besides evaluating climate, a study abroad office must develop contingency plans, particularly toward evacuating students and faculty in cases of emergency. Happily, surprisingly few major difficulties have developed in recent years, though a few apparently criminal attacks on individual American students in Central America have been troubling. More commonly, arrangements to deal with students who fall ill or face unexpected problems back home actually tax the responsiveness of foreign study arrangements.

Few study abroad programs screen students individually, though of course they must be available to inquiring students to provide information and encouragement. Most offices use general criteria, such as minimal grade point averages, to impose some selectivity, hoping of course that these represent some test of seriousness of purpose as well as basic academic ability. Relevant prerequisites, particularly in the language area, may also apply. Some particular programs—George Mason University, for example, has an ambitious summer program taking students to Israel and Palestine for work in conflict analysis—encourage the faculty director to interview students before accepting their applications.

An increasing number of issues revolve around individual students with disabilities, given current American legislation on the subject. Arrangements may need to be made for blind students, for example. In some instances difficult questions about additional fees result as well.

Selection of faculty for particular programs is not straightforward. Offices must decide, in the first place, how many programs must have a faculty mentor, as opposed to sending students into operations run by other institutions, including of course foreign universities themselves. Obvious tensions can arise between the advantages of individual faculty guidance and responsibility, and some loss in range and flexibility as well as resultant costs. When faculty are to be selected, another, more specific tension arises between academic expertise and teaching talent, plus some expectation that a study abroad opportunity should reward loyal service, and the fact that the functions of a faculty sponsor have little to do with pedagogical success back home. Faculty overseeing a program abroad may do a bit of teaching, if only informally, but their real and varied duties more specifically involve chaperoning, troubleshooting, figuring out what to do with students who encounter problems or turn out to be misfits, sometimes serving as tour guides. Whatever the selection process, study abroad offices must provide considerable training for faculty mentors and must maintain close contact. Every program will have some stories of faculty who proved inept or outright irresponsible.

Arranging appropriate housing for students (except for the shortest trips, where hotel or hostel accommodations may suffice) can be a considerable challenge. Many study abroad sites have contractors who can arrange housing with families, but they vary greatly in quality and oversight. Occasionally, an apparently satisfactory agreement collapses, with students left with unsuitable accommodations or hosts. Here is another occasion when study abroad administrators must be available for a repair visit during the course of the program, for problems can accumulate that exceed the organizational or contractual ability of a faculty mentor. A more programmatic decision involves how many students can be housed with a single host family. Some American programs allow two or three students per eager host, which simplifies arrangements and can save money; other programs insist that a single student per family is the rule, because otherwise any real integration with local culture is seriously impeded by American camaraderie.

Not surprisingly, evaluating the quality of an individual study abroad operation involves a mixture of considerations, both practical and principled. The Forum on Education Abroad offers useful facilities in this area. Service to students as (dreaded word) customers, and sometimes rather demanding customers, is one measure. Individual trips may misfire, beyond the reasonable control of administrators back home (and occasionally, refunds must be offered to respond to legitimate complaints), but on average students must feel that they were given appropriate advance information and appropriate attention on the trip itself, so that pledges were fulfilled—promised courses materialized, with the credits that had been stipulated; side trips if advertised were available—and that material conditions and mentoring were satisfactory. A commitment to careful and transparent financial arrangements is essential, and recent disclosures only deepen the requirements here. Additional fees, beyond normal tuition at least at public universities, are unavoidable in many cases, but it is vital to avoid excess—in a situation where cost issues loom so large in student motivations.

Prudent and equitable administration is only a starting point, however. A range of decisions test the thoughtfulness of study abroad officials, particularly around a commitment (within the confines of the varied individual programs) to maximize student contact with local cultures and global issues. No single formula can legitimately be imposed over questions like how many students to house with a host family or how much shopping or sightseeing must be built into an experience to make it attractive; but it is appropriate to make sure that policies are thought through with an eye on basic educational goals. Adequacy of assessment is another legitimate test, with student evaluations carefully prepared and their results publicized and explicitly discussed with the overall academic administration. Imaginativeness is the final, inherently demanding requirement. A good study abroad office, in contemporary conditions, does not rest with a few staple programs, but constantly tries to reach out (insofar as faculty collaborations permit) to additional types of students and, above all, constantly develops new sites, to stretch student interests beyond the West European and antipodal staples.

* * *

Individual offices do not, of course, stand alone in dealing with the current issues in the field. The practical demands on administrator time and the obvious constraints of funding make it essential that wider collaborations supplement the capacities of single-institution programs. Indeed, a further measure of the quality of individual programs involves the willingness and initiative in the collaborative area—including the capacity to send students to programs outside direct institutional control, when the result best serves student interest and educational needs.

The adequacy of the overall mix of advocates in study abroad is worth some consideration. As indicated, the pendulum may have swung too far toward separate programs with built-in interests toward exclusivity. The existence of umbrella organizations, headed by the IIE, aids greatly in larger advocacy. Coalitions that can provide additional options to students, without a massive profit motive, seem to be on the rise as well. There are ample opportunities, certainly, for shared information about best practices and funding sources.

Coordination remains an issue nevertheless, particularly in helping further to address issues such as imbalances in access and interest and the need to persuade larger faculty groups to build study abroad options into their curricular planning and advising.

* * *

Study abroad is a work in progress. It is, on balance, an important contributor to global education, but sober assessment suggests that its results are not always as impressive as its supporters imply or hope—there are breakthrough gains for individuals, but more incremental results on average—and the modest numbers involved raise real concerns. Clearly, foreign study must be only part of a richer mix of global education efforts except on those relatively few, relatively special liberal arts campuses where they become part of regular curricular fare. There are, as well, a number of specific issues to be addressed by American higher education collectively, beginning with the tension between short-term institutional financial self-interest and any real commitment to maximizing opportunities. The exchange options must gain greater attention.

Continued change is virtually inevitable. A host of agencies, on individual campuses and collectively, have a clear momentum toward further growth, and the gains over the past decade have been truly impressive. Trajectories toward modifying some of the classic locations of study abroad are also encouraging, though still somewhat tentative in terms of sheer numbers.

Technology provides opportunities to capture a few elements of study abroad—the experience of international classrooms and contacts with foreign students—through electronically shared course segments and projects. This falls well short of the less tangible benefits of interaction with a culture, but it deserves encouragement for students and programs where literal study abroad is difficult. Coordination here is challenging, but the opportunities deserve consideration not only as a global curriculum item but as part of a study abroad agency broadly construed.

Some authorities hope for further breakthroughs in more classic study abroad efforts, based mainly on proposals for more extensive federal funding. Funding sources have increased over the past decade, and federal officials are not bashful in pointing them out. In 2007 the State Department, touting a "wide range of successful activities," highlighted the Fulbright program for undergraduates, the Gilman Scholarships which reach out to students from lower income and minority groups, and the new National Security Languages Initiative. And there are proposals for more, with legislation introduced to expand financial support as the best means of helping American students deal with the global imperatives of their time and their future. Some tension exists, obviously, between the strong strategic languages interests of some of the best-funded programs, and the more general goals of contemporary study abroad;

and prospects for serious additions to the funding base are unclear at best. But this is an area to monitor for the future.

Other important initiatives rest in the hands of colleges and international offices themselves. A key opportunity involves framing the study abroad experience more adequately in terms of prior preparation for students, along with academic follow-up on return home; both the befores and afters could well include relevant foreign language training and usage, but more besides. In 2007, for example, Mt. Holyoke College, with over 40% of its students already engaged in some kind of foreign study at some point during their four years, unveiled an ambitious plan to expand the pool of participants further and link training more fully to the overall curriculum regardless of major. The plan included new financial incentives, going well beyond the common belief that private schools can assist students with their travel without raising tuitions, given the gap between domestic charges and average foreign tuition; now, charges would more closely approximate actual program costs, and efforts to expand exchange arrangements would contribute to financial moderation as well. Internship opportunities would be fostered, following networking models available from places like Yale and Oregon State.[29] Above all, intensive advising would guide students in relevant course choice before the study abroad experience, while helping them plan to take account of the impact of the experience on course selection later on. Students are to be encouraged to develop portfolios concerning their experience, both verbal and visual, to help cement the experience and encourage further reflection. The goal, which the new plan recognized was already shared by other institutions particularly among liberal arts colleges, was to make study abroad an integral part of undergraduate education, but beyond this, to orchestrate a "quantum leap" in the learning that resulted from the foreign experience.[30]

Obviously, as the Mt. Holyoke discussion suggests, forward movement can be built into the study abroad experience not only by increasing numbers of participants or even expanding the available sites beyond Western Europe, but in promoting wider enthusiasms among faculty and encouraging new links to the overall collegiate learning environment. Limitations will persist, and short of some unanticipated funding miracle there must be caution about relying too heavily on study abroad to meet global educational needs for American students overall. But the experience has met some key tests over time and it can be developed further.

A final confirmation of the importance of foreign study arrives through the well-known flattery of imitation. Partly because of the American example, assumptions about the educational benefits of studying abroad, not primarily to advance technical knowledge but to promote global awareness, spread increasingly among industrial societies by the early 21st century. The European Union, with its special motivations to promote international harmony through non-national study, massively promoted cross-border university attendance throughout its territory through the Erasmus program. Excursions from Australia and New Zealand have already been noted. Japanese and Korean universities began to promote not simply exchanges for small numbers of students, with counterpart institutions in Asia, Europe and North America, but full semester abroad requirements for certain categories. Even short courses were encouraged, despite their limitations. St. Petersburg State University sent groups of political science majors for two- or three-week courses on American culture and institutions, at a few institutions in the United States, complete with an accompanying faculty member. And while most programs operated in a foreign language, usually English, even that was not always required. Moscow State University, building on the resources of the new Russian upper middle class, opened a branch in Geneva, with instruction in Russian and only modest forays into additional training in French. Aside from the European Union's programs, the movement was modest still; only a few elite Korean universities, for example, moved very far. Numbers involved paled before the much larger volume of international students seeking specialized training in science, technology or engineering. Still, the growing perception that the mere fact of exposure to academically organized travel might be helpful in a global environment confirmed, and increasingly rivaled, the longer-standing impulses in the United States. To the extent that study abroad from outside the United States more commonly drew students who had broader linguistic talents, and in some cases greater flexibility in terms of material conditions and less burdensome tuition rates, what had once been an American strength might prove increasingly competitively challenged. Here too, there was every reason to take a new look at making the most of study abroad opportunities as a key part of global education in the United States.

6

International Students and
Global Education

The headlines blared, late in 2007, not only in international education circles but in the national media: the number of foreign students in the United States had finally risen above 2001 figures.[1] (Note: foreign students are consistently called international, to reduce the strangeness implied in the word foreign, a revealing bit of political correctness in this global age.) International student levels had taken a massive hit through combinations of fears about security issues and about xenophobic American reactions after 9/11, and the very real visa hurdles imposed after the same tragedy. But now they seemed to be bouncing back. The 2007 achievement was real, but it raised at least three questions—which in turn underlie this chapter, and which, amid a number of very practical concerns, demand attention from academic administrators.

First, what combination of strategies (on the part of American institutions) and motivation (on the part of internationals) helped account for the rebound—and are there lessons in this combination for even greater future success?

Second, did we have as many international students as we should (most knowledgeable administrators would answer this one with a resounding no, even given their pride in the rebound), and if not, why not, and what can we do about the gap between desirable levels and current realities? Dealing with this question also requires attention to the growing amount of competition from other countries, to which the United States as a whole (some individual institutional initiatives aside) is responding only half-heartedly.

Third, why should we want international students? What relationship do these students have, and what relationship should they have, to other aspects of global education? How can answers to this set of questions help organize not only further efforts to gain more international students in future, but also more imaginative programs to utilize them more effectively, for their purposes and for American global education goals alike?

International students in American colleges and universities might; at first blush, seem simply a counterpart to American study abroad—their yin to our yang. In fact, international students raise a host of different issues, from administrative structure to funding to the questions about basic purpose. More foreign students seek American education than vice versa (in terms of

American study abroad), but their motivations are different and their relationship to overall international education more complex.

This is a special moment in American recruitment and treatment of international students, with interest still high but competition rising and barriers still substantial in the wake of new American global fears. The result is an opportune, possibly even a crucial, moment to take stock of what American higher education is doing and where it should seek to head in future.

* * *

The early 21st-century context for international student recruitment has been changing rapidly, and while some trends continued to benefit the United States the rise of new challenges was even more obvious—despite the numerical successes international education groups trumpeted in 2007.

There were two helpings of good news. First, American higher education retained tremendous prestige around the world. More international students assumed the quality of American colleges and universities than was true for any other area—the only key rivals, in terms of global recognition, were the old prestige universities in the United Kingdom. While many foreign students played ranking games when looking at American schools, easily identifying Harvard or Stanford and sometimes having difficulties picking out a wider range, the fact was that even middle-ranked American schools often enjoyed surprisingly high levels of prestige abroad. Published ratings in China, for example, listed a number of American universities in the world's top 250 that had a more modest standing back home. Reasons for this prestige—even in societies now profoundly opposed to American foreign policy—were varied, and not always in full harmony with the aspirations of American schools themselves. The link to American power and economic success was obvious, even as the national economy faltered in global competition. Specific fields enjoyed particular clout: international students and leaders alike readily turned to engineering, including information technology, and management, at the expense of the broader purposes of American higher education particularly in the area of liberal arts and the humanities. But general prestige was considerable as well, even if the goals of many international students were less broad than thoughtful American educators might wish.[2]

The second piece of good news involved the rapid expansion of the numbers of international students seeking opportunities to study abroad, and the increasing ability of many of these students to pay reasonably steep tuition fees. The rapid growth of the middle classes in places like China and India, given the economic surge of the early 21st century and sheer population size, easily outstripped educational access at home. China committed to provide university slots for 15% of its college-age population, but this still left many reasonably well-qualified students, whose parents had some funds for tuition, unaccounted for. The same was true in India, where university applications soared beyond the capacities of home institutions. Prestige factors entered into demand as well. Many students sought admission to the top schools in their countries, but if their applications failed, given steep competition, they might prefer to seek education abroad over settling for second- or third-ranked institutions back home. This status quest was a powerful driver in South Korea. Here, there were actually more domestic slots than there were students, given a large higher education establishment and low population growth. But opportunities at top schools, like Seoul National or Korea University, were limited, and many students found foreign degrees—particularly, American degrees—preferable to a lesser domestic choice. For the moment, at least, the appetite for foreign study was growing rapidly, particularly in Asia.[3]

But there were generous helpings of bad news, as well. American visa requirements stiffened in the wake of the 9/11 terrorist attacks, and the new complexities and uncertainties reduced real access for many aspirant international students, and annoyed or offended many others. Visa requirements were cumbersome, now involving a need for a personal interview at an American consulate and, often, a second visit to pick up materials if successful. Interviewees were grilled on English language skills, academic qualifications, and adequacy of financial resources, in ways that many found adversarial and others, though more patient, found intimidating, particularly amid fledgling linguistic capacities—facing a demanding consular officer, often either bored or eager to make sure that a student terrorist did not slip through on his watch, was not the best occasion for a first use of English before a native speaker. Sheer cost (there were administrative fees beyond the visa itself), as well as bureaucratic nuisance, kept many foreign students away, particularly if they lived at a distance from consular services, and significant numbers were denied outright. Horror stories circulated about whimsical decisions and outright nastiness on the part of beleaguered American officials. Many students were denied visas with no clear reasons given, with no definable differences from applicants who were successful. Complexity increased for many students who did gain entry but then, returning home for a family visit, found that continued access to the United States required new applications and might be denied outright.

The horror stories here had real basis in fact: almost every major American university knew students from Asia or Russia who lost a semester as they tried to return to their programs after a Christmas break, and again, some who failed to get back at all. For several years, some admitted students felt that the only safe bet was not to risk home visits at all, not a pleasant prospect. Add to the basic visa issues the bad treatment many foreign visitors received at the hands of customs officials in American airports, and concern about xenophobia and safety within the United States, and the prestige of American education could readily dim. Particular incidents of visa denial or expulsion on arrival at a U.S. airport made front-page news in many places, particularly in the Middle East.

Stories about problems doubtless outstripped reality, though reality was difficult enough, but there was no question that American policies kept the number of international students far lower than would otherwise have been the case, from 2001 onward. And, despite urgent representations from universities and higher education associations, there was no sign of significant change.[4]

Into this context came the other piece of bad news: the rapid increase of competitive efforts from the United Kingdom, the European Union and Australia. These were societies, it might be noted, that also faced terrorism threats, but that responded far more flexibly than did the United States. Visas were simply easier to obtain, and the societies involved supported more strenuous recruitment efforts. The aggressive efforts of Australian universities were particularly noteworthy, for this was a relatively new player on the international scene. By 2005 a full 10% of all the students in Australian universities were foreign, paying full tuition fees—mainly from south and southeast Asia but from other areas as well.[5] (In contrast, foreign students counted for 3.9% of the United States college and university total.) Growth rates for the number of international students in Australia reached 15% annually, from the late 1980s onward. To be sure, Australia's aggressive effort brought charges of excessive commercial zeal that, some argued, operated to the detriment of sensible university funding and quality international education alike.[6] But concerns about terrorist potential in the open-door policy did not produce American-style timidity, despite attacks on Australian interests in Indonesia and despite the occasional worried editorial.

And there were other competitors as well, increasingly in Asia itself: Singapore mounted new efforts to recruit foreign students, hosting upward of 100,000 by 2007, often at private institutions.[7] Hong Kong got into the act, seeking to attract mainland Chinese students with what might seem, and be, a slightly less national educational experience. Some of the high-prestige institutions in South Korea, Japan, and even China began to make similar moves. South Korea even projected a new international university center near the Incheon airport, with unrivaled potential access to students from northeast Asia and beyond. A variety of new commercial agencies sprang up to help students win placement in these less-familiar settings. Asian students were gaining new options, and while this hardly dried up sources of American recruitment, some new constraints were becoming obvious and promised to loom larger as time went on.

Reorientation was particularly noteworthy in the Middle East, where nervousness about American intentions was understandably high. A generation of Arab leaders who had been educated in the United States was succeeded by a younger cohort for whom American education increasingly seemed not worth the trouble given opportunities elsewhere. Many students, including a few who continued to attend American schools but many more who no longer bothered, reported on the indignities involved in seeking access to the United

States. Even with visa obtained, arrival at an airport routinely meant a rigorous interrogation in some back room, where students waited alongside drug dealers and passport forgers. As a leader in Dubai put it, in this context, "Australia is more welcoming." By 2007, indeed, Australia had overtaken the United States as a site for students from places like the United Arab Emirates, and reductions of 5 to 25% in the number of students heading for the United States were routine throughout the Middle East. It was not a matter of visas alone. Australia simply pushed its opportunities harder, setting up prayer rooms and *halal* food outlets on many campuses and providing official support for recruitment efforts at local college fairs.[8]

Indeed, collective American efforts to push higher education faltered badly, in relation to the new competition. A State Department tour of the Middle East in 2003 featured American educators eager to urge opportunities at their institutions, but it had little impact because of lack of systematic follow-up; and efforts dwindled further in subsequent years. A huge college fair in Beijing, in October, 2007, saw a massive convention center literally half occupied by recruiters from the European Union, with Australian institutions dominating a full third of the remaining space: both efforts featured eye-catching materials and the latest in marketing techniques. Latin American recruitment was also prominent, with a particularly large booth operated by Chilean educators. American schools were represented by a tiny official display, causing one American observer to note, in a phrase often used in this regard in recent years: "they're eating our lunch." Recurrently the State Department resumed sponsorship of trips by university officials to tout opportunities in the United States, but the trips were sporadic and the visa difficulties presented by the same State Department made many efforts seem confused and hollow. To be sure, American consulates maintained education and cultural affairs offices, stocked with print and on-line information about college opportunities in the United States, and without question many interested international students—the State Department liked to claim not many but most—were motivated or at least better informed by the contacts possible there. But aggressive outreach, of the sort now emanating not only from Australia but from several European countries and some in Latin America, was not a government priority, in favor of lower key business as usual now complicated by the host of new complexities and cautions.

Adding to American woes were relatively high costs for tuition, even at state schools required to charge out-of-state rates to foreigners. Not only did American rates loom much higher than rates back home, but they also surpassed average European or Australian levels—the result of relatively high faculty pay in the United States and relatively luxurious facilities, even with the demeaned dollar. Sheer economics could complicate competition considerably.

Basic trends were not encouraging, though the prestige factor, and continued student enjoyment of leisure opportunities in the United States, as an offshoot of American leadership in global youth culture, must not be discounted. International students paying money to American schools made higher education the fifth largest source of foreign earnings for services in the American economy (at about $14 billion annually), a sign of considerable ongoing strength and a possible motivation for some rethinking about reaching out more aggressively to the market involved. But the fact was, in 2008, that the United States was losing ground in this area, at least in relation to potential expansion and the rapid gains of key rivals. Traditional momentum still counted for something, but only the special efforts of a few schools and a few higher education associations managed to break the troubled surface. Many schools, hit hard in the wake of 9/11, were still struggling to compensate for the significant decline in international numbers.

Overall, American leadership (to the extent that it thought about educating international students at all, even as a factor in the national economy) continued to operate as though American prestige would carry the day, with no special efforts at promotion or marketing—at a time when rivals had adopted a very different stance. The uncertainties introduced by the public and policy reactions to the terrorist threat distracted attention still further. Despite the efforts of some important international education associations, vigorous in their attempts to deal with new barriers, no single entity, in government or out, seemed capable of galvanizing a new collective strategy.

The bottom line was obvious: despite some ongoing advantages, at least in the short run, the challenges facing American institutions of higher education demanded real innovation in response, and absent clear overall direction, at least from the government side in what was a decentralized sector in any event, opportunities for particularly imaginative schools or, at most, consortia, were unusually great. While some institutions themselves maintained a business-as-usual attitude, at most adding loud laments about the new difficulties they faced and possibly adding a few staff members for visa assistance, a significant number tried to break new ground. Their efforts provide obvious models for further action, but they also increased the need to sort out the basic issues of why American schools should want international students, how these students should be handled, and how the whole effort fit into a broader program of internationalization.

Patterns, Trends and Divided Response

American higher education began to attract foreign students by the early 20th century. A number of institutions developed a commendable record in recruiting often small numbers of prominent foreigners, destined for leadership in their home countries yet eager to use American colleges as a means of accessing increasingly desirable Western standards. Wellesley College, for example, established a strong track record with elite women in China. Initial enrollments were small, but a connection was forged that could easily grow with time.[9]

By the late 1950s, over 48,000 international students were on American campuses each year, amounting to 1.4% of the total student population. By this point, despite relatively low overall percentages, the attractive power went well beyond elite levels. Many students from middle as well as upper classes sought in American education a means of advancing their own careers (some of course hoped to stay in the United States as part of this process) and/or bringing valuable skills back home. Emphases varied widely, and there was still some tradition of seeking high-prestige liberal arts undergraduate education, but increasingly international students sought graduate more than undergraduate degrees, particularly in practical fields like engineering, agriculture and science.

Growth was reasonably steady from 1960 through the 1990s, though there was no breakthrough trend of the sort that emerged in Australia after the late 1980s. By 1980 286,000 international students constituted 2.8% of the total student population, and by 2002–3, the highpoint in percentage terms to date, 586,000 international students made up 4.6% of the overall student body in American higher education.[10]

Then, of course, the troubles set in, with automatic decadal growth at the previous 6% levels no longer assured. American institutions began to have to think more self-consciously about their international student policies, in order to decide whether to make the special new efforts needed even to tread water, not to mention gaining ground.

Gains in academic year 2006–7 masked a good bit of variety. Overall, the number of international students increased 3.2% from the previous mark, to 583,000 individuals, after an essentially stable year previously and outright drops the two years before that. The percentage among total college students stagnated, however, at the 3.9% figure. India, and at slight remove China, were the largest sources of international students. Korea was an impressively close third. Japan was the fourth largest source, but with declining numbers presumably as top Japanese institutions increasingly caught up with perceived American quality. Saudi Arabia and Nepal registered big percentages increase, in the middle of the top twenty sending nations, while Vietnamese interest and capacity were growing rapidly as well.[11]

Business and management drew 18% of all international students, confirming a trend visible for some time. Engineering placed second (and if combined with math and computer science, actually topped management), followed by the social sciences (with 8% of the total). Health professions and, even more, intensive English language training were substantial gainers.

International students showed up at all levels of American higher education. In contrast to American study abroad patterns, a substantial percentage were in masters and doctoral programs, confirming the obvious fact that large numbers of foreigners sought special expertise rather than a more general educational experience. At George Mason University, for example, with about 6% of its overall student body from abroad (plus an additional number of internationals temporarily resident in the U.S.), almost twice as many foreign students were in graduate or professional programs as were bachelor degree candidates, and this only with some special efforts on the undergraduate side. But there were undergraduates as well, not just at research universities but at more strictly baccalaureate institutions, and a substantial number of enrollees in two-year colleges—often seeking this venue as a means of gaining English language training or taking advantage of lower costs and greater accessibility with hopes of moving on to four-year institutions later on.

What was additionally intriguing, however, and particularly important in terms of the implications for institutional policy and administration, was the wide variety of experiences among American institutions, at all levels though particularly where undergraduates were involved.[12] Not too surprisingly, the big players in the international student game, in terms of total numbers, were large and relatively prestigious research universities, both public and private. The University of Southern California has headed the list for several years, with 7,115 international students in 2006–7, and in general California scored well because of the size and strength of its overall higher education system and its relative proximity to East Asia. But several Big Ten schools rank high, as do Columbia and NYU, Florida, the two leading Texas institutions, and Harvard, Columbia and Pennsylvania among the Ivies; Boston University and NYU also figured strongly. The top twenty schools ranged from 3,751 to over 7,000, or between 10 and 20% of overall enrollments—well above the national average. Reputation, strength and prestige in the most sought-after disciplines, presumably well-organized international student offices and programs, and by this point usually decades of experience with alumni networks to match, account for unusual success in this area.

But the leaders aside, experiences vary widely, and the gaps are increasing. Thus while most doctoral institutions are now reporting some gains, with only a minority noting declines (67% to 12%, in one survey), the experiences of undergraduate institutions and two-year colleges demonstrate sharper divisions. Among community colleges, only a small majority are registering gains by this point, with a large minority either holding even or (17%) dropping—and since these figures depended on self-report, they were unusually selective toward institutions with above-average outreach interest. Four-year colleges are even more polarized, with 43% reporting gains, 27% showing declines, and the rest barely holding even—a pattern that has been fairly constant since the 9/11 turning point. Masters-level schools, predictably, fell in between, not matching the success of the doctorals but not suffering quite as much decline as the baccalaureate institutions.

Pretty clearly, three factors are now in play in differentiating attractiveness to international students, among institutions of different types but also at schools whose profiles in other respects are quite similar. The first involves reasonably high-level research and professional programs; international students increasingly go to the trouble of coming to the United States for higher degrees, not degrees in general. The second, related to the first, involves prior track record and sheer heft: schools with 1,000 or more international students do much better than schools in general, in part because of informal recruitment networks. But the third, most interesting because more open to adjustment, involves some degree of self-conscious innovation, some new efforts to reach out to compensate for growing difficulties and the growing number of alternatives. And this factor, in turn, involves real choice on the part of the institutions involved. To an increasing extent, particularly beyond the top-twenty research operations with established drawing power, you get what you go after in this particular category of global educational endeavor.

A recent survey, dependent of course on institutional willingness to respond, which always involves considerable self-selection, suggests that over a third of all American higher education institutions (and probably much more; only 700 schools replied) have taken no special steps even to maintain prior levels of international enrollments. This means, of course, that over half (at least of the most interested players) think they have done something, which may be taken as encouraging. But the motives for relative inaction are also important, given the changes in overall climate. Indeed, as administrators who faced enrollment declines themselves noted, the leading reasons for problems— the new complexities of the visa application process (held to account for over 31% of student loss), the rising tuition and fee costs in the United States (23%), and growing competition from other countries (11%)—were not easy to resolve even with a strong institutional commitment; without it, they almost inevitably added up to declining enrollment levels.[13]

A number of schools have clearly decided that increasing international enrollments does not, at least currently, constitute a strategic priority. Given healthy recent increases in the size of the eligible American student population, particularly for the undergraduate category, the international arena may not seem worth the bother. As one anonymous administrator noted, "the college prefers to spend money on marketing and scholarships for local high school graduates and the local minority community." Or from another, more cryptically: "Enrollment is stable and resources are limited."[14] The growing demands on the visa scene increase the realization of the extra difficulties involved in enrolling international students, and for many schools, pressed in other budget categories, providing necessary staffing no longer makes financial sense. New costs, for faculty salaries, IT and other equipment, or other pressing needs, might easily out-compete even maintaining the investment in international students—one institution specifically noted that it had once offered some steep discounts to woo foreign students, but could no longer afford to do so. And of course, there could be some simple hubris: "don't need to [do anything special] when the institution is among the top rated in the world." And some schools, finally, while hoping for some continued international enrollment, were explicitly willing to reduce overall numbers because of the costs and difficulties involved, seeing this as an opportunity to "become more selective in our acceptance practices."[15] American institutions had never uniformly played the international recruitment game, but the new need for some extra effort, and the related need therefore for some special motivation, increased the variety of response.

The Basic Apparatus

Before turning to the most crucial aspects of the international student scene—what kinds of new efforts pay off and what motives might underlie these efforts—it is vital to explore some of the fundamental administrative, pedagogical and fiscal requirements involved in seeking and managing more than the random international student. As many institutions have realized over the past several decades—interested community colleges as well as Ph.D. leaders—a host of special arrangements are required even when the goal is simply to fit international students as smoothly as possible into the overall student population. These arrangements—again, even aside from newer demands—clarify once again the extent to which an explicit commitment is essential in this aspect of global education, and might amply justify an institutional decision not to get seriously involved in the first place.

An Ethics Backdrop. Several American associations have developed codes of ethics applicable to administrators dealing with educational exchange arrangements and with international students.[16] NAFSA: Association of International Educators (originally founded in 1948 as the National Association of Foreign Student Advisors, now with 10,000 members mainly though not exclusively in the United States, at over 1,500 institutions) has been particularly active in this field. Its ethics code urges appropriate professional training and competence for faculty and administrators dealing with foreign students, with a high premium on knowledge about differences in culture and value orientation and the ability to demonstrate related flexibility in actual behavior. Most features of the code replicate standard American thinking about relationships with students—including of course avoidance of sexual harassment or other abuses of power and the maintenance of confidentiality and data security. Emphasis on avoiding personal relationships that might color judgment or suggest undue influence wins unusual attention in the international context. The ethics code also includes comment on the need to receive gifts, in some cultures where gift exchange is a matter of common courtesy, while however seeking to minimize the practice and carefully to constrain the value involved as well as any ensuing expectations (this can be an issue of real complexity in responding to international students and their families where the line between cultural practice and near-bribe can blur). The importance of providing careful and accurate information, though not an unusual criterion, gains special salience in dealing with potential applicants and students whose understanding of American systems may be quite limited, as is the need to provide follow-up data and orientation opportunities. Overall, however, the ethics area embraces only a few special features, though the codes provide a useful starting point in thinking about what international students deserve and require. The big question hinges not on any surprises in the ethical issues themselves, but on whether American institutions and recruiting agencies live up to the standards as well as they ought. The international student can be vulnerable in many ways, and there have been too many cases of misleading information, false claims, and financial manipulation—all covered by codes of ethics but central to responsible administration in practice as well.

Finding the Students. Recruitment efforts for international students have varied widely. Some institutions, quite eager to woo international students, leave it to normal processes of advertising, now of course including web-based promotions, plus any word of mouth to do the job. Some institutions have sufficient alumni in key areas that local networks can also assist the recruitment process. But many admissions offices have long scheduled periodic recruitment trips. Annual forays to east and Southeast Asia have been particularly common, but there are some other targets as well. Large recruitment fairs occur in many regions, in the Middle East as well as East Asia, and these provide opportunities for advertising or personal visits. Particularly in India, a variety of recruitment agencies also regularly seek American business, usually charging a per capita fee for any students who matriculate through their services. A range of possibilities, and investment levels, complicate this aspect of the international student equation.

Another complication, predictably enough, involves developing standards for assessment of applicants. English language capacity is a particular facet of this problem, to be discussed momentarily. Access to SAT and ACT tests varies widely outside the United States, and in some regions, like the Middle East, the whole process of external testing is not widely accepted. This means, for potential students, a choice about how much extra effort to put in to gain access to required tests, and for some American institutions a decision about whether certain standard admissions requirements can be waived in favor of other evidence (including domestic testing programs associated with the end of secondary schooling, the specifics of which vary widely of course from one country to the next). For recruitment of graduate students, variant college practices also pose a challenge. Most Indian students graduate from college in three years rather than four, and this is now the norm in the European Union as well: can the results be accepted as equivalent to an American four-year degree, or must students be required to take a compensatory college year or some additional courses as a condition of graduate admissions? Here again, policy responses vary from one institution to the next.

An unavoidable issue, for undergraduate and graduate admissions alike, involves assessment of secondary school or college records. Larger American universities normally undertake this evaluation in-house, in the interests of speed, but there are private firms available as well. Credentials assessment can be fairly routine if transcripts are in English and/or if the schools have an established track record with the local admissions staff. But the process can be complicated and expensive, and sometimes time-consuming, in many instances—and even with care, uncertainty may persist about the quality of the student record or, in more cases than is desirable, whether the relevant degree has been obtained at all. At the graduate level, competitive American schools usually absorb the credentialing costs, but in other instances these may be passed on to applicants in the form of an additional admissions fee. Particularly with graduate students, eager departments often chafe against the time consumed in evaluations, worrying that they will lose precious student customers.

Assistance with visas is a vital part of the recruitment process. Admitted students must receive Student Exchange and Visitor Information System (SEVIS) documentation, attesting to admission, from the sponsoring institution in order to initiate the whole application process, mainly though not exclusively for the F-1 visa. The institutions involved must be accredited, but intensive English language institutes may also qualify.[17]

Several other issues hover around recruitment, one of them quite new, but all impinging on ethics. The problem of dealing appropriately with gifts (from applicants or their families or from institutions trying to find slots for their students) has been noted already; it's tricky, given cultural nuances, but needs appropriate attention. A number of recruiting agencies operate in the field, charging money sometimes on a payment-per-student-enrolled basis, as is the case particularly in India. Aside from the question of costs, in relation to other admissions activities, the self-interest of the agency in promoting students raises real concerns. A number of commercial recruitment operations have inadequately or inaccurately represented specific American institutions, and some student lawsuits have resulted from misleading promises. This is an area where great caution is needed. Finally—and this is the recent one—some international businesses, seeking to place students most often in American MBA programs, have on occasion appointed school officials to their boards, which is emerging as a probable conflict of interest. The eagerness for American education is refreshing, but it can create dilemmas as well.

Amid some clear hazards, which increase as competition for and impediment to international students expand, there is some welcome experience to share as well. Many schools find that faculty traveling abroad, for instance, on research trips, can often be given admissions materials and spend a bit of productive time as school ambassadors. The result can be one of the most effective recruitment tools available, when prospective students can attach a human face to an often intimidating prospect, and receive more precise, institution-specific answers to questions as well.

Issues of Orientation. Advice on the needs of international students in American classrooms moves a bit further toward some of the core administrative as well as pedagogical issues involved in this aspect of the global arena. International students do not necessarily differ from domestic ones, and of course there is great variety among individuals and, to some extent, among different cultures of origin. Any faculty member who has benefited from the English writing skills of some international students, in comparison with home-grown averages, can attest to the need to avoid any hasty generalization about special needs or compensations in the international student category. Still, experience has suggested some issues that many international students may encounter in American classrooms, beneath the level of basic ethical treatment that must be considered in administering any program in this area.

Heading the list is lack of familiarity with class participation expectations in many American pedagogical settings, and more broadly still, some discomfort with the extent of open inquiry.[18] (Many students are also unfamiliar with the decentralized nature of American higher education, but this primarily challenges their ability to pick an appropriate school; once they are actually attending a college or university, the heterogeneity factor looms less large.) American courses vary widely, obviously, and a few international students actually find some American instructors rather peremptory and distant, in contrast to what they would have anticipated back home. More, however, risk feeling somewhat intimidated by expectations that they will participate in class discussions and challenge professorial views—this departs from their prior norms, and of course may be compounded by linguistic hesitancy and confusion about the apparent informality of dress and manners in the American classroom. As one foreign student noted, "Here, if you speak up in the classroom, they will listen to you. . . . In my country, it is hard to make your own voice, if you are . . . just a student. People don't listen that much." Some international students also report greater American emphasis on backing up opinions with objective data. Certainly, American focus on written work contrasts with higher education norms in some other societies, again a difference often compounded by language challenges. (But there is often unfamiliarity with multiple choice tests as well, and some defendable disdain.) The degree of choice in the American system, coupled with the absence of required advice, can be troubling as well, particularly at the undergraduate level. From some regions also, American standards of academic misconduct seem puzzling, the result surprisingly rigorous. Again a quote: "Everything you say, you have to put someone's name and the date and the page. . . . At home, this was not the case." The fuzzy boundary line between sharing in student groups, and making sure one can demonstrate one's own work, provides additional opportunities for confusion in some cultural settings.[19]

In most of these areas, of course, the problems international students encounter are simply slightly larger versions of problems American students face as well—from the penalties of shyness in class to confusions about plagiarism. And, demonstrably, international students can be extremely successful. At George Mason University, to take one case, their average grades surpass those of domestic undergraduates, partly of course because their smaller numbers suggest greater self-selectivity; and this is not an unusual experience. But there are certain issues of rules and styles that need to be built into appropriate advising and socialization, in turn the responsibility of a sensitive administration.

Almost all international student programs begin at least to tackle these issues with an earlier and separate orientation phase, launched a week or so before general orientations or freshmen weeks for students more generally. Special advisors, with some experience in the kinds of learning issues international students may face, lead this effort, which is also designed to help buffer the sense of strangeness encountered as part of being in a foreign country, not infrequently—at least in the case of student groups like the Chinese—for the first time. Here again there is need for some additional investment. Ideally, the orientation mode is carried over into advising and some special social contacts even as the academic year progresses. Some international student offices also have publications available to provide additional guidance in crucial areas.

Decisions about the Social Side. Not surprisingly, caring for significant numbers of international students—particularly but not exclusively at the undergraduate level—also raises some special social issues, broadly construed. Here too, there is need for sensitivity and concern, some explicit policy discussions, and some special outlays. As with orientation procedures, the potential problems are clearer than the solutions, but some awareness at least launches a responsive process.

Housing is a vital concern. For undergraduates, most universities would expect to provide residence slots for international students, though for dormless community colleges this is a greater challenge. Normally, however, the key issue is not whether to provide housing, but with what level of integration with other students. International houses have been one response, mixing international students from different locations to some degree and sometimes combining them with internationally minded American students. Many housing offices find it convenient to group international students, partly for the convenience of special activities and advising services. Always, however, there is a risk of undue isolation in dorm arrangements that makes it easier for foreign students to stick together and, often, to find informal groupings from their own homeland that will provide a comforting but narrowing social environment.

Study abroad programs for Americans, as we have seen, face very similar issues. In the case of international undergraduates special housing sections also reduce benefits to American students from frequent and informal contacts. Housing integration, with clear supplemental access to necessary international services, is an increasingly vital step. For graduate students, the question of whether institutional housing is available at all may be a more pressing issue. But where students cluster off-campus, they may again emphasize same-group isolation and also tend toward levels of crowding, in interests of saving money, which cause concern as well. And while some international students (particularly undergraduates) bring ample funding for cars (sometimes, surprisingly luxurious cars), dependence on public or university transport is another typical constraint affecting the quality of life and the ability to mix with other students.

Most international student offices or student affairs sections try to provide some social events for foreign students even after the orientation period. Again, the goal is to reduce potential loneliness and isolation and to provide opportunities for informal contacts about problems different from those faced by American students; but these purposes must be balanced by the need to prevent too much separate socializing and too many opportunities for international students to intensify their quite understandable impulses to be with their own co-nationals and to have occasions to revert unduly to the home language.

American vacations pose a potential problem as well, again particularly for undergraduates whose work does not spill over from one semester to the next. Many international students prove quite inventive about using vacation time to explore the country a bit. American students often help, bringing a friend home; and faculty at some institutions provide terrific service, for example, inviting international students to a Thanksgiving dinner (one of those holidays where there's not enough time to do much off-campus but where the sense of isolation from American sociability may seem particularly acute). But for students who don't have a lot of co-nationals around, whose funding is limited, who are newly constrained by visa uncertainties not to go home even in long breaks—there are problems about filling vacation time that deserve at least some administrative attention. For some cohorts of international students, brought over as groups under a particular mantle of institutional responsibility, more systematic arrangements for travel or other activities may be part of providing minimally acceptable service.

Many institutions with significant numbers of international students have also worked to develop international weeks or festivals, ideally designed to take advantage of the special knowledge of the students for the benefit of an American audience (students, staff, surrounding community) and to let the international students express themselves both artistically, through costume, dance, possibly music, and around booths or information sessions where they offer presentations about their home countries. Even appropriate sports events, like cricket, can add to the mix. Carnegie Mellon University instituted a fall international weekend about a decade ago, on the strength of its substantial (largely graduate) foreign student contingent. George Mason has a full week each spring that provides one of the high points of the social calendar. Here indeed is a way to take wider advantage of the presence of international contingents toward educational benefits broadly construed, indulging the identity interests of the foreign students themselves but in a framework that is not isolationist. There are a few common problems with what is a desirable and often successful outlet. Domestic student audiences may be smaller than desired, as international students bustle about to each other's events with more modest American companionship. Or, a slight variant: activities and presentations (as in dance competitions) may rouse more interest from American students of international origin than from international students themselves. The Americans have a more fully developed participatory sense, and less shyness. And, some cynics have noted, they are less committed to working as hard as the actual internationals. Here too, the effort is worth doing, but its effects may not be quite as rewarding, in linking internationals and domestics, as initial sponsors had hoped.

Finally, on the social side, there's the inevitable issue of student associations, so often encouraged but also deplored by student services units. Any campus with significant numbers of foreign students will experience a multitude of national or cultural groups—Korean Student Association, Muslim Student Association, the East Turkistan group—the number and variety can be considerable. The organizations help provide a supportive social framework; they can on occasion be extremely useful in calling problems to administrative attention that might otherwise fester or go unnoticed. They obviously also harbor some downsides. They may isolate. They may on occasion be dominated by Americans of that national or religious origin, leaving actual international students on the periphery. They may on occasion contend with each other, once in a great while even violently. Parades of flags, for example, can generate conflict. The issue once was Palestine, now some of the regional tensions in China. Groups of students supporting independence or autonomy may include their flag in a "national" parade, provoking bitter dissent from students from the nation against which they are protesting. There are ways, of course, to minimize conflict, and it's vital to anticipate; and, as with many tensions about global education, controversy can turn into an educable moment, useful for American students as well as for the disputants. But attention is required.

Associations need, in other words, active guidance and oversight of various sorts, so that they work with each other across as well as within national lines (maintaining an umbrella international student board helps a lot here); so that they interact with other student leaders, reducing the international/domestic divide; and so that they have opportunities to meet with university officials even outside the student affairs domain. Many administrators, including myself as a new provost, were actively assisted, for example, after the 9/11 crisis, by opportunities to talk with Muslim student groups, with the Afghan student association, and with others; we learned a lot, about how we could best reduce anxieties and even provide some educational moments in the midst of tragedy, and of course the groups' existence gave us channels of communication that hopefully assisted student members as well.

English Language. Language concerns, not surprisingly, cut across the administration of international students, from solicitation and admission decisions to satisfactory learning and extracurricular experiences. Obviously, some international students bring fluent English with them—from Canadians to many though not all Indian students to many Africans from former British colonies. But large numbers do not have English as a first or early language, and several types of policies must be in place to respond to their needs and capacities.

An obvious tension underlies this whole area, which helps explain not only the focus but also the variety of policy responses. On the one hand, a wide range of schools seek to welcome students who've made a start on English but wish to advance their ability as part of the American educational experience. They bring diversity, they come often from some of the places we most want to expose to the better side of the United States, and they often bring great intellectual talent. On the other hand, we seek or should seek to make sure we don't put students into educational situations for which they are linguistically unprepared; the cost to them, and sometimes to other students in their classes, can be unacceptably great. A balance between these poles can be struck; it can be facilitated by explicit support programs; but it is not always easy to define or attain.

The basic decision involves language requirements for admission.[20] Many American institutions rely on the TOEFL (Test of English as a Foreign Language) examination to produce data on language competency, though other tests have some use such as IELTS (The International English Language Testing System, based in the UK; IELTS has just set up an American office); and there are some specialized offerings in fields such as management. Where recruitment trips are involved, direct interviews can also play a role in the process.

A host of issues surround any testing program. Many international students have English language work under their belts at home, which proves less adequate than they expect when exposed to actual American standards. Opportunities for confusion are considerable (as with Americans studying abroad). Issues of variety loom large as well. Many East Asian students do very well on written tests, and this at times masks deficiencies in the oral-aural area; it is possible to have a student with exemplary TOEFL scores who does not in fact fare well in the actual classroom, particularly in non-science fields where language is at a premium. On the other hand, many Arab students score rather badly but in fact develop great speaking proficiency fairly readily, and actually can do well in the classroom. And there are innumerable individual variations. Current directions in the testing field are seeking to capture holistic language abilities, moving away from previous reliance on reading and writing alone. The newest version of the TOEFL test, still being implemented along with other versions and other scoring levels, involves four components in reading, writing, oral comprehension and speaking; each area is scored with a maximum possible 30 points, for a cumulative 120-point base. (The older TOEFL test had single but higher numerical scores.)[21]

American institutions vary quite widely in the scores required; this was the case with earlier tests, and remains true.[22] On the new scoring system, for example, Northwestern State University requires a 61 score total, with a minimum of 20 for speaking and for writing; Santa Fe Community College wants a score of 66; but Lehigh requires 85. The University of Washington requires 70; Syracuse and Pittsburgh seek an 80 point minimum, George Mason 88 with minima in each category, University of Virginia 90, Texas at San Antonio 100. Not surprisingly score requirements correlate to a degree with position on the academic pecking order, with community college stipulations characteristically on the low side. But even with this criterion, the range is considerable, reflecting different degrees of eagerness for international students, different levels of tolerance for potential language difficulties. Granting all the variables, it is fair to note that some institutions offer requirements so low as to raise questions about what will happen to the students once they arrive. A few places have developed the dubious policy of accepting students with certain minima subject to further internal tests once they arrive, before full admission, with many applicants unaware of the uncertainties involved. This is a very questionable practice, which is now however more difficult because of the language probes in the visa interviews (there's no bad policy without some silver lining).

The most sensible effort to achieve some balance between the desire to attract and a willingness to work on language issues after arrival, on the one hand, and the need not to put students in an impossible position on the other, involves differential scoring as between students exempt from compulsory language work, and those required to take specific language instruction on arrival with full admission often dependent on satisfactory progress in the language program. The University of Washington, for example, makes a clear distinction between no-bar admissions scores and levels that provide adequate promise but only on condition of some further work. Here too, however, there are problems. Many institutions do not have a particularly well-developed English language training program, and professional qualifications of instructors in this area vary widely. There are only 55 fully accredited English Language programs in the United States currently—the number dropped somewhat in the wake of 9/11, as some schools, probably prematurely, abandoned the investment.[23] Schools that have a good program, or that have access to one, can quite responsibly follow the policy of admitting with the training requirement, often allowing program instructors to make their own judgments about linguistic readiness independent of additional testing (while still allowing renewed testing as an alternative path to full credentials). There are still opportunities for confusion: some international students will think that a semester or two in a program will automatically qualify them; different results for different individuals and various culture groups can also generate frustration or misleading expectations. But at least there is a mechanism for combining suitable requirements with professional assistance. Obviously, however, not all institutions have this system fully worked out, and there is money as well as policy involved. The larger accredited training programs normally make ends meet, by handling students from several institutions, but in the bleak years right after 9/11 some subsidies were essential and the operation is never, or should not be, a major profit center.

Language training issues also loom increasingly large for graduate students in the technical fields, where state laws increasingly press for certification of oral proficiency for people serving as Teaching Assistants.[24] Here again there is a need for training opportunities to supplement testing requirements. Even at the undergraduate level, growing efforts to test learning outcomes, in areas such as writing, place a premium on support mechanisms for English as second language students even after full qualification for admission. Many writing programs now offer special sections with extra training for some second language students (not all need this option), in order to bring them up to speed.

Language, in other words, can be an ongoing issue in the proper educational management of international students. Appropriate requirements, coupled with training opportunities, can be successful—there is no problem that many institutions have not easily and ethically resolved. But the need for attention and some investment is undeniable, and there is reason for concern as well about certain types of American schools whose enthusiasm for foreign students seems to have outstripped sound educational values. Certainly, the language issues—both the requirements and the needed support—must represent occasions for careful and explicit policy formulation.

Money and Organization

Dealing with international students in any number requires some explicit organizational steps. Most obviously, an office of international students is essential to handle visa issues—the service can also apply to faculty and academic visitors, but the student focus is crucial. Admissions offices may require some specialized recruiters (with some travel and marketing allowance); credentials processing also demands staff (most institutions have found that a centralized approach works better than operations within individual academic units), unless the activity is outsourced. Student affairs operations require considerable attention to the distinctive needs and opportunities of international students, including the special orientation sessions; in some instances this is part of the mandate of the international student office.

Money is also central to decisions about recruitment and enrollment, as we have seen. Competition (at least at the graduate level) increasingly presses American schools to cover costs of credentials evaluation, once thrust back on applicants, and some institutions swallow the SEVIS fees associated with visa application—though here too, the charge can be left to the student applicants.[25]

Overall money issues are both intriguing and varied. Few universities tally the costs of dealing with international students, because the expenditures are so diffuse, affecting such a variety of administrative and academic units. Rarely does a careful business plan spell out total revenues versus expenses in this area, and budget offices are rarely asked to generate an overview. This unsystematic approach may benefit the operation, by avoiding too narrow or rigid a fiscal framework, but it is obviously open to criticism.

On the other hand, many colleges and universities view, or have viewed, international students as a revenue stream. The students normally pay out-of-state rates at public institutions—and these are generally seen as an income sources. Financial aid expenditures, essential for recruiting domestic out-of-staters, are sometimes low or nonexistent, particularly at the undergraduate level. Some universities, even highly prestigious ones, have long had a blanket policy denying international undergraduates any institutional financial assistance. Correspondingly, over 60% of all international students in the United States currently cover their costs from personal and family resources, with an additional 4% sponsored by a foreign government, business or university. Only 26% receive any assistance from the American institution, and most of these are graduate students with fellowships or, more commonly still, research or teaching assistantships. Opportunities for other employment, another resource for domestic students, are extremely limited due to the restrictions of student visa requirements; only 4% of all international students report current employment outside assistantship resources. Only 2% receive help from the U.S. government or from an American private sponsor.[26]

It is difficult to determine, given the characteristic laxness in accounting, what the revenue/expenditure tradeoff is, but there seems little question that a number of American institutions make money from their international student operation, again particularly at the collegiate level. Some institutions, historically, have even depended on the foreign income stream as a major motivation for their involvement in the whole operation.

From a larger vantage point, there are warning flags aplenty where money and monetary incentives are involved. A considerable number of international students invest extremely heavily in an American education, and many American officials, even faculty advisors, may not be adequately aware of their sacrifice. Poor living standards in the United States, particularly amid crowded off-campus housing, are one not-uncommon result. Some find themselves extremely hard-pressed to maintain their studies, having hoped for some windfall after the first year or two. And there are more cases than we should have to admit of programs that lure students over with a promise of a stipend, only to pull aid back after the first year or two; the intentions may have been good—the desire to draw international students in—but the end result was often counterproductive, in soured repercussions when a program had to be abandoned for financial reasons, or even cruel as students try to hang in amid real poverty, or both. Even with new visa probes, that seek further information on a student-applicant's financial resources, misleading expectations remain possible.

The financial facets involved in dealing with international students obviously call for careful and explicit attention, whether or not an overall discounting standard is developed. Some costs may be higher than realized, amid the mixture of good intentions and separated administrative units so pervasive in the field. Some profit motives are unquestionably excessive, particularly as the field becomes increasingly complex. There is every reason to reconsider policies that deny aid to certain categories of international students, another issue important at a number of American institutions. And it is imperative to think through the implications of commitment to students whose sacrifices, or whose family's sacrifices, are too often overlooked.

The question of money, of course, has a further ramification, taking us back to one of the basic issues in the whole international student arena: why, if costs are involved or profits less certain than desired, become involved in the enterprise at all?

Disputes and Public Relations

One final topic warrants brief comment, before returning to the current situation and the goals to be sought. Groups of international students on a campus rarely generate significant internal controversy, though we have cited a few periodic bubbles. There are occasional tensions with domestic students, where local prejudices run afoul of foreign student sensitivities. On the other hand, international issues poison intergroup relations surprisingly rarely, in the American campus environment. Pakistani and Indian students, students from Taiwan and the People's Republic normally operate not only amid mutual tolerance, but with some very positive interactions in confronting the strangeness of the American college environment. Issues may arise, however, when a group of international students is caught up in American foreign policy debates. Students from the Middle East (sometimes combining with American Muslim students) may generate or experience tensions with American supporters of Israel, in reaction to specific events in the Palestinian territories or

Lebanon or in duels over invited partisan speakers. International student offices can play a useful role in promoting dialogues and in explaining the need for tolerance and balance as part of the American educational commitment (while rejecting any crude attempt to arrange an opposition speaker every time a given student group organizes its own panel discussion). Most of these issues can be resolved peacefully, often even with educational benefits to the groups involved and to the wider campus community. Not infrequently the greatest lingering problem involves off-campus reactions, from American citizens who fail to understand the university's function in soliciting a variety of viewpoints, even those not congenial to sectors of American opinion. Under the Bush presidency a proposal even surfaced to monitor classes and activities to make sure that foreign policy issues were not presented in a partisan fashion, which presumably meant to assure that too much criticism of the administration did not accumulate—and this could certainly apply to expressions by foreign students. To date, thanks in part to vigorous opposition from higher education associations, nothing has come of this watchdog proposal.

This is not a vast problem category, but it deserves mention as part of the potential considerations in dealing with international students. Interestingly, the efforts to advance tolerance and some grasp of the demands of free expression can be part of an advantageous educational exercise, relevant far beyond the ranks of international students themselves. And the range of understanding international students themselves generate can be truly encouraging.

A somewhat related set of issues gained new attention in 2008. Harvard University and some smaller private institutions began to make adjustments to the cultural concerns of certain student groups, including some Muslim cohorts, in setting aside special opportunities, particularly in swimming and exercise. The idea was to acknowledge gender concerns about privacy from the male view. How widely these concerns should be met, and what public institutions might do given different sorts of constraints, would surely be further discussed. A variety of responses seemed defensible.

The Need for More

The most obvious result of the changing context for international students, with new complications on the American side and new levels of competition, involves the need for more effort, more financial investment and at best more innovative imagination, simply to retain current recruitment levels—and certainly if the goal is expansion. The fall, 2007 survey of colleges and universities—the same one that uncovered the understandable admissions that many institutions just couldn't see the reasons for significant effort—revealed a host of enhancements from that majority of respondents who had decided to stay in the game. Over 20% of the colleges involved had designated new funding for marketing and promotion; 22% had sponsored further international recruitment trips (the greatest number to east and south Asia, with

25% of the total to China alone). Over a quarter had added to staff or provided for additional staff time. A full third had ventured new international programs and collaborations.[27] Many had done all of the above.

Additional investment was a common theme. Simply to maintain enrollments, further staffing was needed to keep pace with visa requirements. Many international student offices, previously responsible for advising and programming as well as visas, had been so distorted by the new regulations that their non-visa functions fell off, requiring compensatory personnel. Competitive pressures, plus the unpleasant fallout from the visa snarls, prompted many institutions to pay for the SEVIS I-901 fees, mandated by Congress to require international students to cover the cost of the automated system that keeps track of students and visitors during their stays within the United States—though other schools tried to pass not only this fee, but the costs of their own tracking systems on to students. Decisions about whether to pay for credentialing services might be rethought, with more schools taking on the costs in order not to discourage foreign applicants. Money, always a looming issue in the care and feeding of international students, would almost inevitably become an increasing burden in any of these responses, and this helps explain the growing separation between schools that upped their ante and those willing to accept the results of a stand pat approach.

A number of schools went beyond enhanced investment in established operations, beyond even compensating for the costs of some of the new federal requirements. The several hundred colleges and universities that sought new kinds of collaborative arrangements to help supply international students were often breaking new ground, while reflecting additional needs for imaginative applications of funds. Efforts ranged from student exchange agreements with individual schools abroad to larger cohort recruitments of various types.

Exchange arrangements had long been popular, but interest has increased in the new setting. Many foreign institutions and their number expanded rapidly, particularly in the various parts of Asia) were eager to send students to an American counterpart, in return for accepting a similar number of American students. The goal, usually, was a semester or year abroad, without significant additional costs to either the individuals or the institutions involved. American students paid tuition back home, but simply took courses at the exchange school, with local housing and board rates added on, and the reverse applied to the international student. Opportunities to negotiate agreements of this sort grew steadily, and the result could help sustain international student populations within the United States. A key problem, however, as we have seen, involved the fact that international eagerness for these arrangements outstripped American student interest (and in many cases, except where instruction was offered in English, linguistic capacity). Even exchange arrangements with established European centers often went begging. A number of American institutions, faced with the embarrassing (and costly) disproportion of foreign exchangees, had to terminate some initially promising arrangements, and often became more wary of signing additional agreements. Most sensible collaborations did not insist on absolute parity in exchanges each year, but some kind of balance over a three- or five-year span, but even with this adjustment the mechanism did not always flourish. It was often more constructive to discourage eager administrators from some foreign institutions, even relatively prestigious ones, or to limit numbers pledged, than to encourage unrealistic expectations.

Amid these limitations, a smaller number of American schools negotiated opportunities for groups of qualified international students to spend a semester or more on their campus. No exchange was involved, but identification of a cohort might allow a collective rate below the normal tuition level—taking $5,000, or 20%, or some similar figure off the tuition and fees of the standard out-of-state student rate was a common arrangement. (There were tentative indications that the international students' share of costs was dropping in favor of other sources of support amid these adjustments—from 63% of the total in 2005–6 to 61% in 2006–7, though any trend must be monitored over a longer period of time.) In essence, but in return for adequate numbers, American schools were entering into scholarship arrangements beyond what had previously been seen as necessary. Cohort agreements were possible on both undergraduate and graduate levels. In some cases, formal joint degree programs emerged from these kinds of deals, most commonly at the graduate level. In these arrangements—popular also between some European and some Asian universities (Seoul National and the Sorbonne, for example)—students spent at least a year on both campuses involved, presenting a dissertation to faculty on both campuses as well. Large numbers of students were rarely involved in these particularly elaborate undertakings, and the programs served research collaborations among faculty as much as student internationalization; but the innovation suggested the imaginative interest now involved.

Articulation agreements constituted another path, now more eagerly explored than ever before. Here, usually with the help of American admissions officers and relevant faculty committees, American schools agreed in advance with specific foreign institutions on the acceptance of certain courses for credit, assuming satisfactory performance, so that students admitted in transfer would be relatively assured of the course load that would remain for a degree (most commonly here at the undergraduate level). The advantage for the foreign schools was an American connection, which could serve to attract students for at least the first year or two who would then seek access to professional expertise in the United States (as always, popular targets highlighted engineering and management). Two-year institutions in South Korea, but also some mid-level colleges there and in the Middle East and Pakistan, sought arrangements of this sort. Iowa State, for example, negotiated articulation opportunities for technology students at the (Indian) Bits Pilani branch in Dubai, while some other arrangements focused more on general education credits. For American institutions the plus was access to additional numbers. Drawbacks included the considerable amount of time that had to be invested in curricular negotiations and evaluation of foreign courses, and (sometimes) confused expectations on the part of students whose enthusiasm for transfer obscured the need to meet qualification standards including those in English. But the collaborations did present advantages, and there were other possible variants. In 2007 George Mason and Cheju University, in South Korea, sketched a Pathways program in which students would be directly admitted both to Cheju and to Mason, but would take their first three semesters at Cheju, transferring then seamlessly for a Mason degree on the assumption of satisfactory performance.

One of the most elaborate arrangements to deal with the supply issue, ultimately involving several American schools, was brokered by the National Association of State Colleges and Universities and the Chinese Ministry of Education. Troy University, in Alabama, was the pioneer on the American side. The program was called 1–2–1, in which students began at a Chinese university (several dozen institutions enrolled, with numbers steadily growing; participants included mid-range to relatively high-ranked schools, though not the national status leaders), then were admitted to an American counterpart in an agreed-upon undergraduate program for the second and third years. They subsequently returned to China for the final year, in some cases doing an extra project under the direction of an American faculty member via the Internet; and, when all was successfully completed, they would graduate with two undergraduate degrees simultaneously. Participant American schools commonly offered a discount on out-of-state rates, but in return received groups of usually highly qualified, enthusiastic Chinese students in fields like computer science, management, economics but also a fair smattering of other disciplines. Cohorts of 30 to 40 students per sophomore year were quickly achieved, not only at Troy but at other American participants like George Mason and New Mexico State. Again, there was extra effort involved: the students had to work extremely hard, usually staying for two summer terms as well as the normal load; the need for some compensatory English language work was sometimes an unexpected burden; and of course the Chinese parents shouldered a considerable financial obligation. Decisions about housing were challenging: how much should the students be mixed with the mainstream, how much allowed to enjoy the comforts of compatriots, a balance particularly complicated when cohorts were involved. American schools normally hired special advisors for the Chinese students, to deal with issues ranging from orientation and advising to making sure social and travel opportunities were available for vacation periods. And vetting the Chinese credentials was no small task, though it became easier with growing mutual familiarity. The advantage was, of course, significant student numbers from one of the countries that promised to be particularly influential in the global future; and there was some financial return despite the discounts and the extra investments required (at least assuring that the results were fiscally neutral). The program also reduced, though without eliminating, visa hurdles, as American authorities had greater confidence that students would not remain in the United States beyond the agreed term, since failure to return to China would sacrifice both educational degrees. Growing interest in both countries reflected the program's mutual benefits. And the program served as a model for at least some explorative discussions with educational authorities in places like Vietnam and Malaysia.

Clearly, some American institutions proved both venturesome and imaginative in responding to the new challenges of seeking international students, and their ventures could be more widely imitated. The results could go well beyond maintenance levels, positively increasing international student numbers even as overall national rates tended to stagnate. Troy State's achievement in upping its percentage of international students is a case in point. George Mason more than doubled the pace of its overall student growth in the first eight years of the new century, with a 53% international surge comparing to 26% for students of all sources. And there were other success stories, involving students at various levels. At the same time, the innovations necessary to reach these gains involved real costs and complications, far beyond waiting for applications from abroad with only the most modest recruitment efforts. Explicit policy commitments and financial investments were essential, and clearly not all American schools, even those with successful prior track records, were interested in joining in.

Motivation: Why Seek International Students?

Reasonable administrators can and do disagree about the importance of seeking international students: there is clearly more debate, if largely implicit, here than in the study abroad field. Cost-benefit calculus is complicated, particularly in the new climate where additional funding may be required. Some of the clearest benefits of seeking international students accrue not to the specific institutions involved, but to the United States more generally—but there is (and perhaps there should be) little public support to reflect this fact. Institutional benefits themselves were varied, not always easy to pin down.

The most obvious reason to urge serious commitment to the recruitment and nurturing of international students, particularly in a time of growing tensions around the standing of the United States, involved the belief that access to American education and experience in the United States, for students whose talents and, often, family backgrounds offered leadership potential for the future, would improve opinions about things American and increase contact with positive American achievements and values. This was not an easy proposition to test, but on balance its accuracy seemed at least highly probable. While American education has not made relevant alumni Arab leaders blindly partisan, it has helped cushion relationships with countries such as Jordan or the United Arab Emirates where a substantial segment of current political and business/technical elites spent time at American schools. A key reason for the enthusiasm about recruiting Chinese students obviously involves the assumption that this will improve relations with Chinese leadership and middle-class opinion later on. National interest does not, of course, always translate into institutional interest, and a university administrator could well agree with the overall proposition while hoping that it will be other schools who respond to the need.

Some schools would amplify this general point with a special commitment to seeking, and helping to fund, students from particularly disadvantaged parts of the world, like many countries in Africa. Here, hopes to burnish the national image are combined with a real desire to contribute expertise and educational enhancement to the larger struggle for economic and political progress. The idealism is sincere, though funding constraints limit its expression. Still, a number of colleges and universities have managed to develop a real stake in the recruitment of significant numbers of African or other students (particularly in undergraduate programs) without relying unrealistically on familial resources.

Idealism aside, there may be a national interest as well in the sheer earnings that result from the spending by international students, not an insignificant contribution to an economy otherwise suffering badly from the balance of payments gap. Here, there may be a link to institutional advantage, for those schools that continue to find ways to make international students a modest source of profit. We have seen, however, that this calculus becomes steadily more problematic from the standpoint of individual schools, so even here the connection is complicated.

From the school standpoint, a visible percentage of international students might be a badge of prestige, something to brag about—though there's an obvious question of chicken-and-egg, with many of the most successful units already high up the national pecking order. Clear advantage accrues to graduate programs, in the science and technology fields, that face a shortage of American applicants. The most obvious academic wounds after 9/11 involved severe shortages of students, and with them research and teaching assistants, in vital areas—and many universities have been actively and self-interestedly working to repair this damage, with some success. National interest is involved here as well, insofar as some international students may seek to remain and improve the talent pool. Australia, New Zealand, Canada and the United Kingdom have been cited for their use of foreign students as part of a deliberately-cultivated pool of skilled immigrants. American policy, particularly given new visa strictures, has been less engaged in this area, but some benefits may flow from institutional efforts even so.[28]

National interest, possible institutional profit, and dramatic needs in the STEM fields add up to significant impulses for responsive attention to the flow of international students. Most of the schools most heavily engaged, however, particularly those committed to innovation and to undergraduate as well as graduate populations, would make another, more sweeping claim: direct contribution to the larger mission of global education for domestic as well as foreign clientele.

Troy University, whose constructive ambitions in this arena have already been noted, states the case this way, perhaps with a bit more flair than usual but along lines that would be generally defensible. The University in the 1970s had a deeply segregationist past, and in this context what diversity there was linked entirely to African Americans. A new chancellor in 1989 (a native Alabamian) brought a truly international vision into this mix, seeing global education as a vital contemporary component and international students a vital aspect of this in turn. Deliberate attempts to recruit foreign, particularly Asian students yielded a student body now 10% international. This means that almost every undergraduate class has at least one international student, transforming the nature of academic discussion no matter what the curricular subject. As the Vice Chancellor puts it, "Faculty phrase questions differently and students consider responses in terms of the changed composition of the class." Investments have been considerable, not only in recruitment and discounting but in a new International Center and special support activities. But the results transcend the classroom. The new Chinese student association not only holds a public New Year celebration, but also encourages its members to participate in many aspects of campus life; the Chinese dragon now chases the university lion through the town square as part of Homecoming. The presence of some African students amplifies discussion of other kinds of issues on campus. A bit of extra push, but also the sheer numbers of international students have a definite educational impact, though one that is difficult to measure precisely.[29]

Even schools with different specific contexts might tell a similar story. George Mason University has an unusually diverse student body as part of its regional draw. But it still has many American students who have never been out of the country, never interacted with foreigners, and they too find their educational experience affected by the presence of international colleagues. The consequences are not easy to pin down, because one hesitates to burden international students with special obligations to communicate with American peers. But an impact on classroom discussions and on some extracurricular contacts seems clear enough. Individual international students have played a leading role in campus activities, including Habitat efforts in New Orleans as well as specifically international programs; a Chinese student, for example, holds a leadership position in the National Society of Collegiate Scholars. Their achievement levels and points of view embellish courses from economics to dance. Many international students bring exceptional work habits and intelligence along with distinctive backgrounds. Many share their culture actively, not only in international weeks but by pairing with

American language students as "buddies." Some participate actively in outreach, participating in sessions in high schools and making contacts with local families.

Several community colleges could also point to direct educational ramifications. The Northern Virginia Community College, with over 9,000 international students from over 150 countries (including large contingents from Ethiopia and Iran, as well as Latin America), not only reacted with a multi-level English language program, but also an international studies degree with specializations in several of the regions involved. These developments in turn sparked a more coherent effort to define a global education program overall. From students and regional student groups, to individual curricular and festival activities, to a major planning process—not an insignificant sequence of building blocks.[30]

In general, as these examples suggest, there is growing interest in going beyond reliance on the informal contacts international students make, toward somewhat more systematic attempts to benefit, educationally, from their presence, at least at the undergraduate level. The increasing reliance on cohort approaches facilitates these efforts, by identifying groups of students, whether from China or elsewhere, which can be solicited for various kinds of educational collaborations. It remains important not to presume too much—the international students have their own purposes, and are often making significant sacrifices to fulfill them. But the goodwill and talents of many of these students allow some utilization without contradicting the core institutional obligations.

Cohort groups, particularly, also feed further connections. Several dual-degree Chinese undergraduates are already planning to return through applications to graduate programs. Alumni groups are forming—a longstanding strength for some American universities—in ways that will maintain connections and help promote further undergraduate enrollments. Undergraduate experiences feed additional linkages and exchanges, for example, of sports teams as well as faculty visits, and new summer study opportunities for American students. Officials at home institutions, in China and elsewhere, gain further knowledge and appreciation of American opportunities through the experiences of their undergraduates. Successful efforts, in sum, continue to reverberate, with clear benefits to the goals of global education more widely.

Intelligently organized, groups of international students can complement study abroad efforts in bringing vital perspectives to American students—given the fact that so many of the latter cannot manage more than a brief trip at best beyond the national boarders. The fact that many international students cluster in the very disciplines that are most impervious to study abroad can be an advantage here, which faculty and administrators should organize more intentionally than has usually been the case to date. Both emphases are necessary: as in so many aspects of global education, it's a diversification of effort, not undue complacency about a single sector, that really matters.

* * *

A mixture of motives, and no small amount of hope, justify the efforts of many American institutions to try to meet the challenges in the international student arena. Administrators and faculty committed to the recruitment and nurturing of international students believe they are helping the students themselves, building connections important to the national interest now and in future, serving narrower self-interest particularly in filling needs in science and technology, and—most optimistically of all—contributing directly to a broader global awareness on campus. A few institutions have not only increased their investment in this field, but have launched additional efforts to connect international and domestic students even beyond familiar venues such as international houses or extracurricular showcases for national cultures. There is every reason for continued attention to the connection between the international presence and the broader educational goals of American institutions, to make more certain the linkage between sincere hopes and at least some degree of reality. More pragmatically still, in a changing environment, there is every reason to keep tabs on best practices and the still-growing number of recent success stories, if the national stake in international recruitment is to be maintained.

7
Branch Campuses and Collaborations:
A New Frontier

Not a terribly funny story, but worth telling: it involves the number of American university presidents who see each other more often in Chinese or Indian hotels than in any domestic venue.[1] The enthusiasm for international ventures, plus the staggering procession of foreign delegations to American institutions, has reached new heights during the past five years. Some of the activity involves arrangements for study abroad or international recruitment, but much discussion goes beyond this. Shared degree programs, collaborative research ventures at institutional as well as faculty-to-faculty levels, and the effort to set up American operations directly abroad shape an increasingly varied and ambitious agenda.[2]

We're dealing, admittedly, with a somewhat narrower band of American schools than in the previous discussions of study abroad and international recruitment. There are some diverse windows, however, and the issues involved are informative beyond the specific efforts to date. The arena is difficult, with numerous failures to report along with some tentative successes. For some institutions, however, the activity constitutes a significant component of the future. It also illustrates some broader issues in global education, most obviously the challenge of emphasizing American values while fulfilling needs not only for mutual benefit but also for mutual responsiveness. Equally important, an interesting range of institutions are involved. While the Big Cats, the Ivies and their emulators, have a special toehold in some outreach efforts, given their negotiable prestige abroad, there are other types of entrants as well, with some proposals even including community colleges. Particularly noteworthy arrangements, sometimes involving significant funding, should not obscure the wider mix. The range suggests additional promise for the future, at least in some types of global implantations.

Not surprisingly, the phenomenon—which as we will see is not American alone—draws increased attention as part of globalization itself. The World Trade Organization seeks to promote what many call "borderless" education, particularly higher education, as part of free trade opportunities in general, and various drafts of legal guidelines have circulated.[3] Some pressure has been applied to certain countries, like Taiwan, to open to foreign institutions as part of a demonstration of commitment to free trade—the Taiwanese have only partly acquiesced, burdened by an overlarge educational establishment of their own. Sponsorship of educational "free zones," most notably in Qatar and the United Arab Emirates but now prospectively in South Korea as well, further testifies to the link between educational outreach, commercial exchange, and global interaction more generally.

* * *

Study abroad of course has generated the largest number of institutional outcroppings, mainly in Europe, in which a whole variety of colleges and universities maintain facilities where they can offer programs to American students. A few of these have opened to locals as well. Some expansion continues, as landlords continue to dangle the odd castle in Germany or mansion in Provence as sites for American activities; though a number of ventures have failed as well, because of high fixed costs against a shifting student clientele. These activities, whatever their merits, do not constitute the kinds of global ventures that currently draw the greatest attention. Some may form links with local universities, to enable the linguistically talented American student to take a course or two or to build some social activities. But these are, for the most part, activities not only by Americans, but for Americans, which is not the most interesting recent emphasis.

An effort to plant American higher education outposts abroad, with foreign students as the target, actually began even earlier than the study abroad establishments. The Lebanese American University, for example, originated as the American School for Girls in 1835. The late 19th and early 20th centuries saw the formation of a number of American colleges in China, Korea and Japan as well as in the Middle East. The initial impulse was strongly religious, as part of the wider Christian missionary effort, but there was always an interest in advancing higher education as well, amid often limited access to locally traditional higher education and frequently with some particular interest in women's advancement. Many of these early schools have since been taken over by national governments. Several major provincial universities in China, for example, point to American origins around 1900, often with a charming cluster of original buildings now dwarfed by recent campus growth. In the Middle East, however, several key institutions remain, now with largely if not exclusively secular purposes. The American Universities of Beirut (a mid-19th-century creation) and Cairo (post-World War I) have strong standing, with many prominent graduates.[4] They are heavily supported by scholarships issued by the United States government. USAID gave 1,250 scholarships to the American University of Beirut and the Lebanese American University in 2006–7. A newer program awards a smaller number of grants for Cairo, to male and female graduates of leading public national schools. These are significant efforts, and one might argue that their model is still valid. But they differ from the more recent institutional initiatives from the United States, in that they do not have direct sponsorship by American schools nor do they award American degrees.[5]

The field is also complicated by the rapid growth of "American" colleges and universities, particularly in the Middle East and Central Asia.[6] These schools are locally generated and run. They may or may not form any significant connections with institutions in the United States. They offer programs in English, with varying standards of language competence, and they mirror standard American curricula in some respects. Many emphasize management, a smaller number add technology and IT fields. Some are quite successful, even financially profitable after a few years, because of the prestige of the American label and the opportunity to claim competence in English (spiced in some instances by scattered employment of American professionals), because of real academic merit, and in some cases as well by quickly earned reputations as party schools. (One American University is located right next to a Hard Rock Café, an interesting juxtaposition.) While most of these self-styled American universities have no institutional links to the United States—though in some cases individual American faculty and staff participate—there are a few instances of dubious extensions from home base. A Hawaii University project in Lebanon—an outgrowth of an unaccredited institution in the U.S. with a potentially misleading name—drew some interest in ways that suggested local unawareness of the fact this was an American operation in little but label.[7]

This chapter focuses on a narrower slice of the wider international enthusiasm for American educational cachet. From the standpoint of American higher education and its global outreach, the crucial development centers on various new efforts at direct outreach, from individual institutions, to connect with global audiences and launch a growing array of collaborations with regional governments and programs. Explicit branch campuses are the most straightforward, and most ambitious, expression of these initiatives, but shared degree programs and guided consultancies deserve some attention as well. All of these extensions follow, at least in some measure, from a mix of motivations, which in turn combine several elements of the global education agenda.

Reasons to Innovate

Several spurs developed toward innovations in American educational outreach abroad, particularly in terms of activities by individual institutions.[8] Opportunities to tap expansive student markets played a key role. As countries emerged with new economic capacity but also new educational need, the idea of establishing branch campuses or direct educational programs of a more modest sort gained growing appeal. The rapid expansion of English language abilities in many parts of the world also fed a novel audience that might prefer local options to the risks and costs of going abroad. Two motives might intertwine in this appeal to students on site: the possibility of earning money might seem very real (though hopes often outstripped realities), but the interest in tapping types of students who probably could not, for financial and cultural reasons, come directly to the United States was keen as well, independent of profit. This mixture of motives emerged first for targets like Japan (where by now, however, domestic educational strength largely precludes new American efforts), but more recently has developed for south-east Asia and the Middle East (with some appetite as well for the rich but challenging markets of China and India). New constraints on direct recruitment of students to the United States, particularly in the aftermath of 9/11, added greatly to this impulse. Simply to retain access to students in some regions, particularly in the Middle East, new approaches seemed essential. Interest in recruiting international students, then, anchored most of the innovations in American institutional outreach. In some cases, novel ventures held a direct promise of bringing students ultimately to the United States as well: a branch campus or some similar operation might help facilitate a student's attending school in the United States for a semester or a year, cushioned by the training received in the home region, or it could whet appetites for further graduate education.

An even more obviously self-serving motive, often mentioned but hard to quantify, involved the role of new kinds of outreach in bolstering institutional prestige. A number of the more venturesome American universities are indeed on the make reputationally—even when already boasting reasonably high standing—though there are high-prestige entrants as well. Increasing awareness of international ranking systems, particularly from the United Kingdom and China, may increase this motivation.[9] Along with the profit incentive, this kind of self-interest helps explain why some observers, both at home and abroad, brand much of the outreach effort as "neo-colonial," an attempt to milk foreign enthusiasm for narrow institutional gain.

But innovative outreach also highlighted opportunities to serve a region directly, on the assumption (which needed to be considered and stated with care) that American professional training and larger educational values (now usually stripped of specific religious impulses) could help various countries on the path toward political, economic and social development.[10] Here, some of the motives that encouraged recruitment of international students were in play, but with more elaborate and more deliberately institutional focus. Goals resembled those that had supported earlier efforts like the American universities in Beirut or Cairo, but now they extended from individual American colleges. Assumptions that American education could encourage a more democratic politics, through the overall atmosphere of an American campus as well as through explicit training of new leaders; or could provide new kinds of management and technical expertise; or could contribute to the process of offering new opportunities for women—these were some of the impulses that, beyond access to additional student audiences, could build enthusiasm—on the American side, and hopefully among potential foreign collaborators as well—for new efforts. This was the context in which a sympathetic Crown

Prince in the Middle East urged how important it is for the United States to send something besides guns to the region. (Note also, unsurprisingly, that interest in American educational presence often embraced some local factors: in the United Arab Emirates, initial construction of higher education involved what many saw as undue reliance on Egyptian educators, and inviting some American outreach was intended to counterbalance.)[11]

Many efforts, as we will see, also held promise for new kinds of opportunities for American students, essentially extending study abroad but through intermixtures with international students rather than stand-alone programs. Campuses or programs designed primarily for foreigners can nevertheless provide locations for American visitors, studying the same subject areas as the international students or using the occasion for work on regional topics and language. In parts of the world where more standard study abroad may not seem too attractive, because of real or imagined fears about local hostilities, for example, these facilities may promote opportunities for desirable regional exposure otherwise not widely available.

Outreach sometimes offers faculty opportunities for research projects in a more global setting, or for additional collaborations with colleagues abroad.[12] Team research across borders is hardly a new item, and it does not necessarily bear very directly on global education. The rise of big science and big technology has increasingly grouped scholars from many countries within projects dealing with physics or chemical engineering. The rise of international science and technology communities (and to a lesser degree, social science clusters) is an important aspect of globalization. Where institutional outreach enters in, within this larger context, is in facilitating global extensions of the research endeavor, in several different directions. First, an institutional outpost can promote research on comparative or international issues from disciplines less routinely involved in team projects. Rhetoric scholars thus, around an international branch campus, study writing processes for students with first languages other than English. Management professors seize opportunities to think about comparative approaches or regional management adaptations to global networks. Second, outreach efforts can facilitate connections even in the sciences on global issues, such as climate change or the international aspects of information security. Collaborations on these topics may develop without specific institutional outreach, but the latter can draw in a wider involvement and can on occasion bring in regional scholars (for example, from Africa) not always included in the more standard networks. Third, certain kinds of collaborations, particularly around joint or dual degree programs, build more detailed levels of contact among faculty and graduate students that create a basis for interactive research in a variety of fields—often with the added merit of recognizing the growing parity of cutting-edge scholarship in places like India and China.

The basic point, obviously, is that institutional outreach can frequently respond to a variety of otherwise somewhat separate motivations in the global education field. Expanding access to international students and developing regional impact head the list, but a single operation can also legitimately address other key interests as well, helping both to serve and to coalesce an overall global agenda in ways that may inform the home campus quite directly. And a final point—though also obvious. Institutional outreach increases the number of faculty and administrators encouraged (in some cases prodded) to learn more about regional and global issues beyond their comfort zone. A few authorities are beginning to recognize that teaching abroad (and not just to carefully transplanted American students) has direct benefits to the individuals involved and, by extension when faculty return, to the institution as a whole. A persuasive recent article notes how teaching abroad widens one's research perspective, simply because of the need to think about topics in a different cultural context, while obviously acquainting the scholar with specific regional differences in education and student dynamics—often encouraging innovative thinking not only on global issues but on other matters such as interdisciplinary teaching and scholarship. (Institutions like West Virginia University are even beginning to help with airfares for faculty teaching even short courses abroad, precisely because of these unexpected benefits.)[13]

The newer kinds of outreach activities are immensely demanding, a point to which we will now turn. They may be justified, however, by the mixture of benefits they provide, by the strength of the combined motivations involved. Prioritizing these complex experiments is not an easy call, because it does place demands on such a variety of human resources at the home institution. Clearly, a number of quite different types of American institutions are deciding that the potential gains are truly compelling.

Collaborative Degrees

Most accounts of American installations abroad do not include collaborative degrees, which we have already referred to in considering sources of international students. The approach, which is rapidly gaining popularity at least at the discussion level, nevertheless deserves consideration as an outreach mechanism, with its own special promise and problems. A brief summary here will warrant inclusion in the chapter's conclusion, precisely because of the inherently mutualist approach.

There is no tally of the number of joint or dual degree programs involving American institutions (and as noted before, other countries are busy with this approach as well). Yale University seems to have a number of arrangements with Chinese universities. Several leading centers in South Korea are openly courting collaborative degree arrangements.

The basic idea, of course, is to provide students opportunities to study in two sites (for our purposes, one American, one foreign) and receive more than a conventional degree for their efforts. Collaborative degrees encourage both study abroad, but in a focused discipline, and the recruitment of international students. They often promote faculty interactions as well—these are essential simply in designing and running a mutually acceptable program, and they can blossom from this into further educational discussion and/or shared research projects. Unlike some of the more ambitious outreach efforts, collaborative degrees can also emanate from faculty initiatives, though they ultimately require administrative involvement and blessing; in this sense they provide a particularly decentralized and relatively spontaneous way to encourage global connections.

Collaborative degrees can operate at several levels. Some offerings can encourage undergraduates. The University of Aachen, in Germany, has arranged several collaborative degrees in Management, allowing German students to spend a year abroad (including at American partner institutions), and Americans to do the same at Aachen. The result is a more diversified and internationally sensitive undergraduate experience—and, of course, two degrees rather than one. Negotiations are currently underway between an American university and a Korean counterpart, in tourism. Both have strong undergraduate training in this field, but with somewhat different specific emphases; and obviously, in tourism, simply having a year's worth of international experience and perspective is a career plus, at least as clearly as in Management.

Master's and doctoral programs win interest, with more specific attention not just to international experience but to the sharing of research specialties and strengths. Several doctoral programs in climate dynamics or environmental change are in the works, involving Asian or Turkish and American collaborations. Opportunities to study at two institutions capitalize on the specialized strengths of particular faculty, and in this case the chance to study in two different regions of the world enhances student research scope as well. The University of Malta, eager to build its offerings in conflict analysis, proposes a joint Master's degree with an American counterpart where the field is somewhat more fully developed. The result will be some prestige enhancement for Malta, but also an opportunity for students from both countries to gain wider perspective in a field that has obvious international dimensions. The list of existing arrangements, active negotiations, and further possibilities is considerable. In the long run, this relatively simple mechanism may prove to be the most useful and durable of all the new efforts in global outreach.

There are, of course, complexities and drawbacks. Harmonizing two curricula takes work, and some negotiations founder on the difficulty. The programs can be costly: each requires, for example, two separate admissions decisions, to assure both partners that appropriate standards are being maintained. Most programs are inherently small, a fact which may limit the bureaucratic investment but by the same token does not distribute it over a wide funding base. Some programs face the difficulty, already discussed, of international imbalance: fewer American students may be interested than their more venturesome foreign counterparts, and this can drag down an otherwise promising initiative.

Accreditation issues loom large on the American side. Dual degree programs, in which students complete the essential requirements of an American institution (taking all the required courses in an undergraduate major, for example, even when they do not cover the whole undergraduate program) while doing separate work abroad, may pose only limited difficulty. They must be reported to accrediting agencies and sometimes, for public institutions, to state offices, but since they do not really alter the core American degree they may not involve elaborate inspection. Joint degrees, which particularly at the graduate level are much simpler for the student than having to fulfill two full sets of requirements (and which also provide more impetus for faculty globalization), are more complex. They usually build on an approved American degree but by definition they alter it to include a year or more on a foreign site and, where a dissertation is involved, some kind of joint production as well. Many accreditation groups, and state agencies, require that these be treated as new programs, with all the paperwork and approval process these entail. These are hurdles that can be jumped, but they are not simple and, again, they do involve both faculty and administrative investment. These are hurdles that also, in my opinion, might be revisited as agencies recognize the desirability of global engagement and find more flexible means of maintaining contact with appropriate standards.

Then there is the challenge, accreditation aside, of eating one's academic cake while having it: how to capitalize on the advantages of collaborative degrees while providing some assurance that students are not getting an unwarranted academic bargain. Here, dual degrees, though easier to arrange, are the real problem. Joint degrees (a single degree issued by two institutions) are hard to arrange, but they can leave all parties satisfied that the student will earn whatever single award is conferred. But dual degrees provide two sheepskins for, often, little more than the price of one—few additional requirements beyond a single degree, except for working in two places. Each American institution involved must decide what extra assignments it wishes to impose—up to, in the case of the Ph.D., two separate if cognate dissertations—in order to avoid a sense of unjustified shortcutting with the dual-degree approach. The issues here are difficult in principle—for at the same time one does not wish unduly to discourage interested students by making the path too convoluted—and they can involve extra faculty time in monitoring an additional project of some kind. All of this may be quite manageable when there are other advantages involved, from access to international students to setting the basis for cross-border faculty research projects, but there is no question about the additional effort needed both to complete an initial arrangement and then to maintain its effectiveness.

Consultative Relationships

Individual American faculty have contributed to the development of institutions abroad since the 19th century, helping to plan curricula, serving on the faculty or in administration. Recently, however, the enthusiasm for American higher education and the desire by institutions to find methods of additional international engagement have generated a number of formal consulting arrangements that go beyond these individual involvements. These in turn form another aspect of college and university outreach, with clear and hopefully mutual advantages without, however, the level of commitment which actual branch operations entail.

One of the leaders in this endeavor has been American University, in Washington D.C. In the late 1990s American partnered with the government of Sharjah,[14] an emirate in the United Arab Emirates, to establish the American University of Sharjah. The ruler provided substantial funding, and built an imposing campus, for an operation that opened its doors in 1997. American University's guidance helped develop curricula in a number of key areas, both graduate and undergraduate. It promoted the hiring of a large number of Americans for both faculty and administration (by no means primarily from American University itself; an early president, for example, had previously served in a similar capacity in Arkansas, while the business school recruited leadership from places like the University of Arizona). Sharjah carefully stipulated that its programs were based on American-style instruction, in the English language, but modified by articulation within Arab and Islamic values—"thoroughly grounded in the Arab culture of the region in which it is located"; not a branch of American University in Washington, it nevertheless was able to claim a "close affiliation" with that school in its promotional materials. Its affiliation doubtless facilitated its unusually rapid attainment of American accreditation (from Middle States Commission on Higher Education) as well as disciplinary accreditation in engineering from the American ABETS organization (one of only two institutions in the Middle East to gain this prize).

Backed by generous financing and the American collaboration, which went well beyond the vague and sometimes misleading claims of more ordinary "American" universities in this region and elsewhere, AUS advanced quickly. By 2008 it had 5,000 students, drawn from the entire region and not just the emirates, and it had graduated a number of promising leaders in the UAE itself—including the first female government minister. There seemed little question that the formal consultative relationship was helping the institution meet its goal of becoming a major educational force in the region.

What did American University gain from the deal? There was obviously a financial incentive, though how much this exceeded the costs of sending advisors and providing consultation time is not clear. Individual faculty and administrators seem to have profited to some degree. The University was also able to send students to the new facility, thus promoting study abroad in what was otherwise a challenging region, while attracting students from AUS for visits, semester stays, or graduate school applications. Opportunities for providing further training for some regional faculty also emerged, a common theme in consultative discussions here and elsewhere. The enterprise thus both reflected and enhanced AU's international mission, and its striking success contributed new prestige as well.

Flush with this experience, American University turned to a second consultative opportunity, this time with Nigeria.[15] ABTI-The American University of Nigeria was formed in consultative partnership, opening its doors in 2005 with the goal of bringing American-style education to sub-Saharan Africa. Nigerian partners were presumably able to provide significant funding, based on unexpectedly substantial oil revenues in recent years. Consultation focused not only on curriculum but on facilities design and IT infrastructure. Even more than with AUS, the new institution formally emphasized the provision (in principle—this aspect is still under construction) of student and faculty exchanges with the American home base, with research cooperation down the line as well. The hope was that the first AU student would visit in 2008, to set this cluster of goals in motion. American University directly provided a vice president for international affairs, who oversaw the mutual coordination. And, as with AUS, American's involvement facilitated the vetting and employment of other American academics and administrators. AUN seemed to be progressing well, though its recency precluded significant evaluation and progress may turn out to be slower than in Sharjah. Still, this second model at least tentatively confirmed the utility and the potentially mutual benefits of consultative outreach.

There were some downsides. Consultation did not assure standards, and there were some rumor-level concerns that Sharjah students did not uniformly maintain the level of English language proficiency that would allow them to take full advantage of their classes. Accommodation to regional customs raised potential dilemmas, as in the fairly strict separation of the sexes not only in student life but in classrooms in Sharjah. There was always the danger of confusion, for student applicants and the American institution alike: materials that carefully disclaimed the actual provision of American degrees might be misunderstood given references to the close affiliation amid enthusiasm for precisely such credentials. Some concerns surfaced as well about potentially excessive financial rewards, at least for some top administrators. Inevitably also, some local participants worried about the bossiness and insensitivity of some of their American partners—an issue that has emerged even more strongly in some other settings.

At the same time, the apparent success of this kind of consulting relationship, in advancing the emergence of major new higher education centers, plus the relative absence of significant risk for what might be regarded as a limited liability American partner—financial risk, certainly, but also exposure to any accreditation concerns—plus the obvious contributions to internationalization goals back home, made the model potentially appealing.

Consultative networks, though less focused than the American University initiatives, have also involved several historically black institutions in the United States and partners in post-apartheid South Africa, where a number of struggling universities, such as Transformed University in the Eastern Cape Province, sought guidance on curriculum development, teaching methods and other issues. Michigan State University's African Studies Center also developed advisory relationships, with particular attention to the cultural sensitivity needed to make consultancy effective across boundaries.[16]

And there were wider possibilities. A number of initiatives in Pakistan involved approaching American universities about a similar kind of consultative relationship, though to date the instability of this country has precluded the closing of any firm deals. Institutions in China and in Saudi Arabia have floated the idea of setting up affiliate schools with a consultative American partner.

Interesting opportunities also involve community college planning. American success in this field, and the deep educational needs of some societies that lack this intermediate higher education level, have drawn a number of proposals for consultative relationships to develop campus networks in Brazil, in the Kurdish area of Iraq, and most recently in Sierra Leone. Funding presents a challenge, even to support significant consultation, but opportunities for real interaction, as opposed to preliminary planning, may yet emerge.

More limited but still institutional consultative relationships include sponsorship of Chinese administrators spending a month with American counterparts, and inviting return visits, or more systematic multi-year administrative collaborations, complete with mutual visits, for expanding higher education institutions in places like Montenegro. The University of Pittsburgh and other American centers provided consultative services in the emergence of new business schools in various parts of East-central Europe after 1991. George Mason University played a similar role in sponsoring conflict resolution centers in Ukraine, Georgia and other regions in the same time frame. Arrangements of this sort, often funded by the U.S. government, were far more limited in scope and duration than the American University models, but they had similar implications in terms of facilitating student and faculty exchanges even after the duration of the formal relationship (including faculty training and degree work).

It seems likely that the consultation model will spread, quite possibly along the fuller lines sketched by American University. The University of Arizona has recently announced a service agreement with the Jiangsu Provincial Department of Education, in China, to provide academic content for several degree programs at a new (yet-to-be-built) Nanjing International University.

This will involve extensive visits and consultations by Arizona faculty, as well as training for Chinese academics in the United States. The arrangement in fact goes beyond the Sharjah model, in predicting actual Arizona degrees for some Nanjing International students who take an outright Arizona curriculum in their senior year. Sparked by this model, a new international university venture in Vietnam, at Ban Tre, is also looking for an American consultative partner. The pattern could be catching, at least as international education operations gear up in many countries, precisely because of the combination of benefit, cultural flexibility and delimited responsibility for both partners in an arrangement. Current discussions involving agencies from China and private consortia in India also enlist several American community colleges and associations, with some shadowing arrangements in the Chinese case; but to date the consultancy models here are more diffuse.

Branch Campuses

The most striking kind of outreach involves setting up actual American degree programs on foreign soil, aimed primarily at an international student audience and in collaboration with some regional partners, either private or governmental or both.

In recent years, over 82 institutions have set up campuses or programs abroad (up from 22 in 2004), and over half of these have been from the United States (Britain and Australia are the most eager participants outside American ranks, but India has important technical outposts in the Gulf).[17] All sorts of places and schools are involved. Webster University has a bachelor's program and an MBA in Switzerland; Suffolk offers an initial two undergraduate years in Madrid after which students can complete studies back in Boston. Carnegie Mellon specializes in focused programs, in management, IT, and entertainment technology, with different particulars in various places from Qatar to Australia. A host of offerings are available in Singapore, from Carnegie Mellon in Information Systems, to Cornell in management and hotel management, to the University of Illinois (a joint degree with the National University of Singapore) in chemical engineering, to UNLV in hotel administration (bachelors) and hospitality (masters). A large grant from the government has facilitated a number of institutions based in Qatar, including Cornell's medical college, Texas A and M in undergraduate engineering, Georgetown in foreign service, and Virginia Commonwealth in design. Hong Kong is another cluster center, with particular focus on business programs from a whole range of institutions from Northwestern to the University of Northern Iowa to South Florida; some more general bachelors programs are also available. The University of Indianapolis has a wide-ranging, though controversial, set of undergraduate offerings in Greece. Some undergraduate or two-year programs are available in China, and here too there are several technology and business degrees from several American institutions (some in conjunction with Chinese university partners).

Georgia Tech offers specific degrees in France, Singapore, Italy, South Africa and China, with plans for India. George Mason University has opened a set of undergraduate and masters programs in Ras al Khaimah, in the United Arab Emirates, and is developing a more limited global affairs masters curriculum at Cheju, South Korea (plus the entry-level two-year undergraduate curriculum, which assumes later completion back in the United States). New York University is another ambitious entrant, with a dual-degree law program in Singapore and now plans for a liberal arts curriculum in Abu Dhabi.

About a third of all branch campuses offer only one degree program, and several others (like Carnegie Mellon in Qatar, with business and computer science) specialize strongly—but there are wider-ranging initiatives as well, as over 66% of the branches have developed more than one subject area. Over 70% of all efforts include business, IT, or both; 23% offer only bachelor's degrees, 58% include (or are confined to) the master's level. Granting the complexity of data, in a rapidly changing and only informally censused field, current estimates see average enrollment standing at 1,083.

In terms of recent geographic preferences, the Arabian Gulf (Qatar, but also increasingly the Emirates), Hong Kong and Singapore obviously have pride of place, because of considerable openness to international initiatives and a great deal of local support. China has drawn huge attention, because of the compelling size of the student market, but actual engagement is more limited because of constraints on investment offerings by potential partners (typically, physical facilities are discussed but not initial operating funds) and regulations by the government that may be interpreted to require an active Chinese educational partnership. (The most successful foreign ventures to date come from Nottingham and Australia.)[18] India has focused a great deal of recent discussion, because of the possibility of changes in legislation that will permit the creation of educational free zones in which international programs might locate. Currently, only shared degrees with Indian partners can even be discussed, and they remain quite limited in fact. There are over 30 twinned programs (some estimates go as high as 66) with private universities in India, but none can offer an explicitly American degree without transfer to the United States. As noted, South Korea, in several locations, is developing free zones that may host a number of American institutions and consortia, the most ambitious one near the new airport in Incheon; but these have yet to mature beyond the talking stage. Vietnamese authorities are discussing an international university center as well.

The recent flurry of activity succeeds a decidedly cautionary past. In the 1980s over 30 American institutions set up operations in Japan, building on an apparent appetite similar to that now anticipated in China and the Gulf, and of course on the nation's growing prosperity.[19] Only one of these ventures survived, an impressively successful program from Temple University that continues to operate with a wide range of undergraduate and masters-level degrees and certificates. All of the other efforts perished, most rather quickly, the victims of government hostility (which fell short of outright bans, but which discouraged any kind of local accreditation or encouragement) and the increasingly successful competition from Japanese schools, plus often high costs (with tuition levels above what students wanted to pay, but which were compelled by the expenses of doing business), plus limits on the English language capacity of many enrollees (despite years of training). Temple did manage to overcome the obstacles, though there were many crises and alarums; but the failure rate was obviously more impressive still. More recently, a Johns Hopkins initiative in Singapore collapsed, when student interest and funding did not meet needs. A widely trumpeted proposal by Kean University to have the "first American university to open an extensive . . . university campus on Chinese soil"[20] seems to have been stillborn; while a similar University of Montana initiative has simply not won government approval. Besides failures or embarrassing delays, there are hosts of decisions not to bother, as when the University of Washington (which claims to receive a proposal a week) turned away from a government-encouraged invitation in China. This is difficult terrain, with a shaky past; caution is abundantly justified.

Institutions that have been established operate mainly with investments either from university partners, as in India and several places in China, where facilities and some administrative infrastructure are provided in return for the prestige and shared offerings available from the American side. Or, as most notably in Qatar and the Emirates, they open with investments from government or a business partner or both. A few ventures have relied on American investment funds, mostly for very specific programs where substantial fees can be charged, as in some business school initiatives; but this approach is rapidly declining. Public universities in the United States indeed must typically demonstrate that they are not using domestic funds at all, an understandable limitation particularly in tight budget times but which imposes obvious burdens on negotiating power.

Direct foreign operations involve a number of other challenges as well. Interviewed by the *New York Times* about George Mason's operation in Ras al Khaimah, I blurted the truth: "I will freely admit that this has all been more complicated than I expected,"[21] and I'm assured that many colleagues would say the same. International partners not infrequently seem to change arrangements that, to American eyes, have been firmly contracted, because of shifting political or financial circumstances. This was the experience of an American business school operating a mixed on-site and distance MBA program in a southeastern European city, for example.

- Recruiting students is typically more difficult than expected, requiring at the least a longer lead time before satisfactory enrollments are accumulated. While the idea of directly earning an American degree without the full cost and displacement of going to the United States is immensely appealing, potential students in fact have many options to choose from, and often know little or nothing about any American university short of Harvard or Stanford.

– Cost may be a factor: to operate with at least some American faculty, whose pay runs much higher than that of most foreign counterparts, tuitions typically surpass local levels (or those of international branches from other places).

– English is a perennial challenge, as in dealing with international students generally. Setting scores too high discourages applicants, though many American branches offer language training to bridge the gap. But going too low produces students who cannot operate effectively in class. American institutions in the Emirates currently display a range of policies, seeking to balance attractiveness with effective learning; and some local institutions, like the (unaffiliated) American University of Dubai have actually moved their own requirements up, because of the effectiveness issue. But some newer American entrants, prestigious back home, are low balling in terms of English standards. (Language issues are more complex in a branch campus setting than for international students in the United States, since outside of class students can more easily return to a non-English setting. This can make reliance on scores or a carefully prepared transition from exclusive language training more pressing.)

– Organizing student life at an American branch, particularly with undergraduates involved, raises obvious issues of providing an appropriately open academic climate while respecting local customs—the balance can be struck, but it requires effort.

– Even determining appropriate programs is a challenge, particularly for undergraduate ventures that go beyond the ever-popular management and IT staples. Biology, for example, hot stuff back home, is a less easy sale in some parts of the world, though a bit of patience may pay off over time. The complexities are intriguing, but they can be daunting as well.

The international operation places significant burdens on faculty and staff on the domestic campus. Admissions authorities must evaluate foreign transcripts, often amid considerable variety. Registrars must help determine class schedules. Faculties must vet any new colleagues, including some with degrees from places other than the United States; and they or their departmental staff must provide sample syllabi as well as basic degree curricula, with regular updates as needed. And there must be some arrangements for monitoring the quality of student work, through periodic visits as well as the provision of experienced faculty from the home campus. Assessment activities must reproduce American levels and standards. Faculty interest in direct participation will typically vary, as stereotypes about many foreign locations, security concerns, as well as the standard range of professional and family constraints come into play. Accreditation issues are manageable, in that the programs derive from the domestic source and have already been approved; but of course there must be additional reports and site visits. But there is no question that, overall, a whole range of people, on the spot but also at the home campus, have to devote considerable time to the initiative, and while some prove devoted, even excited by the new venture, most can legitimately note that they were not adequately informed about the responsibilities amid the excitement of doing the deal in the first place.

Financial issues inevitably loom large. Even exploratory trips, like a recent courtship visit to potential Indian partners by Cornell's President, can cost $50,000 or more.[22] Once established, particularly given current problems with the dollar and considerable inflation in many parts of the Middle East and Asia, costs almost always surpass expectations. (Faculty housing outlays in the Emirates, for instance, have recently been increasing by about 15% a year.) A few ventures have been so abundantly cushioned—the Education City project in Qatar is the most striking example—that concerns may be limited, but even here there are unexpected surprises.

Money and perceived political stability constrain many current branch campus projects, which in turn becloud the future of this kind of activity outside of a few identified centers. Carnegie Mellon University is in some stage of considering a project in Kazakhstan, but results and timetables are unclear. Proposals for branches in Iraq or Pakistan shop for American interest, but at least foreseeably it is difficult to follow up.

The biggest challenge, of course, both in current terms and for any prospective projects, involves balancing the necessary American standards of quality with local expectations, and particularly the expectations of active partners.[23] Issues range from the sublime to the (from a liberal American standpoint) ridiculous: establishing American educational presence for an international audience, some officials and some prospective students and their parents alike, involves producing staff and faculty who "look" like Americans, which means white and unaccented. It takes some time and effort to generate greater realism. Adjusting to local habits, as in the Gulf or India, of referring to students as "boys" or "girls," or seeking tactfully to modify the habits, can be an interesting challenge, with significance well beyond the nomenclature involved. Some foreign partners, private investors most obviously but even some governments, will hope for quick returns on investment, which puts pressure on enrollment as well as costs. Where active partnership with a foreign university is involved, compromises over programs may be difficult—as in a Chinese case where a religious studies course had to be significantly modified and relabeled.[24]

Many of the countries American institutions most seek to court, precisely because of the desirability of exposure to American values at a time of foreign policy tension, also have authoritarian governments and constraint on the free movement of books and internet access. Blatant interference with free inquiry obviously cannot be accepted, but it may be permissible to urge faculty to be a bit prudent. And the need to change a biology book, in the Middle East, to one that did not emphasize lab work on fetal pigs might be regarded as a harmless concession. Meeting local government standards in other respects can be challenging—as the earlier Japanese experience already demonstrated.[25] Establishment of free zones in principle exempts foreign institutions from local regulations. But in many places local accreditation is still essential in practice, for example, to recruit students who might wish government employment in the future. The task is usually manageable—in many places in the Gulf, for example, accreditation standards themselves are based on American example—but the additional bureaucratic investment is considerable. Research expectations form another intriguing challenge. While major research institutions operate in several sites, indeed forming the basis for some partnership programs particularly at the graduate level, a modern research tradition is less clearly established in many parts of the Middle East— and an American presence in this regard might help a bit (a point on which American outreachers and local partners often agree); but developing this kind of agenda, amid the press of setting up a teaching operation, is not an easy task.[26]

Partners often want American education but emphatically, and understandably, do not want local students to become American. American instructors, even as they carefully encourage change in such areas as gender relations, learn for their part that they have a role in making students the best professionals possible—but not Americans. It's not an easy dance.[27]

The obvious point, despite recent and ongoing enthusiasm, is that branch campuses constitute a major undertaking. Some current ventures will surely fail, though the earlier Temple example, from Japan, reminds us that with tenacity and imagination some may also succeed, to regional and institutional benefit alike.

Even as we must await longer term outcomes, there are significant interim rewards. The chance to see a first class or two, after the detailed effort required in launching an operation initially, can be deeply moving. A young Saudi woman, part of an initial English language class and then successfully matriculating as an undergraduate, almost dances with excitement: "I'm gonna be a businesswoman." A collage of young men and women (though more men), ranging in origin from India to Egypt, seriously debate the need for a better student government constitution, so their representatives can be more conscientiously chosen; and enthusiasm for the idea of outlets for suggestions and (yes) grievances (food complaints seem to unite students across borders) runs high. American faculty, serving, for example, in Qatar, note their own unanticipated enlightenments, as stereotypes are modified and both teaching and research gain new perspectives through the challenge of addressing a more truly international audience than has ever been achieved back home. "I believe that Texas A&M made the correct decision in choosing to become a part of Education City, and we can make a positive difference in that part of the world. . . . My learning curve was deep, [but] I developed a profound respect for Arabic culture and for the Islamic religion [and] made some lifelong friends . . . in the community."[28] American students, spending a semester in the same settings—a key benefit of the best-designed branch campus efforts—similarly report important new learning and a network that, they think, will pay off in the future.

Other, less tangible benefits can accrue. Precisely because the effort is difficult, a branch operation or ambitious joint degree or consultative project can pull people at the home campus out of conventional constraints, forcing them to think about broader international issues in ways that redound to the benefit of other facets of a global education program. The gains range from learning that a "strange" place is actually quite congenial and interesting, to gaining new vantage points on shared global issues. The experience can be informative in unexpected ways, and students are not the only ones who learn.

Where Are We Heading?

Objections to branch campus experiments, of any sort, are numerous, and from various quarters. On the American side, particularly where public institutions are involved, some legislators have worried about possible uses of taxpayer funds for foreign benefit. A few at the federal level complain that providing higher education access simply heightens the potential for foreign economic competition, and possibly strategic–military competition as well, by giving away secrets to American success.[29] No major regulatory movement has been mounted, because the whole area is so new and because there are clear policy advantages to American educational outreach as well, but the issue could rise up more strongly in future.

Foreign authorities have reason to worry. American (or other cross-border) campuses can spin out of any reasonable monitoring control, which is why some countries, like Taiwan and after a brief flurry South Africa, remain extremely nervous while many others surround the initiatives with hosts of requirements including co-participation by a local institution. There have been cases not only of failure but of probable fraud. The Indianapolis University effort in Greece has been dogged by accusations of quality shortfalls, deliberate falsification of student credentials in order to boost enrollments, and illegal collusion to keep students out of the military draft.[30] Whatever the merits here, there is unquestionable pressure on many international operations to consider shortcuts to boost treasured enrollments or delay failures.

The question of greed cannot be ignored. There is no doubt that many American institutions have looked to foreign operations as a new source of domestic funding—as in Montana's (apparently stillborn) plans to tap China. A University President recently boasted, in an arguably unseemly fashion, about the $50 million gift received from the government of Abu Dhabi, in return for opening a campus in a few years: "It's like earnest money; if you're a $50 million donor, I'll take you seriously. It's a way to test their bona fides."[31] There are some fine lines here: a branch operation is a huge undertaking, and it typically costs more than anticipated. Some profit may be an essential component of motivation (and it certainly refutes the criticism about misusing American funds), and some earnings may eventually be plowed back into global education efforts. But there can be too much zeal, and certainly it's hard to shake off the perception that profit allure displaces claims about more benevolent and complex global goals. Charges of neo-colonial exploitation ring out on all sides of the waters, and they may increase over time.

Yet the other, nobler motives do flourish. Most branch campuses are supported by a real commitment to global education and to mutual benefit for faculty and students, back home as well as regionally. The American schools involved, for the most part at least, realize (or soon realize) that there are easier ways to make a buck, even in hard domestic times; the real international effort has to be founded on educational goals. The flurry of branch campus interest may flag, though this has not yet occurred. But it represents an important extension of the broader interest in using innovation to enhance global connection.

A few probabilities exist. Some of the current initiatives will fail, particularly as competition (from other American institutions, and from foreign entries) heats up, though a few will likely take root and flourish. It is in fact vital to acknowledge the possibility of failure, in efforts justified by appropriate institutional goals but undeniably chancier than more conventional, domestic endeavors. Opportunities to blend branch campus outposts with more distance learning provision, only lightly ventured thus far, will surely increase. For most interested American institutions, collaborations, rather than solo operations, will probably deepen, as a means of truly combining local interests with American contributions, meeting the genuine goal of global value added.* This is why joint degrees and consultations must be considered along with branch

---

* Growing collaborative mutuality, virtually inevitable as educational disparities lessen in many parts of the world, has one other crucial corollary: so far the United States has hosted virtually no cross-border educational initiatives, a revealing comment on the range of institutions already available but also, perhaps, on some smug insularity. It would be great to see some American universities reach out to foreign collaborators for some shared degree programs on domestic campuses—and American students in areas like global studies could benefit hugely as well.

campuses outright, for their long-range future may be more promising. Whatever the formulas—and a mixture of endeavors may prove suitable—the effort to widen student audiences, to provide American students and faculty with global experience beyond the more conventional boundaries of study abroad, and the desire to use American educational values to contribute globally and to counterbalance some of the less appreciated national policy initiatives—will surely sustain and widen the effort at innovative outreach.

One additional point is abundantly clear. The regulatory climate for cross-border efforts, for branch campuses but even for more modest joint degree initiatives, must further mature. Assuming the global goal is accepted—and we still might see a nationalist backlash, either from governments abroad or from our own—further thought must be devoted to meeting the complex challenge of quality assurance amid flexible collaborations. Partnerships, which will probably constitute the most attractive future option, are actually impeded particularly from the American side, amid accreditation approaches better suited to the past than to the future. There is every need for continued discussion and exploration, in the American institutional interest and, one hopes, in the interest of a global community as well. For, whatever the precise shapes and the ultimate tally of successes and failures, the push to create global campuses has solid foundations and will only grow with time.

* * *

The final statement for this chapter is simple enough: how does one decide whether a global venture is worth pursuing or not, at least at a fairly general institutional level? Whatever the decision process, whether by committee or administrative officer, the question is crucial, and it must and can be answered, drawing together various elements covered in this chapter already:

- The project must promise, at least in the medium run if not immediately, some educational benefit to students at the institution.
- It must have, or be capable of winning, interest and active participation from at least some relevant academic units—even if other units will have to be persuaded down the line.
- It must be affordable, which usually, pending some philanthropy, means it must be revenue neutral at the least.
- It must involve an interesting part of the world, often where policy issues or probable future trends indicate the importance of American involvement. It must be framed in terms of mutual collaboration.
- It must, of course, be manageable, in relationship to everything else going on.
- And it should often, if not always, promise possible innovation for the institution, through novel types of exchange, novel mixture of disciplines, new learning opportunities for faculty and staff as well as for students.

The checklist is easy enough to state, less simple admittedly to apply in advance of an actual initiative. But the list does distinguish among projects, providing sorting opportunities that are essential given the abundance of available proposals and ideas.

While cautionary, the checklist raises questions that can be answered affirmatively—at least affirmatively enough to justify moving ahead. The challenges of international collaboration or outreach must not obscure the huge potential benefits—to the students involved, to faculty and administrators who can grow through the experience, and to the institution and the region involved alike. When the project does advance, the sense of achievement and the outright excitement are hard to match in academic life.

8
Leadership and Administration:
Bureaucratic Innovation without Bureaucratization

As global education initiatives proliferate, often covering a wide range of activities, issues of structure inevitably emerge. Historically, as we have seen, many institutions long avoided a fully articulated global strategy: study abroad was encouraged, under one office; recruitment of international students was a matter for admissions; faculty groups dealt with curricular issues. The result could be fine, but it could hardly be called coherent. And often there were (and still are) gaps, for example, as between curricular emphases and carefully considered frameworks for study abroad. International students, once on campus, were regarded as a province of a Student Affairs office, apart from their explicit academic studies, and again while this might work well it hardly tied this element to other aspects of global education. Coordination and interrelationships remain key concerns on many campuses.

Another organizational challenge focuses on the international research connections of individual faculty. It's difficult, in the first place, simply to keep tabs on who's doing what where—not for purposes of regulation, but to try to maximize the value of relationships. Most international education officials now judge the value of faculty research links in terms of enhancing campus internationalization above all. They want faculty to use their ties to bolster the global prestige of the university, to enrich course offerings back home, and to recruit more international students. But these goals are not foremost in the minds of many of the scholars involved. As a William and Mary global education official recently noted, "We have hundreds of faculty who do international research, but it's unclear to me how to translate that into international development work."[1] Greater campus coordination (plus more money for international offices; remember the source of the comments) is the obvious response—but how to do it? There are important cases where a single initiative, thanks to good school organization, blossomed into fuller payoff: a University of Pennsylvania project on HIV in Botswana, from the School of Medicine, led to undergraduate research and study abroad opportunities; Delaware State, with scant international track record, used a small grant on malaria in Uganda to build coursework on global public health and a cooperation agreement in principle with a Ugandan university. But these examples could easily be matched by promising projects that had no wider echo at all, because of lack of campus awareness and lack of adequate organizational push.[2]

Coordination challenges often apply as well to discussions of relationships with different parts of the world. It is not easy to develop the strategic apparatus that will allow an institution to decide that, for the next period, some parts of the world will be given more attention than others. Curricular decisions in this regard are often the provinces of individual departments and centers. Outreach efforts, orchestrated by singular programs or faculty groups, appropriately follow particular interests, without explicit regard for their potential in stretching a university too thin in relationship to other regional priorities. A school may decide on special emphases on, say, the Middle East and east Asia, but individual campus segments may also clamor for responses to needs and opportunities in Africa, or south Asia—and it is not easy to identify the mechanisms that will sort out the claims. The flip side of the coordination challenge, also quite real, involves different initiatives applying to the same region, operating however in mutual ignorance. Simply collecting information on programs and relationships with China, for example, is not an insignificant task. And while some data quests may prove unnecessary, as the involvements have little fruitful connection, there are other cases where several units are even dealing with a single Chinese or Korean university, but without taking advantage of their potential coordinated strength. It is not unheard of to show up at a foreign university and be greeted with a proudly displayed MOU with your own institution, signed a few years back by a unit leader who did not bother to report his achievement centrally.

The sheer burden of international interactions, however pleasant and engaging in principle, is an organizational factor as well. An institution like Carnegie Mellon, with over 60 international operations or collaborations, some major, others quite narrow, with over 40 different responsible faculty, needs an elaborate chart just to keep track of things. Foreign delegations and proposals proliferate widely. Many American institutions are pressed to sign a number of Memoranda of Understanding each year, and there is always the danger of overdoing the politeness, signing more MOUs than can possibly be actualized or even signing arrangements that actually conflict. The whole issue of coordinating MOUs and figuring out which ones should mean anything, which ones are harmless expressions of fleeting friendship, is an organizational challenge in itself. Dealing with these matters, plus the necessary travel abroad that is essential to maintain relationships in places like China and Korea where American institutions need to send not only representatives, but periodically representatives of a certain stature, raises staffing needs that easily surpass what seemed necessary even a few years previous.

Questions of this sort figure into another obvious administrative response: figuring out how to follow up on the reports of the proliferation of task forces that have dotted American campuses during the past decade. The task forces themselves mobilize impressive faculty and administrative talent. Some, like the Mt. Holyoke group discussed earlier, focus on particular problems, such as improving the context and impact for study abroad. But many—examples recently include the University of Pennsylvania and Boston University—are intended to translate new presidential interest in global advance into more specific, integrated recommendations ranging from curriculum to projects in developing nations.[3] In the fall of 2007, a new president at the University of Delaware (a school with a well-established record in key global areas) similarly announced a new strategic planning group—the pattern has become widespread as part of the inception of a new central administration.[4] And the results of the planning exercises are typically most impressive, calling forth widespread faculty and stakeholder interest and addressing many facets of the global challenge; but the exercises also raise the issue of who, if anyone, or what office, if any, is going to be responsible for overseeing the next steps, particularly when these imply unusually intense cross-unit cooperation. Again, there are some prosaic questions about administrative structure that simply must be addressed.

The key issue, in figuring out what organization makes sense to optimize global educational initiatives, involves the tension between centralization and more localized action and decision. Centralization helps deal with problems like inadequate knowledge of potentially complementary (or even worse, contradictory) efforts, and properly done it might help knit the various facets of global education together. Without some central sorting mechanism, centers and programs appealing to the word "global" easily proliferate without any rhyme or reason, to the confusion of outsiders trying to figure out how to identify the appropriate location for their particular interest. Even the creation of clarifying websites can be difficult. Central voice is essential in major undertakings, like branch campuses (though there is the delightful recent story of an Australian university that managed to found a branch in Dubai without the president's knowledge; the branch did collapse, however, when the president found out). And central representation for many international negotiations— even some launched by individual units, but which for prestige reasons need to be confirmed by a presidential or vice presidential visit—is unavoidable. On the other hand, as many faculty can eagerly attest, too much centralization can stifle promising initiatives. It risks seeming to locate global concerns in one unit, where for success they must be accepted by a wide variety of disciplines and programs. Some degree of messiness, even cases of temporary overlap or duplication, may be desirable in the interest of attracting the widest possible buy-in to a fundamental global agenda.[5]

Certainly, leadership in global education can and should come from a variety of sources. We have seen important cases where a new president spurred a significant new commitment to global activities, to the great benefit of the institutions involved.[6] Troy University, with its outreach to international students, is a successful case in point. New York University, with its recent ambitions for branch campuses and an impressive emphasis on global relationships in the law school, is another example. Institutions that want to jump forward in global initiatives, for their own sake as they contribute to the contemporary academic mission of higher education but also, in some cases, as a means of advancing a larger educational and reputational agenda, almost invariably depend on leadership at or near the top. President Byker of Calvin College, a former international lawyer with direct experience in Beirut, has helped spur his school toward impressive levels of activity in study abroad and the recruitment of diverse international students, with significant curricular change as well. The list of top-down but deeply rooted inspirations could easily be expanded, with examples from every type of institution from community colleges onward.[7] And there are other important instances where a top administrator, not initially a global advocate, becomes one because of the various advantages involved—Carnegie Mellon University seems to be a case in point, where a long and frankly desultory discussion of building a global university finally took fire when the central administration saw the significance of new links to India, the Middle East, and elsewhere.

On the other hand, vital efforts come from leaders in single programs or departments. At George Mason University—and the example can be repeated in many other places—what is now a thriving program in central Asian studies resulted from the interests of a few scholars dealing with Islam, plus the head of the undergraduate Global Affairs major, some programs developed in the region by the Institute for Conflict Analysis and Resolution, plus a successful grants officer. Initial forays into China stemmed from deans (and their own close associates) in policy studies and in computation and earth observation (entirely separately). The results were sufficiently rewarding, while pointing to other opportunities, that a China officer was hired—but even now, while information about most initiatives at least reaches her desk, a number of key collaborations remain entirely independent. The result is a bit chaotic; the ability to sum up what's being done with China remains less facile than might be desired; a few opportunities for mutual coordination may be lost. But the vigor of actual interactions with Chinese counterparts, for research efforts, training programs, and provision of students, easily compensates. More recently still, a promising venture in international research and training on information security, though now involving some central support after the fact, resulted from the imagination of a single faculty member and an outside collaborator. And all this is quite apart from the unusually successful and ambitious connections forged by the study abroad office and other individual agencies within the university.

The need for leadership operates at many levels, and it does not predetermine a single organizational approach. Any university with serious interests in global education must now have the involvement of top leadership, and their central impulses may be crucial. But the same serious interests require a host of imaginative players amid faculty and staff ranks. A number of institutions, including the University of Illinois and the University of Florida, have been working actively on issues of defining organization, with interesting but diverse, often tentative, results. Small wonder that there are various models of administrative structure, and that while each has some drawbacks many seem to function adequately.

A Decentralized Approach

There are doubtless hosts of organizational arrangements, or lack thereof that do not involve a clearly designated, central international office and officer. George Mason University may nevertheless be taken as an example, with a brief gloss on the resultant plusses and minuses.

The University is deeply engaged internationally, and this has long been the case. Various academic units have research and training collaborations literally all over the world. There is of course the outright branch campus in the Middle East, and a more limited engagement in South Korea. The study abroad office is extremely active, and the University ranks high on the numerical scale here. The number and percentage of international students are substantial, and there was no measurable retreat in the wake of 9/11. The undergraduate Global Affairs program is large and growing, in just a few years of existence; there are several strong, relevant graduate programs. A global category was built into general education six years ago. Undergraduates rank high on their awareness of international issues. Delegations from institutions and governments in various countries visit with considerable frequency, and the president and provost, as well as hosts of staff and faculty, do business abroad with considerable regularity.

But there is neither an international school nor an overarching international office. Several academic units boast strong core faculty who deal with international policy issues—Humanities and Social Sciences, Public Policy, and Conflict Resolution head the list, and each offers at least one relevant program on both masters and Ph.D. levels, the source of some confusion to outsiders on occasion. A Center for Global Studies was set up to provide some scholarly coordination, and it has had measurable success in developing cross-cutting initiatives in areas like international migration; but it does not offer degrees and has only limited centralizing power. Study abroad and the processing of international students are separate (though friendly), and an effort to put them under a single umbrella met with political resistance internally.

There is a global affairs coordinating committee, with representatives from each of the international units and from each school and college—the Provost's Advisory Committee on Global Research and Education. It was the existence of this body, both in its role as connector and in its representation of wide commitments to global education from literally every academic segment of the University, that won a Heiskell award from the Institute of International Education a couple of years ago. Indeed, at its best the Committee does share information and help align initiatives, sometimes adding strength to the efforts of individual units. It can help focus policy discussions, for example, about goals for expanding the numbers, sources and levels of international students. Certainly, the ability to engage the engineering college or science along with explicit international relations faculty is a genuine strength, in rooting global education quite broadly. Faculty can talk about making better use of international students, or relationships between student life functions in International Week and curricular goals.

Other institutions have pursued what might be called this kind of diffuse model, while moving ahead with clear global momentum. Tidewater Community College rests internationalization with a faculty International Education Committee, which oversees initiatives and assures academic leadership along with a Chief International Education Officer. Faculty members serve on the committee for two-year terms, in addition to regular teaching duties, so the approach comes with clear cost. But the College has successfully acquired state and federal funds for faculty study tours abroad and curriculum development efforts focused on different regions of the world, so the lack of a central administrative focus does not retard significant initiatives. The State University of New York at Binghamton advanced a new commitment to global education on the basis of a broadly based International Education Advisory Committee, though there is a Director of International Programs under a Vice Provost, to help draw the threads together.

Too much decentralization has obvious downsides, which is why even institutions that rely considerably on a faculty committee structure often supplement administratively. Diffuse structures place substantial burdens on officials who play de facto coordinating roles. It allows a great deal of information to slip through the cracks. Actively engaging members of Mason's Advisory Committee is not always easy, and too many meetings center on around-the-table, slightly haphazard reports about personal initiatives. Interaction between key offices is not always optimal, allowing issues like integrative housing arrangements for foreign students to escape attention for too long a period. Figuring out what university official will take on what international visit is doable, but ad hoc at best. While it is clear that the university can and will follow up on all sorts of international opportunities, often quite swiftly, each occasion requires that a new response and new group be brought together.

What the decentralized model *does* demonstrate is that great success and rapid growth in global engagement are possible without a highly rationalized administrative structure. What it *might* demonstrate is that success and growth owe something to this very structural incoherence, which promotes local unit initiative, encourages flexibility, develops little by way of constraining bureaucratic rules. What it *might* demonstrate, as well, as the Heiskell award implied, is the relationship between lack of central administrative apparatus (as opposed to representation) and wide participation in global efforts across fields. An outside observer has recently commented on how much awareness of global initiatives deans, admissions officers and other administrators maintain, partly because they're spontaneously interested, partly because the university is unusually active, but partly because decentralization forces attention upon them—and this is almost surely a good thing, a solid basis for the global education effort overall. Unfortunately, these important relationships are possible but not provable; it is not clear that the gains implied cannot be achieved alongside a somewhat more focused and efficient administrative arrangement. It can be argued, as well, that while minimally adequate coordination and oversight have developed, they involve too many committee structures and too many unfunded mandates to faculty and administrators in principle assigned to other duties. Over time, the downsides of the lack of more formal organization will probably force some further, if limited, moves in the direction of a central office at least for the purposes of information gathering and symbolic representation to foreign visitors, plus probably some planning coordination as well. Even doing usable inventories of existing programs turns out to require not only a central officer but a level of expertise that goes beyond well-intentioned amateurism. Decentralization has its charms, and there's no question that any modifications must attempt to retain the entrepreneurial vigor and wide buy-in of the decentralized model; but decentralization also displays vivid limitations.[8]

It is even being argued now that, on many campuses including community colleges, having a physical space dedicated to coordinating global efforts and with a staff available to answer questions and steer suggestions is an important gain. Here too, the signs point to some formalization of administrative arrangements, because so much is otherwise bubbling up without direction and because questions and concerns sometimes race ahead of decentralized expertise.[9]

Models of the International Office and Officer

All sorts of institutions have established overarching international offices, often quite recently. Northern Virginia Community College, developing a new mission statement after 2005, vowed to leverage its existing role in serving over 9,000 students from around the world "to create learning experiences that build greater global awareness across the college." The institution not only had large numbers of foreign students, including 2,000 from Latin America: it had consequently established a major English as a second language program and an area studies degree program, with emphases on Latin America and Japan, plus a significant menu of foreign language options; and it had many intercultural celebrations and a wide array of study abroad offerings. But, as the mission focus developed, the lack of coherent overall organization emerged strongly. Even a guiding website was lacking. There were also potentials for expansion, for example, in encouraging faculty to take advantage of international opportunities or in partnering with larger consortia on relevant issues. And strong emphasis emerged for extending study abroad beyond European targets, with particular interest in India. Even a satellite program in China seemed worth consideration, though this remained at the concept level. Finally, there was recognition/hope that global programs might prove attractive for outside funding.[10]

What, then, to do next? Step one was a major college-wide task force, to turn promising thoughts into fuller plans. A new blog was set up, to solicit thoughts and suggestions from around the campus. Quickly, as well, a new Office of Global Studies and Programs was set up to begin to provide both the coordination and the sustained encouragement that the various goals seemed to require. The Office was charged with bridging among the many existing components, for example, in linking course offerings with co-curricular activities and in doing more to assimilate international students into the campus community (with a new agency established to help in this regard as well). The Office was also responsible for developing coherent budget requests, again a first, so that larger intentions and coordination needs could be considered as part of central funding priorities for the first time. The Office would also help develop new links to business, amplifying opportunities for language study— again, there had been no previous assigned responsibility for outreach in this area. And the office could assist in the ongoing process of monitoring course offerings, in terms of quality and potential interrelationships.

The move toward an Office was both recent and somewhat tentative, an example of a fairly cautious change but a recognition as well of new administrative needs and potential benefits. It is an interesting example of a first step beyond decentralization.

Another approach that has recently emerged involves extending the functions of an existing office, not to cover the whole global front but to offer a growing level of coordination among several activities. The University of Minnesota thus established a "curriculum integration initiative" administered by its Learning Abroad Center, in addition to a large international programs office. The initiative involved workshops for faculty members and advisors on global initiatives, with training in best practices for study abroad while also working with the Center for Teaching and Learning to help faculty create international components in their classes. The initiative specifically addressed the need for all colleges and departments to participate, and it also built in an assessment component.[11]

But the current wave of the future probably involves an even more elaborate move, creating an international office with official direction, often at a vice presidential level, reporting variously to the Provost or to the President. This is what Arizona State University did in 2006, translating one of the characteristic strategic planning initiatives of a dynamic new president into organizational change.[12] The new Office of the Vice President for Global Engagement acknowledged the growing level of global research and education by faculty, the increasing number of international students (a major initiative area for the University), and the rising need for student awareness. The new office was charged with encouraging innovative approaches to global problems and developing global application to programs of various types. The office was responsible for advancing the university globally "by establishing and maintaining strong relationships," supporting globally focused programs of study, research and student mobility; and creating international strategic partnerships with key institutions around the world." The office obviously encourages study abroad and also a growing array of relevant internships, directing the International Program Office; it also promotes faculty exchanges. It works hard on collaborative arrangements both in Latin America and in China (including participating in science programs for Chinese high school students), with specific initiatives in both cases. It oversees ASU's MBA programs in China and Mexico. It hosts international visitors to the University. It organizes raffles to support schools in Malawi. The new Vice President was also charged with working with all deans, academic administrators and faculty members to encourage international projects and initiatives of all sorts. A prominent career Foreign Service officer was hired for the position, bringing the benefit not only of elaborate international experience but also significant federal contacts. This was a major administrative venture.

Indiana University at Bloomington is another successful case of change through centralization, suggesting perhaps the particular importance of decisive new administrative structures in large institutions. The school created a centralized office across the institution, with its multiple branches, to handle international services, overseas study, and international research and development, with the chief international officer reporting directly to the President while working with academic units throughout the campuses. Under this umbrella, a specific Center for Global Education at the Bloomington campus works with schools and faculty members to create specific academic programs such as a new international studies minor.

And the idea spreads. East Carolina University advertises for an Associate Vice Chancellor for International Affairs, charged with implementing the University's international strategic plan; aiding in the expansion of agreements with international institutions; encouraging study abroad and faculty exchange and "other activities related to promoting an international community at the University"; preparing students for citizenship and "successes" in a global environment; working with university units but also an external audience (community groups, national organizations) to promote global activities; encouraging relevant short- and long-term goals for each of the functional areas under the office, while ensuring compliance with relevant laws and regulations; and representing the Office of International Affairs both on and off campus.[13] A large assignment, and how the actual process of internal coordination will work, given diverse faculty interests and initiatives, will need to be tested over time. But the goal is clear enough: international now needs its own oversight operation, with a high-ranking official to match. And the requirements include not only internal issues, but external arrangements and, increasingly, engagement with potential supporters and participants from outside the university proper—not only internationally, but also in the local region.

The movement toward more central officialdom is still tentative, quite apart from the fact that not all globally engaged schools have yet taken the plunge. Titles vary, from associate provost to executive director to vice president. Responsibilities vary greatly as well, frequently with a considerable mixture of assignments given the need for cross-unit coordination. Thus even an executive director position, serving under a Vice Provost for International Initiatives, is supposed to oversee study abroad and international student services (with a staff of 20), while also doing budget work, working with staff and faculty across campus and with international branches, managing Fulbright scholars, and coordinating with outside agencies and corporations; and assessment is tossed in for good measure. A growing number of positions also require public relations work, to communicate global activities to legislators, friends of the school, and a wider public—another good addition, but a potential distraction as well for a single official. There is a danger of moving too many items into the position specs, as opposed to diffusing them among other offices (like media relations, in this case). Sources of potential recruits are diffuse as well. Training requirements are vague of necessity, including degree in the field and "relevant experience" in higher education—or independently strong international credentials without the academic background. This is a specialty still taking shape in the United States.

Further oscillation is inevitable. One central international office points with pride to the connections it has developed between conventional study abroad and undergraduate research with global links: interaction helps both prospect areas. And it contemplates pulling in academic programs, such as area studies majors and minors, as well. But William and Mary has just decentralized, putting academic programs back in the units, because their inclusion in a central operation reduced interactions with relevant disciplines and introduced a host of practical coordination issues. Clearly, it is hard to strike a proper balance, even with the growing sense that some enhanced linkages must be developed; there is no one best model at this point. Whatever its structure, coordination and flexibility—the capacity to react quickly to new needs and opportunities—must both be served.

One final point: it's worth noting that a growing number of foreign universities already have an international officer. In some cases the official boasts only modest rank, and is around mainly because of terrific English skills and the capacity to show visitors around. Increasingly, however, a more senior figure is involved as well. The international vice president at St. Petersburg State University, for example, is only one of three major administrators under the president (the other two overseeing education and research, respectively). International officers at Chinese and Korean universities often have significant influence. Dealing with them, from the American side, often requires presidential or provostial stature—unless there a ranking dignitary of one's own to put in the mix. The pattern does not require the kind of organizational thrust that many American universities are beginning to introduce, and it does not predict how many services and programs should merge into a central international office, but it can be an additional spur toward some formal, central arrangement.

Fundraising

An increasingly important issue, whatever the administrative structure for global education, involves the organization of fundraising. Obviously, many facets of global education would benefit from some outside funding, beyond normal tuition revenues; use of state monies, for public institutions, is frequently constrained in the global arena, and the support trend is downward in any event. Study abroad often suffers, as we have seen, from inadequate resources to help cover travel costs, and international students far too rarely gain access to scholarship funds. At the same time, conventional development offices are not always highly attuned to global issues or some of the special funding channels that might apply. A few large schools do organize international alumni. A few, like Stanford, have tapped into significant endowments for global studies initiatives. Dickinson College has an endowment dedicated to its international activities. But there is commonly a gap between aspiration/need on the one hand, and the organization of solicitation efforts on the other.

It is not easy terrain. Government sources, such as US AID, offer real potential. But relevant federal funding has been cut back in recent years. Proposals that were generated two years ago by the Department of Education for curricular efforts in the global arena were turned back because of budget limits and expenditures on noncompetitive earmarks. US AID staff on the ground, for instance, in Africa, often eagerly encourage initiatives, only to discover that central directives focus attention on other specific regions. Many of the big foundations are not particularly open. The Mellon Foundation, a vital asset in the humanities, does little international work outside a few South African projects plus some support for information technology initiatives. Ford has displayed interest but mainly in very targeted projects. Globally involved corporations, whether U.S.-based or not, in principle a logical target for appeals, do not to date offer a particularly systematic track record in philanthropy for higher education. Finally, projects directly linked to operations abroad frequently encounter a lack of a relevant philanthropic tradition where higher education is concerned.

This means that fundraising must often appeal to diverse and lesser-known foundations; to federal offerings that are sporadic and widely scattered; and to a welter of private donors whose international ties and interests are not always easy to uncover. Including global projects in capital campaigns is another promising avenue, but it is just beginning to be deployed. And the federal offerings, though sporadic and often frustrating, must not be ignored. The simple fact is that while the federal government devotes very low funding to the global education or education outreach area, in percentage terms, the monies that are available can be considerable in institutional terms. The further fact is that federal efforts are so scattered, among agencies and sometimes among different policy directions, that it takes considerable institutional initiative to ferret out what the opportunities are and how they might be addressed. There is no easy federal clearinghouse, despite some State Department forays, though a project in this direction might be very worthwhile.

In this context, a growing number of schools are employing fundraisers specifically attached to the international education office or in more decentralized settings to a relevant administrator. The staff works with the conventional development office, of course, but with enough separation to retain the special focus. Frequently, global education offices or more specific programs also develop advisory boards (around Middle Eastern Studies initiatives, to take one example), sometimes with international membership, aimed at the usual mixture of advice and funding support. Fundraising is also being added to the responsibilities of the new international directors—to the tune of 20% of their time, according to a recent University of Idaho personnel ad.

Most of these operations are fairly new, and it may be premature to assess their results. Several, however, already pay for themselves and more, through mixtures of usually small grants adequate, however, to get a number of promising initiatives off the ground. There are at least a few more substantial successes. Stanford has gained its impressive endowment for its international studies center, but even some slightly humbler institutions have broken through—like the State University of New York in Binghamton, which has endowment funding both for study abroad in general and for study in Spanish-speaking countries. Finding not simply useful but sustained support remains a challenge. Too many international initiatives, including many funded by the federal government, have developed really promising collaborations during the life of the grant, only to disappear as the support ended. We need more institutional commitment, on the American higher education side, to think about life after specific project funding—collaborative degrees offer a promising route that I hope will be increasingly considered. But more than attention and intention are required: more systematic commitment to fundraising is a vital administrative component.

Advisory Boards: Faculty Input and the Role of External Groups

The increasingly formal organization of global education efforts, and the hopes for more active fundraising, both invite attention to wider steering committees and advisory boards of several sorts. Particularly with a centralized office for global education, it is vital to develop a faculty group, drawn from diverse units, devoted to guiding the administrative officers and communicating their concerns in turn. Where there is a global education faculty, attached perhaps to a global affairs major, this can provide a part of the faculty constituency, but greater breadth must be sought, with units treating participation by faculty members as the chief committee responsibility. Beyond a steering committee, a wider advisory group of interested faculty, convened a couple of times a semester, remains desirable to provide information about unit-based opportunities and initiatives and to help transmit knowledge of the wider global education efforts back to the units in turn. This is compatible, finally, with at least an annual global assembly, with a speaker and social activities attached, at which key developments in the global education program can be highlighted and discussed. Communication and inputs, in other words, become increasingly vital when programs become more formally organized, and a concentric circle approach will hopefully do the trick.

The external advisory boards have a clear role as well, in offering advice, in promoting activities from student recruitment to internships, and in providing fundraising assistance. Some parts of the United States offer wider range to this kind of external support than do others, but nowhere, now, is it impossible to find external friends or alumni with relevant global experience including, in some cases, global corporate connections.

As in other aspects of global education, both internal and external board structures are new to the global enterprise. Smaller offices, for example, for study abroad, and discrete disciplinary programs in languages or international affairs have neither required nor encouraged these more diffuse structures. With wider range and greater formal organization, however, the need increases both for channels for input and for opportunities to communicate, and here too organizational innovation is an essential response.

Collaboratives

Much of the current effort in global education stems from individual institutions, and we have seen that a great deal of commendable energy and imagination results. There is room, however, for pooled efforts of various sorts, and given the challenge of the global arena more attention might usefully be paid to this channel in future—particularly if the governmental climate for global initiatives remains schizophrenic at best.

As noted in an earlier chapter, some existing university consortia have gingerly dipped toes into global waters. The Big Ten academic collaborative (the Committee on Institutional Cooperation or CIC) has long helped member institutions share strengths in less commonly taught languages, enhancing options available to students. The Colonial Academic Alliance (complement to the Colonial Athletic Alliance) brings study abroad officials together to help pool some programs and thus both expand student options and increase program viability; there is also discussion of shared language resources. A few consortia have been approached about providing collective consultation for new universities abroad, for example, in Saudi Arabia—offering the kind of services American University has provided in two instances, but taking advantage of the greater range of subject expertise that a group of schools can generate. Collaboration of this sort is difficult, because of institutional barriers, the limited experience of most collaborative activity, and outright competitive rivalry (an obvious issue). Still, the approach has promise and it may help respond to the complexity and range of global possibilities. Some new collaborations may also be forged as a result of solicitation from the field: efforts to respond to the educational free trade zone being developed in Incheon, for instance, typically involve several American institutions, each emphasizing a set of programs (in technology, for example, or social science) that picks up on particular institutional strengths. Finally, some federal funders, like the Fund for Improving Postsecondary Education (FIPSE) in the Department of Education, for its international program support, require partnership or consortial linkages.

To date, the efforts of several of the higher education associations to move into the global arena, or expand their effectiveness, have had more impact than more spontaneous collaboratives. The most obvious entrants here are the societies explicitly devoted to international education issues, some of them now more than a half-century old. Groups like the Institute for International Education provide immeasurable service in urging more attention to global issues and providing regular updates on categories like study abroad and the numbers of international students on American campuses. Prizes and newsletters alike offer not only encouragement but concrete illustrations of best practices, while annual meetings provide committed international educators opportunities to exchange experiences. The IIE also, of course, administers some relevant funding, and though support for the Fulbright program has declined the organization has been nimble in finding special resources to encourage goals like support for study abroad by minority students and engineers or to promote student exchanges particularly with regions involved in economic development or political change. Other groups play important roles, for example, in providing forums for study abroad coordinators. The Council for the International Exchange of Scholars (operating within the IIE frame-work) strives hard in promoting faculty visits both from and to the United States, recently extending its efforts to the community college arena.[14]

At least as important, since the mid-1990s, has been the growing involve-ment of more generalized higher education associations, after some sporadic efforts in earlier decades.[15] These are steadily gaining expertise—the American Council on Education has a growing staff in the international area—and has the advantage of a wide general membership not predicated on prior commit-ment to global education. These groups can, in other words, reach newcomers to the field. The American Council on Education has been tireless in dissemin-ating publications and organizing leadership dialogues, conferences, "webi-nars" and workshops on a host of subjects. They have materials on integrative approaches to internationalization, on involving faculty across the campus, on assessing global education results, on seeking support funds, on balancing central administrative with wider involvements; they have paid particular attention to leadership issues, from presidents and provosts to the faculty more generally. The specialized publications but also more general newsletters offer numerous examples of best practices, from a wide variety of institutional types—appeals for involvement by community colleges, for instance, have been visibly effective as ACE tries to encourage efforts well beyond the most familiar cast of higher education characters. Specific pamphlets like *Internationalizing the Campus: A User's Guide* (2003) and *A Handbook for Advancing Comprehensive Internationalization: What Institutions Can Do and What Students Should Learn* (2006) are models in the field. The ACE is pushing some approaches, notably the synergy between multiculturalism and global education, that may be open to criticism, in merging rather separate goals to the detriment of the global component. But there is no question about overall effectiveness. ACE conference invitations and collaborative discussions and laboratories have directly spurred about thirty institutions, such as Northern Virginia Community College, to take a fresh look at their inter-national engagements and come away with a far more comprehensive plan.

On the motivational side, several reports from NASULGC (the National Association of State Universities and Land Grant Colleges), particularly offer-ings in 2000 and again in 2004, have tried to rally attention to the diverse facets of global education, from curriculum to the recruitment of international students, noting troubling lags in American institutional response to global issues and advocating leadership from several levels in the academy. The efforts both reflected and encouraged the growing attention to key issues from the late 1990s onward.[16]

Other groups provide powerful assistance as well. The role of the American Association of State Colleges and Universities in negotiating student recruit-ment with the Chinese Ministry of Education has been crucial, and the organ-ization earlier provided similar service with regard to programs in Japan. Even specialist organizations grouping institutional researchers and budget officers increasingly provide international education panels at their national and regional conferences, again generating vital information and spreading knowledge of successful practices. As the global education momentum swells, collaborative organizations provide impressive assistance in motivating individual institutions toward further engagement and in offering guidance in a host of specific areas, from study abroad to budgeting to curriculum to assessment. Given the absence of systematic government involvement, relevant associations help compensate for the current unevenness of commitment by individual institutions and, in some cases, for lack of individual bargaining power. Several associations have also consistently championed universities' interests at the level of federal policy, as in the visa crisis—without, of course, consistent success at least recently. There is, to be sure, rarely much money involved in the collaborative approach, and funding for new initiatives remains a crucial issue. Institutions indeed often have to ante up a bit to participate in conferences or to join in other ventures such as AASCU's discussions with Chinese officials. Still, the strength of collaborative activity, particularly but not exclusively for some of the newer-comers to the international education field, is crucial at the present moment, and there may be ways to expand the associational approach in future.

Consortia play a vital role as well in representing global education issues to the federal government. The American Council on Education and other groups help support the Coalition for International Education, which in turn advocates for funding for foreign language and international studies programs. If the federal government develops further interest in this vital area under subsequent administrations, this kind of effort may become more important than is currently the case, further relieving some of the current dependence on individual institutional effort.

For individual institutions, of course, most current collaborative opportunities play back into specific decisions about administrative structure. Without a clear international officer, some of the associational initiatives are hard to follow up: even deciding whom to send to an attractive conference can be an issue. In turn, in their quest for leadership involvement, some of the associations may be calling for more time from presidents and academic vice presidents than is sustainable over the long haul. The question of how much to trust to a specialized administrative unit, how much to distribute over an institution more generally, remains challenging.

Conclusion

Greater consideration for planning in the administrative organization of global education is increasingly essential for three reasons. Most simply, it is abundantly clear that proliferation of separate offices and initiatives fails to take full advantage of the effort being expended. Too often, among other things, faculty interests—underpinning curriculum—and administrative bailiwicks like study abroad are functionally divided, to the disadvantage of both. Second, the sheer magnitude of the needs and opportunities in global education call for a more thoughtful approach to organization than many institutions have heretofore expended. This applies most obviously to decentralized structures, but it can apply to international vice presidencies as well—when these involve gestures to global criteria without much substance or when they are assumed to absolve other administrative and academic units of their own global responsibilities. The obvious plea is not for any one administrative model, but for careful consideration of what model will most adequately assure the desired mixture of coordination and initiative.

A recent report drove the point home: "Many plans fizzle at the implementation stage because there is no campus coordination or accountability for outcomes."[17] Good intentions and even elaborate plans do not suffice. Leadership is vital, and this means, over time, a clear organizational structure; and increasingly, in all probability, this will come to entail the appointment of a senior official with oversight responsibility in the field, and a coordinating infrastructure (including a fundraising component) under this official in turn.

The final reason for more widespread attention to the issue of structure involves the impulses of the majority of global educators themselves. Globally committed leaders tend to be eager to take advantage of any opportunity that comes their way—after all, the cause is so significant, current arrangements often so ill-developed, that any innovation may be welcomed. It is hard, in this field, to establish priorities and think strategically, because of the ways that the field's scope and the enthusiasm of the most devoted practitioners intertwine. And of course rigid marching orders, in a global arena that does change rapidly, would be a mistake. Still, mechanisms must develop—more commonly than is currently the case—to sort out the range of options, to see how they relate, to provide bases for choosing some over others. Faculty and administrative involvement in this process is essential, but organizational and planning arrangements must be clarified as well.

9
Assessment

A Swiss company reportedly defines global competency as follows: "Globally competent managers parachute into any country and get the job done while respecting cultural pathways."

To which an American international studies administrator suggested a more modest modification: "A globally competent person can drop into another country and function adequately while not making too many waves."

* * *

Growing emphasis on assessment in higher education inevitably, and properly, spills over into the global arena.[1] The heightened focus on global education, and the newly competitive international environment, generate their own pressures on individual institutions to take stock of global activities. Moves toward formalizing leadership and organizational structure bring questions about outcomes in their wake—and also, hopefully, facilitate the development of an assessment process. Simply generating a single census of global initiatives provides a vital basis for speaking about global education in general, and not just particular components. Not surprisingly, the most common approach toward assessment involves this kind of enumeration, which also has some of the quantitative potential so dear to assessment gurus. Imaginative suggestions have also emerged concerning applying assessment to faculty and staff, to chart changes in competence at these levels. But the real challenge of global assessment involves learning outcomes, from specific activities like study abroad but even more from the student experience as a whole. Here, given the newness of the global priority and the greater attention lavished on areas like science or writing, talk has exceeded action. Global education leaders expound about what global competence means, and their conversations have moved forward a bit; but systematic action remains elusive.

Assessment must reflect the basic goals of global education, an obvious point but essential in a field that too often breaks down into discrete activities, all worthy but not always integrated into a larger vision. Assessment must thus include a sense of what global activities are contributing to a wider world, with principles of mutuality front and center, and a clear grasp of the kinds of habits of mind, above and beyond fleetingly memorized factual content, we want to be able to demonstrate in our students.

Assessment must also weave together various facets of global education. Activity surveys help, but efforts focused on student outcomes must grapple with obvious differentials, for example, in types of majors or access to study abroad. It is easiest to assess students with considerable global exposure. Efforts to date reflect understandable difficulties in recognizing serious but more modest outcomes—one of several targets for considerable work in future. Discussions have also focused more actively on cultural comparison and intercultural competence than on awareness of global factors and their evolution in recent history—with a real resulting disparity that must be addressed, in a contemporary world that is partly a cultural mix but involves more than that.

General Approaches

At first glance, some of the suggestions about global temperature-taking can seem rather predictable. They gain heft, however, when we realize how new serious global commitments are at most institutions—novelty sometimes compels the obvious—and how often the addition of global goals to institutional strategies lacks real specificity or measurable content. George Mason's first thrust into inclusion of global goals among university priorities—not that long ago, I blush to say—talked glowingly about making sure that all students gained "an understanding and awareness of themselves as citizens of the world and the ability to thrive in a global environment." Specifics were sparse in this overall five-year plan, though numerical targets were set for study abroad and numbers of international students (both goals were met) along with a vaguer injunction to teach the global perspective "across the curriculum": "all programs will incorporate a worldview into their materials and approach." This last, worthy in the extreme, had no particulars attached, which meant it could not really be assessed, which meant in turn that it was not accomplished. The injunction to develop some clearer benchmarks to translate noble intentions into actual, annual steps forward remains, for many institutions, an essential project.

Two thrusts can be suggested, and they are complementary. Both have won a familiar place in the general literature on global education. The first approach, pushed hard in recent years by the American Council on Education, urges a review process based on questions that can guide a deeper evaluation of institutional strategies joined by a student learning outcomes and assessment process. The questions can vary, of course, but they combine to produce a meaningful list of items with which any committed institution should be engaged.

Thus: are president and provost explicitly committed to leadership in global initiatives; is the faculty engaged, and does the institution provide rewards for international activities; is internationalization explicitly noted as a priority in the institution's overall strategic plan, and is there a specific strategic plan for the global education sector itself; what are the main strategies used to achieve global education? The American Council on Education also delights in referring to an "ethos of internationalization," though what this adds to the more specific guidelines is not entirely clear. The approach also includes a question about the commitment to assessment, and the involvement of the assessment office, which means that something beyond the checklist itself must be developed.[2]

The next stage in the review process involves more focused targets, about which a fair amount of specific information can be developed. Again, this is fully compatible with the intentionality checklist, but it offers more quantifiable or short answer components. Questions here include: the inclusion of internationalization in general education; the involvement of academic departments in internationalizing their majors and in promoting study abroad; ways in which faculty engagement in internationalization is encouraged; the number of globally rich courses that are available, and what enrollment patterns over time reveal about levels of student interest; what if any is the language requirement and what are the enrollment patterns in this category; the co-curricular activities that are available, and the levels of student participation; the governance structures of internationalization and how well they are working; and the level of financial resources available for internationalization, along with plans for the next targets for further investment.[3] Actual reports increasingly include evaluations of relevant library holdings and consortial arrangements for materials in the global arena.

The questions are good ones, and most, without too much monitoring effort, should be answerable. Only the checklist for general education and departmental involvement fail to provide reasonably clear categories of evidence, but the data could be developed. Issues of faculty involvement, which crop up in both stages of the general approach, are intriguing; but it should be possible for colleges and universities to cite what encouragements are available, in the form of inclusion of international initiatives among the items that support promotions and study leaves plus explicit research grants for global activities and the like. The challenge formally to list factors of this sort, rather than leaving them to ad hoc responses, is a good one, and obviously links this assessment approach to the need to tie down overall strategic planning into more concrete, measurable policies. This kind of census-taking approach can readily be supplemented by the even easier task of counting numbers and types of students engaged in study abroad and the levels of international students at various degree levels, where quantifiable data, and targets, should become routine parts of institutional reporting.

Even this second approach begs the more probing questions about student outcomes. Dutifully, this second list admits the fact, and adds the necessarily more open-ended items: "How does your institution review and evaluate the global dimensions of undergraduate education?" And: "To what extent has your institution developed learning goals associated with the global and international dimensions of global education? How do you assess student achievement of these goals?" Unfortunately, the census-taking approach conduces more readily to asking these questions, as part of a longer list, than to seriously examining how they may be answered. There is no escaping the need for a more elaborate analysis of a learning-centered, rather than activity-, intention-, and organization-centered assessment strategy.

Checklists have been amended to include additional information about faculty, and global transformations thereof. Without offering quite such a specific set of questions, some assessment discussions include evaluations of numbers of faculty involved in global research opportunities, attending international scholarly meetings, leading study abroad programs, developing and modeling international scholarly collaborations—as well as introducing global materials into their courses. These measures gain interest given the findings that American faculty are much less likely than their foreign counterparts to travel widely or connect with scholars abroad. The idea is to develop and measure "global competence" in faculty and staff, before one can expect too much from students, without developing an unduly standardized approach that would confine and antagonize faculty members unnecessarily. Establishing campus awards for faculty and staff achievements in the global arena is a way both to motivate and subtly to model and measure a greater level of engagement.

Even the checklist approach, however, is going to be a challenge for many institutions. It implies some kind of office—perhaps, the increasingly common international studies center, complete with high official—charged with and capable of doing the information gathering and resultant tallying. It is certainly possible to count global courses, policies toward internationally active faculty, financial investment and so on; and some estimate of leadership commitment and inclusion in strategic planning can also be ventured. The University of Cincinnati is developing a web-based approach to the institutional census, with interesting application to the global checklist. But this effort is just emerging. Few of the sprouting international offices at other universities are yet equipped with the formal mandate or, more importantly, the staffing to do this job. Applying measurements to faculty, collectively, would be more ambitious still. Even the easier approaches to assessment in global education require commitments beyond current routine.

Assessing Student Competence

Discussions about possibilities for learning assessment in the global arena—as opposed to activities and organizational censuses—began in the early 1980s, a testimony to the quick realization that a new push in curriculum and co-curriculum had to be justified by some willingness to probe learning results. A few of the early inventories mixed cultural diversity goals with global understanding, but there was independent focus on international education as well. While language achievements figured into the process, most discussions of inventories did not emphasize this area too strongly—though easy enough to measure, most authorities were probably not too hopeful that many students could advance to a worthwhile level. Emphasis rested, as a result, on newer kinds of knowledge, attitudes, and skills. While discussions were active and varied, no clear set of protocols emerged. Even established test-builders, like the Educational Testing Service, though they offered some ideas, did not find a sufficient clientele to build actual programs. The field, even today, continues to lack the concreteness that actual, routinized assessment requirements would generate.

It is not surprising that discussions of the desirability of global learning outcomes assessment have surpassed much concrete result in terms of actual measurement. This tends to be true in assessment generally, and given the higher priority of targets such as IT competence or writing, and the sheer novelty of the contemporary global education enterprise, one would not expect the global arena to be a pacesetter. The term "global competence" has become increasingly current, but details remain elusive. The exordia are stirring—"what competencies do students need to become world citizens and succeed in today's global workforce?"—but the realities are less advanced. Discussion is additionally complicated by the interdisciplinary nature of the global field, which inhibits easy agreement on how to proceed. World historians, to take an obvious case, would have a noticeably different list of essentials from international management experts.[4]

A host of categories have been advanced, all of them defendable but none terribly carefully defined. Knowledge of a foreign language might seem an obvious item, except for the fact that it's hard to agree on how widely, and to what level, this should be required. (There is also more to communication capacity than foreign language, despite the latter's centrality: many American collegians need practice in confining themselves to the forms of English foreign colleagues are likely to understand—an unexpected issue, for example, in electronic classroom collaborations.) Knowledge of world geography and understanding of historical forces that have shaped current global patterns certainly should enter into any factual compendium—but at what degree of detail? Few experts have actually taken the plunge to identify manageable, top-priority fact lists that cover all the fields involved (and if, as should be the case, some global public health and environmental topics enter in, beyond the standard social sciences and history, the complexity increases still further). A few lists, quite reasonably, seek to insist on a "state of the planet" awareness, about major current world issues from population to human rights to trade arrangements. Dispute inevitably arises, at least implicitly, about what types of global topics should gain priority. A few lists call for particular knowledge of different political structures along with some awareness of international systems, possibly with a bit of geography and economics tossed in.[5]

Emphasis on "heightened awareness" is promising, particularly when it can be partly tied to measurable curricular requirements such as world history or a global affairs course. But actually testing gains in learning, as opposed to checking off prerequisites, is challenging.

Attitudes often feature prominently in global assessment discussions, such as the American Association of Colleges and Universities global citizenship list. Students should learn to tolerate ambiguity and unfamiliarity, while respecting cultural differences—"managing stress when dealing with difference" is an extreme statement of this quality.[6] It is certainly fair to insist that students emerge from even a rudimentary global program with the understanding that not everyone around the world thinks the way they do, and with some sense of strategies to cope with this fact. These invocations obviously go beyond knowledge goals—students should know that the world displays different values and beliefs—but they are correspondingly extremely hard to test.[7] And what degree of achievement should be insisted upon? At what point can students return to a belief in the superiority of their own values, even while recognizing that other regions display different if more questionable standards, without losing points?[8] The area is intriguing, indeed unavoidable in the cultural diversity aspect of global learning, but its susceptibility to any kind of standard assessment may be questioned. This is particularly true when requirements push even further, to ask for empathy about others. On the fringe of attitudes, more testable but probably less common as a curricular item, several assessment proposals include awareness of different forms of etiquette.[9] On the fringe also (in my opinion) but on the more touchy-feely side, some authorities want strong self-esteem and awareness of one's own culture and place to figure in as well, assuming that this provides a basis for taking responsibility for one's own actions in a global context.

Bentley College, among others, has actively utilized a management probe, The Global Competencies Inventory, developed by the Kozai Group, to test its business students about openness, tolerance of ambiguity and experience with other cultures. (This test also involves qualities like self-confidence and emotional resilience.) A scoring device allows results to be communicated to individual students, after they have taken the "Global Openness" course.[10] A few ventures probe an even more focused values agenda, including not only "ability to look at and approach problems as a member of a global society" but also a cooperative approach to work: nonviolence; and a willingness to change "one's lifestyle and consumption habits to protect the environment."[11]

Analytical skills or habits of mind may well be a more promising category, ranging from the ability to look up global data to the capacity to engage in serious comparisons. This, at least, would follow from the earlier curricular discussion, if not from some of the global assessment literature itself. And in fact we know something about how to evaluate comparative abilities, by generating new scenarios for student analysis, and even about how to promote these abilities explicitly. Established capacities to relate global and local developments is another reasonable entrant, often evoked, though there is less experience about how to test skills here on new materials. Historians (and sympathizers) would add an interest in checking for analytical experience in dealing with significant change and continuity over time, in basic global systems such as migration or cross-cultural contacts.[12] A few authorities have tried to relate critical thinking skills—undeniably, a good general analytical category for successful undergraduates—to the global arena, possibly around the ability to explode purely ethnocentric thinking or, more grandiosely, to understand "the hidden complexity that can alter the interpretation of world events."[13] But it is not clear how some of these more general aptitudes, however desirable, can be precisely defined, much less evaluated.

Much of the thinking about assessing global understandings, in other words, stumbles on overambition, excessive if well-intentioned vagueness, and the sheer multiplicity of learning categories. Again, the faults are understandable in a new and vast field, but they unquestionably complicate the process of coming up with real, manageable, affordable assessment standards.

As with assessment generally, substantial discussion has also focused on various modalities for evaluating learning outcomes. Purely factual testing mechanisms do not seem relevant—memorization, so far, is a means and not an end in the global education arena. Portfolio activity, however, including e-portfolio tools for assessing international learning,[14] seems highly appropriate. Journals, that help students deal with their encounters with international issues and activities, may help account for some of the more attitudinal components of the global exercise, including reactions to cultural difference.[15] Specific skills, as with comparison, can be probed through short essays that respond to new data or constructed scenarios provided as part of a testing process independent of particular coursework; here, student learning gains can be measured against earlier tests administered with similar materials but prior to the additional analytical exposure. Here, sampling mechanisms can allow some sense of the impact of a global curriculum without massive cost. Even exit interviews can help, for lack of more sophisticated apparatus: seniors can be asked a couple of questions about the impact of their overall undergraduate experience on their awareness of and sensitivity to global issues.

All of this, admittedly, remains fairly abstract. One of the most concrete discussions of assessment feasibility in the global arena has come from the state of Georgia, appropriately held up as the closest thing yet available to a gold standard for evaluating global learning outcomes. The effort is recent, with full implementation yet to be realized—but the advance is real.

The Georgia University system's office of international education has drafted standards both for community college and for four-year college results, after reviewing the overall global competency literature and gaining input from institutions at both levels. Two-year college graduates should:

- be able to identify global issues and major geographical and cultural areas,
- know major historical and scientific events that have shaped today's world,
- show appreciation for different ethnicities, perspectives and cultural beliefs, and
- have basic cross-cultural and foreign language skills.

An interesting addition involves demonstration of knowledge of a current event that reflects more than one national perspective.

Four-year graduates should:

- know current international affairs and understand global interdependence,
- demonstrate intermediate cross-cultural and language skills,
- know international elements of their particular academic area,
- of course show adaptability to different cultures and cultural contexts, and
- be ready for lifelong global learning.*

To reach the competencies, specific courses should develop international learning objectives; a foreign language should be required; global-themed learning communities, study abroad and globally relevant service learning and internships, various international co-curricular activities and speakers, and internationally focused degree programs, minors and certificates are all recommended. For assessment strategies, Georgia recommends relevant exams and research papers, portfolios, language competency tests, reflective essays on international topics or projects, cross-cultural awareness inventories, surveys of graduating students and alumni, and feedback on study abroad programs.

Georgia does not stand alone in trying to move beyond recommendations to some actual assessment criteria. Michigan State, in summer 2007, ventured its own list of assessable objectives, including knowledge in language,

---

* Many assessment experts would prefer that this list include future reference to "knowing," because of its low position in Bloom's Taxonomy of the Cognitive Domain, aiming instead at higher order thinking skills with goals like "critiquing," "comprehending and demonstrating," and "analyzing" or "assessing." They would want students to be able to "apply these skills" to the pursuit of lifelong global learning.

geography and history, and the kind of cultural self-understanding that would allow effective work in diverse settings. Students should know about interdependence from a multi-disciplinary standpoint and should see their place in the world in relation to global historical and geopolitical trends. They should have second language proficiency and understand how language relates to culture, and how culture affects communication and behavior; they should be able to engage with people of difference perspectives. They should be able to understand other identities, and "question explicit and implicit forms of power, privilege, inequality and inequity." They should be able to use analytical thinking to understand how global processes are interconnected, and apply science and math literacy to knowledge of global processes in areas like health and the environment. They should see, in the effective citizenship category, the relationship between personal behavior and impact on global systems. The challenge, of course, was to move these various goals into the actual content of undergraduate education. The Michigan State group also recognized that it had not made an explicit decision about requirements, particularly in foreign languages (interviewed students expressed great hesitation on this one). Faculty concern, about internationalization as just the latest of a string of objectives in undergraduate curriculum, also had to be acknowledged; some minority clusters preferred more attention to issues at home. But the working group hoped that the administration would press forward to weave the global competencies into both curriculum and study abroad, and would reflect the priorities in promotions systems and budget priorities. The next step, clearly, was to figure out what combinations of courses, activities and study abroad would move the goals into practice and "connect with other initiatives on the campus related to student outcomes assessment." Here, more than with Georgia, key questions obviously lingered about gaps between goals and reality on the one hand, and goals and measurement on the other. The field remains a work in process.[16]

Finally, though obviously more focused, assessment standards in the foreign languages are also gaining new attention. Emphasis on literary mastery and appropriate style remains, but it is now joined by tests and portfolio requirements that allow language majors to show that they can command popular idiom, can communicate orally, and can demonstrate appropriate knowledge of cultural issues. Portfolio work helps assess cultural mastery and fluency in different writing styles, and many language departments, including those at Weber State University, are working to develop mutually understood scoring rubrics. Oral examinations, including now computerized oral proficiency tests that seem to work fairly well, increasingly factor into the mix. Weber State at least found that most of its majors (in European languages) averaged an advanced-low rating when the various scores were combined. George Mason is training select faculty in assessment according to ACTFL guidelines. Less agreement exists, obviously, on appropriate exercises in some of the less familiar languages, where fewer students, other than heritage learners, have a running start before college; and on what if any competency tests, beyond course exams, might be visited on non-majors.[17]

In sum: lists of the components of a global competence as a learning outcome vary, inevitably. Some are too long; some unspecific in an area rife with more talk than testing; some involve too much liberal correctness. Collectively, however, the better efforts include three components, and this may help in developing a good composite picture. They all want some knowledge, as in the ability to discuss current global issues and, possibly, a foreign language. They all want some analysis—the habits of mind—including comparison, the learned talent of seeing a topic from perspectives of other societies, and I would add some experience in relating the global to the local and back to global and some experience in interpreting global change. They all seek, finally, some capacity to combine awareness and analytical skill with appropriate attitude, with sensitivity to global complexities and diversities. Appropriate though not limitless knowledge, usable habits of mind that extend beyond a particular course of study, and sensitivity to different perspectives and communication needs—not a bad list, and hopefully one that can be both developed through education and assessed as its result.

At a Minimum

Given the current push toward all sorts of assessments, often involving unfunded mandates from state agencies or accreditation groups, the addition of global to the assessment list demands a prudent discussion. After all, in contrast to writing or math, there is no big external push, and while this reflects the unfortunate weakness of official support for global education goals it may be taken as welcome relief. Groups like the American Council on Education regularly ask, as part of their checklists, about assessment, and whether the formal assessment office is involved, and this is an understandable question from consultants eager to accelerate the global commitment. But for assessment offices themselves, already overburdened, the task of taking on yet another set of activities, in a field that is not conventionally well defined, may be one obligation too many. Globalists may wish that their field might replace, say, competence in information technology (given the fact that the latter is actually well established among most students, whereas global is not), but they are unlikely to prevail anytime soon. So too much emphasis on assessment, in the global arena, may be whistling in the wind.

Three points do seem inescapable. First, any institution seriously engaged in global education should venture at least a biennial checklist, to determine the status of study abroad, global content in the curriculum, and so on, and to combine these indices in a single document that both administrators and faculty (and interested students or applicants) can use to evaluate progress or regression. Many of the necessary data—for example, on international student numbers—are routinely available through Institutional Research, so the only chore is the combination—not an overwhelming task. Pushing beyond, for example, to consider annual efforts at teacher training and outreach to the schools, involves a bit more work, but not at an unrealistic level. Libraries should be able to tally relevant holdings. Having both an international education office, and a faculty (and possibly external) advisory committee expected to look at and render public comment on the checklist, in a peer review process, is a vital aspect of contemporary academic pulse-taking. And of course the results should go to the top levels of administration, and to trustees or their equivalents, to help inform their ongoing involvement with the global priorities and their basic assessment of the institution.

Second, the checklist approach should fold into a five-year review process for internationalization, where a more formal task force should take the annual/biennial data but explore more fully the state and trajectory of the whole gamut of global education and outreach efforts. Appalachian States, for example, returned five years later to a global strategic plan, with excellent results in terms of assessment and further planning alike. Where steering and/or advisory committees exist, they can be part of this process, but a discrete group should form for this periodic assessment, with appropriate bells and whistles from central administration. Many institutions have recently seen the strength of the task force approach, when the assignment was getting a coordinated effort started in the first place. We need now to pledge a recurrent commitment of equal seriousness and stature, to make sure that directions are appropriately defined and maintained—and adjusted.

Third, any globally serious university should at least be discussing (again among faculty and administrators together) the kinds of learning outcomes sought among undergraduates, when general education, across-the-curriculum and major programs are combined. Resources for actual value-added or outcomes tests or portfolio evaluations may be lacking, but at least criteria are in view, to help orient the academic and study abroad programs themselves. A question about global perspective can easily be added to seniors'exit questionnaire, again a process well short of formal learning assessment but at least a move in the right direction. Some sense of what students think they got out of the global portion of the curriculum is at least a first step, even though the questionnaire hardly probes what if anything they actually learned. The larger exercise of constructing outcomes goals will in itself be salutary to those involved—as other competency outcomes groups have discovered. It can encourage vital self-assessment in global gen ed courses, to make sure they connect with wider perspectives and analytical goals. The fact that the discussion must take place across normal unit and disciplinary lines, given the range of specialties embraced by globalization, is admittedly an additional challenge, but also an additional reason to undertake the task.

There are ways, in other words, to make some commitment to global assessment even without the capacity for a more formal program. If some institutions can experiment with the formal aspects as well, others should be ready to learn from their experience. But the checklist and engagement with discussing intended outcomes are available to all, and further movement in these directions is both possible and desirable.

10
General Observations:
Some Underlying Issues

Much of the work in global education involves specific projects and project categories, each with its own policy issues and administrative demands. Study abroad, a global affairs major, recruitment of international students—each area involves some shared assumptions and faith, about the importance of emphasis on global activities and contacts, about the centrality of global experience in contemporary higher education. But each area can readily narrow in on very specific problems. Even systematically connecting global courses with study abroad is not always easy, because the study abroad office is somewhat separated from standard academic departments and academic endeavor and because student availability varies so much from one category to the other. We have seen that the focus in recruiting international students often stands apart from other aspects of the global education agenda. A key issue in organizing international programs involves generating the maximum possible interconnections, without dampening localized initiatives and enthusiasms.

Linkage is only part of the issue. One of the truly intriguing aspects of serious engagement in global education—at times, one of the challenging features as well—involves the range of basic issues the field tosses up, from appropriate roles for faculty governance to the connection between institutional policy and foreign policy. Thinking this broader compass through is part of the backdrop to effective administration.

This chapter returns to some of the general concerns and challenges that international education produces, cutting across particular areas, preparatory to a conclusion about global education and its future more broadly. The topics embrace but transcend particular activities, and they merit attention from faculty and administrators as they lift their heads from the task of adding a global component to an environmental course or trying to figure out how to recruit students for a study trip to Egypt. We need to attend to certain underlying tensions and certain basic values, even in confronting daily administrative tasks in the global arena. Four areas stand out, as underpinning most if not all global efforts, culminating in the inherently contested question of prioritization; and of course there are links among the four, with no tidy boundaries.

I. Mutualism

The book's introduction talked already about the importance of approaching global education through a mutualist lens. Particularly in developing programs abroad, certainly in study abroad and increasingly in recruiting and pleasing international students, it is vital to learn from others even as American educational values and achievements are highlighted. Many activities have to provide mutual benefit or they will fail outright. More subtly, any assumption that global education means simply taking American systems overseas without adjustment or flexibility, or providing rigidly American educational standards as the framework within which foreign experiences must be carefully nestled, simply contradicts what global education is all about.

At this point, having explored the key specific areas, these general injunctions can be handled with greater complexity. The future of American global education depends on increasingly ample and explicit recognition of the importance of mutuality and reciprocity. Growing strength of educational operations outside the United States, growing concern about the myopia of American foreign policy, both push against Ugly Americanism on the higher education front.

Achieving the desired balance, however, is not easy, both because of ingrained American parochialism—even among faculty members who would like to regard themselves as cosmopolitan, and because of the fact that some global operations depend on a certain, though carefully limited, sense of American distinctiveness. There is a juggling act here that has to be acknowledged.

Certain examples of national arrogance in so-called global education efforts have simply been wrong, though this does not mean that they have entirely disappeared. The careful insulation of "study abroad" students under the tutelage of American faculty using the same curricula as those back home is an obvious case in point. There may be a small amount of educational value in efforts of this sort, as opposed to simply staying home in the first place; but the efforts also mislead students into thinking they have gained serious insights and they certainly constitute wasted opportunities.

But there are a number of much more nuanced situations, where the proper balance is far more difficult to prescribe. Accreditation raises crucial issues, as American institutions expand international programs and enter into a growing variety of collaborative arrangements. Though different regional accreditation branches impose different strictures (the Southern Association of Colleges and Schools seems more rigorous than some other analogues, for example), all accreditation operations seek to make sure that claims of equivalence to domestic standards are matched by realities. This will in turn lead them into often elaborate probes of the nature and quality of foreign degrees held by some of the faculty in a branch campus or into inquiries about the adequacy of Chinese or Indian universities who are sending student cohorts to obtain American degrees.* The tension between providing informed assurances and making invidious assumptions about foreign teachers or institutions is not always easy to manage. There are a number of heartening cases in which accreditation bodies have displayed real flexibility—as in countenancing the joint degree programs in the Chinese 1-2-1 consortia, without disruptive investigations into the participating Chinese universities. And there are certain examples of accreditation inquiries that have played an important role in assuring that certain international ventures hew to crucial standards in areas like library acquisitions. But the interplay between assessing quality in American terms, and acknowledging value in international alternatives, can be a complicated one—even aside from the massive paperwork and costs the accreditation efforts inherently involve.

Individual institutions face tensions of their own. Faculty will divide in their assumptions about the quality of foreign colleagues recruited and partially evaluated abroad, rather than through comfortingly familiar domestic procedures. There may be suspicion as well about the preparation of international students, not only in English but in mathematics and other fields—though obviously there are regional variables here. Some faculty harbor beliefs about international students that are simply not borne out by the facts—as in confusing accents and some stylistic inelegance with overall poor performance, when the data show that international students often do better than average.

Branch campus operations and recruitment of international undergraduate students both typically assume some special merits in American technical training but also in liberal educational values and teaching strategies. After all, there's no point going to the trouble of establishing activities abroad or making the sacrifices many students endure to come to the United States if there's not something distinctive involved. But these claims must be softened at least through sufficient recognition that foreign contexts can add value as well, that international students can do extremely well without becoming exactly like American students. Discussions with foreign officials must similarly balance essential claims about what an American education "must" involve (including freedom of inquiry) with acknowledgement not only of local customs but of local educational merits that can be embraced in a collaborative enterprise.

These are not easy deals to strike, whether the subject involves credentialing an individual foreign student or negotiating a branch campus with a local

---

* As a related aside, new requirements in some accreditation regions that faculty with international degrees teaching in the United States not only produce evidence of the terminal degree but have it formally evaluated, reflect some unfortunate and mistrustful trends, hardly designed (whatever the minor problems at the margins) to win international educational friends.

sheik. There are no hard and fast rules. The main point, as a backdrop to appropriate flexibility, is to recognize the problem, to avoid over-shrill or over-general claims about American superiority and to use mutuality to guide educational efforts that may be a bit different from the home products without losing recognizability and with opportunities for gain through collaborative adjustments. Foreign operations of all sorts, including again the recruitment of individual international students as well as larger endeavors, must be seen as benefiting "us" as well as providing advantages for "them," and they must be defined in terms of cross-fertilization, not unilateral Americanism.

II.   Disciplinary Balances

Global education raises complex issues about disciplinary involvements. On the study abroad side, we have seen that crucial issues of differential interest and opportunity continue to bedevil the field. Though individual faculty in technology and science fields may be deeply committed to internationalism, collectively they and their students see far less point in global exposures than do their counterparts in the humanities and social sciences. Assumptions about the inferiority of things foreign may enter in here quite explicitly. It is often harder to recruit faculty to spend time teaching abroad in these fields than in the liberal arts, for a host of reasons including research facility needs but also including attitudes.

The same tensions enter into curricular discussions. Most of the components of global education come from the humanities and social sciences, though the growing involvement of environmental and public health faculty provides some useful balance. "Globalization across the curriculum" is a noble goal, but it requires far more experimentation and imaginative leaps (along with faculty development incentives) in some fields than in others. Maintaining a wide commitment to global education, across different schools and faculties, is possible, but there is undeniable challenge.

On the other hand, American global education in other guises leans disproportionately strongly to the technical disciplines along with management. Foreign authorities negotiating for American operations or articulation agreements most commonly rivet on these fields, rather than the social sciences or, even more, the humanities. International students vote with their feet in similar fashion, at both graduate and undergraduate levels. Crucial discussions occur, in branch campuses, articulation negotiations, or even the advising of international students, about the purposes of American general education, with its social science and humanistic components. It is not easy to clarify, or at least to persuade, concerning the importance of certain fields of study and the spirit of critical inquiry they engender.

Obviously, issues in this area can benefit, once more, by some flexibility. Requirements of deep exposure to English literature or the history of Western civilization can surely be modified to take into account other cultural traditions and interests—while preserving, possibly even enhancing, a humanities component in general education. And there are some truly heartening breakthroughs. A Korean educational leader, soliciting American participation in a venture in the IFEZ educational free trade zone in Incheon, deliberately courts a strong general education component and an emphasis on critical inquiry as exactly what Korean education needs at this point, far beyond technical competences in which their better universities are fully equivalent in any event. And we have to acknowledge that many American students themselves have trouble figuring out the value of general education—international disdain may be a bit more pronounced, but it is not unique. It hardly takes a global education framework to generate worries about the future of the humanities in American higher education.

Still, there is a problem. Many aspects of the global education effort may, if allowed to play out without imaginative intervention, reduce the balance that many American educators believe is a signal strength of the national tradition and, most crucially, limit opportunities for generating a spirit and capacity for critical inquiry. There's every reason not only to be aware of the problem, but to encourage inventive efforts to figure out new combinations of cultural materials (as part of a global humanities component) as well as new collaborations between Americans and foreign scholars in these fields and not just in science and technology. Opportunities to define and defend the ways American higher education generates and sustains critical thinking are needed at home as well as abroad, but the global context generates some particular challenges that faculty and administrators should try to meet.

At a simpler level, the issue of disciplinary balance may seem to work out. Humanists and social scientists staff the global curriculum and send students abroad; scientists and technologists woo the foreign students and operate the programs abroad. But this apparent equilibrium masks some very real tensions in degrees of commitment and levels of cultural awareness, to which a college or university, in coordinating global education overall, must actively attend.

III.   Where in the World

Any school developing global programs must ponder geographical balance. At the curricular level, this means thinking about developing courses, or more desirably minors and in some cases majors, in African, Latin American, East Asian, South Asian, Middle Eastern, and European studies. Decisions about how many faculty can be afforded, and what kinds of regional niceties can be accommodated (what about Central Asia, for example? are we taking Canada and Australia for granted?) are crucial. They can be carved in various ways, depending in part on resources, but they should be considered explicitly and not left to chance. A key issue in coordinating international studies, over the usual welter of schools and departments, involves trying to make sure that different regional strengths are adequately represented and adequately available for the various levels of instruction. (For instance: a graduate unit finally hired a strong researcher on South Asian economic issues, even as the university overall lacked good South Asian coverage; the challenge, not easily met, was spreading the benefits or doing some supplementary hiring across units.) Balance issues loom also in the modern languages area. Progress in representing non-European languages is obviously considerable, but it remains troubling that Farsi, Hindi and even Arabic are offered on so few campuses. A similar globalization act is underway, as we have seen, with study abroad, but while important gains move students from an excessive European focus the national aim still does not match the targets.

Other kinds of regional disparities impinge. Recent projects for outreach and collaboration have focused massively on China and India, with some attention left over for South Korea, Singapore and Japan; Vietnam, with its own vigorous attempts to forge new connections, may soon enter the mix. The emphasis is understandable, given the new monies these economies are generating and their population size. But the emphasis, along of course with continued European ties, does raise questions about the rest of the world. A number of specific American institutions, particularly but not exclusively in the southwest and Florida, have strong links with counterparts in several parts of Latin America. A few years ago Monterey Technology Institute, in Mexico, launched an ambitious program of student exchange with various American counterparts, which met with some success. Collaborations in Costa Rica, Chile, and to some extent Argentina and Brazil are also significant; and Latin America continues to exercise considerable attraction for study abroad. But the region clearly does not command as much attention as its potential future importance and its current development needs might warrant. The same applies to parts of central and Southeast Asia, where some significant initiatives do not yet add up to an overall higher education strategy for American universities.

Russia also raises questions. A flurry of collaborations developed in the 1990s, when American interest was high and national barriers low. But as the political situation became less friendly, and as quick profits did not materialize (and as some key funders, like the Soros Foundation, found their efforts frustrated), American interest turned, probably disproportionately, to other targets. American sources of funds dried up, and Russian institutions, not well supported in their own right, had little to offer. The European Union remains active in contacts with major Russian universities, and there are some interesting individual American projects, including student exchanges and some collaborative electronic classrooms. But the linkages are surprisingly sporadic. Here is a clear case where interesting educational possibilities and a longer term national interest have not managed to win through.

The most obvious orphan, however, amid the flurry of new collaborations, is Africa. A delegation from Burundi, headed by its Minister of Education, visits an American university, where a faculty member originally from that country has forged a tie. The nation is poor, recently emerging from devastating civil war. Its educational needs, particularly at the primary and secondary levels, are vast, and the College of Education at the American contact is eager to develop a collaborative program to work on teacher training and curricular standards. But there is simply no money: Burundi has none, the American institution has none to speak of, and despite on-the-ground enthusiasm from US AID there's no current federal priority as well. It looks like the project will founder. There are some brighter spots. Nigeria, with recent oil money, has been able to stimulate collaborations in the area of technology education, and of course is developing its American university with guidance from American University in Washington D.C. A few fledgling private schools have formed on-paper collaboratives with American counterparts to provide guidance in areas like management training as well as IT. Some American foundations have opened to Africa, though most commonly primarily to South Africa in the wake of apartheid. A few historically black universities, headed by institutions like Howard, have vigorous African connections and a decent flow of students. But the number of opportunities for useful and mutual interaction vastly exceeds the resources available, and, even more than in the case of Latin America, there is no sense of overall strategy in American higher education; and there are too many stories of mutual interest sparked, sometimes with funding initially suggested, only to see hopes ultimately dashed. Whether disparities and vacuums of this sort are in the national interest is worth discussing; certainly, it is hard for individual higher education institutions to right the balance.

Whether the issue is curricular coverage, study abroad, or educational collaborations, many American universities need an active sense of overall strategic planning with global geography in mind. Some kind of institutional foreign policy may be essential. It is legitimate, indeed virtually unavoidable, to select some targets over others. Adequate curricular representation can be given to many areas, except in the smaller colleges, even when strongest emphasis goes to a couple of regional programs. Language selections may be mitigated by opportunities for students to work on other languages through local consortial arrangements. Obviously, institutions striving for branch campuses cannot possibly be everywhere at once, though there are some interesting efforts to develop operations in the Middle East, East Asia and possibly South Asia almost simultaneously; and as noted, American University is seeking to replicate its successful Middle Eastern initiative in Africa. The obvious goal is to be purposeful about strategic geographic decisions, at whatever level, while also seeking to minimize undue disparities. If at the same time an openness can remain to other cases of great need and opportunity, where some funding might reward earnest effort, American educational strengths and needs might be well served.

IV. Faculty Interests

Any serious global educational initiative has to involve faculty, and many initiatives will emanate directly from faculty ranks. The relationship between faculty and global education has its complexities, however, and this is the fourth area, transcending individual categories of endeavor, that warrants comment.

One issue, involving faculty but also student affairs staff, involves the relationship between global education initiatives and efforts in the area of diversity and multiculturalism. Many colleges and universities most eager for advances in global education are also unusually committed to multiculturalism in the American context, both in curriculum and in student life. This applies to open-minded faculty and administrators as well, for whom broadening beyond national parochialism can produce a single liberal lens. In 2007, the American Council on Education presented a persuasive set of conference papers on the constructive links between the two endeavors. Unquestionably, dealing with international students and issues promotes some of the key behaviors and habits of mind one wants in the multicultural field as well: a willingness to be flexible, an openness to the validity and manageability of cultural differences. Similar emendations of Eurocentrism and unthinking commitment to American exceptionalism may additionally be involved in both endeavors, a substantive as well as analytical link. Some minorities provide important clientele for area studies programs or language learning, as they seek to recapture knowledge lost in the American generational chain. As we have seen in discussing study abroad, involving certain groups of minority students more equally in global educational opportunities is or should be a key goal—another important connection. Unquestionably, further discussion will reveal additional means of promoting both causes in American higher education in mutually reinforcing fashion. Still, however, there are differences that go beyond the distinct historical and political origins of the two agendas, and too much well-intentioned blurring can be risky. Minority groups in the United States have heritages from regions of origin that can and should be explored. These origins have, however, even in the case of fairly recent immigrant groups, been modified by the American experience. The groups are not fully international, and they should not serve as surrogates for more systematic international inquiries. Because of the deep importance of minority concerns, and in some cases their political support, there is always some danger that global exercises will be preempted by American multicultural displays. This already happens in many international festivals, as we have discussed, where minority groups, familiar with American participatory styles, take the lead in presenting costumes and folklore from a global region, leaving actual international students on the side. This blurring may be trivial. But the need to deal directly with global cultural differences and overlaps, in curricula and in active outreach, and to add the global economic and political issues to the cultural, must be held separate from multicultural endeavor. Confusion is understandable, and bridges can be built after distinct approaches are established; but the distinction is essential.[1]

A rather alternative set of tensions affects global educational initiatives in their own right, where problems may involve not how to embrace global activities but whether to do them at all. Various faculty members will differ, of course, on the importance of any global enterprise. A few years ago—I think this is less salient now—faculty in some units resisted the whole idea of even modest investments in foreign language training, on grounds that everybody worth anything spoke English. At my current university the idea of global research and education as one of five or six key emphases for the future has not been frontally resisted, but I'm sure there are those who disagree. We have noted tensions that arise between faculty who assume the superiority of their programs, and serious commitments to study abroad even if, heaven forbid, some technical or scientific training occurs offshore. Certainly the more ambitious overseas projects will always, and understandably, encounter faculty who worry that resources are being committed at a time when funding for core local projects is already inadequate—the fact that in most cases the bulk of the investment is not from the university does not necessarily prevail against these concerns. It is important to provide forums in which these issues can be discussed, and appropriate priorities established with due faculty voice. Faculty advisory boards can play a vital role here.

It is also true—and here, despite my faculty background, I know I'm an administrator—that some kinds of international engagements do not easily lend themselves to full faculty input. Negotiations with a foreign government or university, beyond a specific research collaboration or individual degree program, almost inevitably must be carried out at the administrative level, even if, as is sometimes the case, a faculty contact spurred the discussion. The idea of a branch campus must of course be presented to faculty (as to university trustees and, as relevant, appropriate state agencies) but rarely will it be possible to scrutinize details in a fully collaborative fashion. One collaborative venture my university has sponsored was presented to a faculty forum, sponsored by the Senate, where it received fairly cursory comment and enthusiastic approval; later, however, it turned out that other faculty were not fully aware of what was going on and chimed in with considerable grumbling. Particular tensions can arise over degree programs to be offered. Faculty in individual units have considerable reason to argue that, even when a university has approved an overall collaboration, they have deciding rights over whether their offerings are included; but the larger institutional good may push in another direction. These issues can be resolved, with adequate mutual discussion and candor, but they are not necessarily easy.

Faculty also become involved, again perfectly properly and understandably, in what can only be called foreign policy disagreements, when it comes to recruiting certain kinds of international students or, particularly, entering into collaborative arrangements with overseas institutions. There may be specific concerns, varying with individual faculty or groups, about the policies of individual countries. I have been lobbied, quite appropriately, by faculty about China's human rights record and its treatment of members of the Falun Gong religious group, as the university furthered various arrangements with the Ministry of Education and with Chinese universities. Activities in the Middle East often provoke comments about policies toward Israel or toward women or, again, human rights records more generally. At times, I must confess, the extent of stereotyping about certain regions of the world, the resistance to more accurate and nuanced analyses, has surprised me, on the part of otherwise discerning academics. And I must admit as well, for my own part, a certain diffidence about putting the United States forward as a consistent standard of probity, for example, in the human rights arena. There have been times in recent years when I've felt grateful that certain foreign officials have continued to be willing to deal with us.

There is no question, however, that a university's global activities are quite likely to put it into contact with countries of whose policies Americans do not entirely approve, and that some faculty (and other friends of the university) may be uncomfortable as a result. Here too, obviously, there must be opportunities for frank and, one hopes, civil discussions. There are unquestionably regimes and particular collaborations with which we should not become involved—I was at one point persuaded, I admit still somewhat reluctantly, that one proposed enterprise should be withdrawn involving a country with which American policymakers were at odds. The State Department often muddies issues as well, encouraging scholarly exchange with one hand (currently, for example, in some outreach efforts to Iran), while raising barriers and objections with the other. And it is always vital to make as sure as possible, in any collaboration, that core institutional values are not sacrificed, from equal opportunity regardless of gender or ethnicity to open inquiry. The whole point of global activity is to blend greater global connection and awareness with these principles, even though the principles are not universally embraced.

On more straightforward opportunities for collaboration across disputes of policy and national interest, however, the situation is different—though again, not all faculty will agree. I believe that, overall, most academics can be persuaded that extensions of American educational values and operations, in a mutualist and collaborative framework, beat smug assertions of moral purity in isolation. This was, I believe, our experience during the Cold War, as we gradually learned that scholarly connections with the Soviets and their allies improved situations mutually, even though they involved dealing with regimes Americans found distasteful. I believe the principle still applies. Educational connections may be especially important to societies with which the United States operates in some tension—precisely because we stand to learn more from these connections and also have the greatest opportunities to stimulate discussion, whether through individual international students or larger activities. It is a question of hope and belief that can be candidly presented for faculty discussion and that, I think, will usually win the day. The conviction that, in most circumstances, educational connections will do more good than harm, that they do serve student, institutional and national interests properly construed, can be deeply held. It leads of course to the broader issues of global educational priorities, with which we conclude in the next and final chapter.

* * *

The need to have a "foreign policy," at least at institutions with a wide global agenda, referred to several times in this chapter, may seem grandiose. Here is another area where global specialist administrators and wider faculty groups will not share a similar sense of scope and urgency. Yet there is considerable reality involved. Deciding on regional focus, discussions with faculty about the reasons for engagement with a particular initiative despite some political concerns, simply managing the various foreign delegations that seek contact (with appropriate protocol and some possibility of mutual benefit, and not just another hollow signing of a MOU): all of this commands real attention from various university officials and faculty leaders. One of the reasons to consider carefully the organization and coordination of international activities is to facilitate coherent management of the types of decisions involved. Initiatives and contacts sprout far more rapidly than opportunities to follow up, but this is another reason for a genuine policy capacity, for the ability to make and justify strategic choices. The complexity can be daunting, particularly since, even in the more globally oriented institutions, there are many other issues to contend with. But there's no reason to conceal this aspect of administrative life: the opportunity to participate in policy discussions, where student interests and institutional outreach are both involved, is a privilege, a source of continuing stimulus and a widening sphere of contacts and knowledge alike.

11
Conclusion:
The Global Mission

Any reasonable list of challenges for American colleges and universities over the next several decades—some ambitious pundits even say for the 21st century, but centuries always turn out to be longer than early-years seers anticipate—includes the need to develop appropriate global orientations central to the core mission. Lists can vary a bit otherwise—some would note lifelong learning as another key challenge, others perhaps accessibility and diversity (related to global issues but, as we have seen, not by any means identical). For some, lists would still include educational technology; and I think we have to keep the difficult balance between teaching and research in the mix. But global is going to show up on the top-five priority list without much question. As we have seen, virtually every institution over the past 15 years has brought new urgency or range to its global agenda, with few places yet comfortable that they've achieved the desired level. An intriguing aspect of the field, as discussed before, is the significant involvement of so many different kinds of institutions, with leadership and innovation coming from many sectors—there are only a few top-down advantages in global education in terms of the standard institutional pecking order.

As part of the new prioritization, a great deal of ink has been and will be spilled about creating the global university. Interest here grows in institutions of higher education literally around the world. It involves consideration of a range of activities and connections but also new learning goals. It requires serious innovation. It must engage the full range of American institutions of higher education—well beyond the current vanguard.

At the same time, it becomes increasingly obvious that the global university emerges from no single formula, no one dramatic gesture: not just a study abroad office or a new global course. The globally responsible university requires a reorientation of purpose, deep and lasting commitment—but also a wide array of specific actions and activities. It is the combination of commitment at all levels and the wealth of detailed effort that produces the global outcome. Even the most global university is still in process of development, but the need for a rich mixture is already clear.

Happily (I think) explicit efforts to rank universities in terms of global achievement have not yet fully developed, but there's no question that a certain degree of competitiveness can emerge, as institutions compare their global facilities. Up to a point, the spur may be healthy. At the same time, it is unclear how highly the various components of the college and university clientele rate global education in assessing institutions. Accreditation agencies and state boards of higher education may welcome signs of global outreach, but they do not (yet) require them—which is both a relief and a caution, as nonglobal criteria may win an undesirable level of priority simply because they have to be assessed, however mechanically. Corporate leaders increasingly note the desirability of global competence (particularly striking of course is the support for study abroad); but there is a gap here, as with liberal education, between what leaders say and what personnel offices actually emphasize, where global credentials are less systematically sought. Undergraduate applicants now seem to pay fairly close attention to study abroad opportunities, as one of their criteria for institutional choice—even if, in the event, it turns out that many of them do not themselves take advantage of the facilities available. We have seen as well some recent polling results that suggest growing public awareness of international education goals. On the other hand, my institution recently did an opinion survey about what matters, and found that among most groups global achievements fell well down the list—noticeably below research, graduate programs, critical thinking gains for undergraduates, and a few other items, and above only athletic success among the seven criteria available (and my guess is that respondents did not tell the truth about their real valuation of athletics). Of the groups surveyed, only undergraduates and applicants themselves placed high value on the global, an encouraging sign for the future, and an indication of awareness of where not only the world, but many careers, are heading. Overall, however, the global area has yet to enter the general evaluation of schools as firmly as might be desired. And, as we have seen, faculty divide over the priority as well.

Complicating the situation still further, as we have also noted, is the inescapable fact that developing an ambitious mix of global endeavors takes an immense amount of work and, in some cases, operates amid undeniable uncertainties. Money is an issue, though happily a serious engagement with global education does not involve costly equipment or facilities—in this sense it's an easier addition than programs in science or technology. Unrealistic or undesirable expectations for profit sometimes complicate the financial picture, making even moderate costs seem unanticipated. And of course it may be easier to find political support for science or technology goals than for global initiatives, even though the former are much more costly, given the less decisive economic return on global activities and, frequently, some concern about foreign values or policy disputes.

Still, costs are not usually the main point; effort is. Overseeing the contemporary array of global initiatives can be fascinating, but it takes time and mental energy. Decisions about organizational structure are not easy, because of the various offices typically involved, the need to balance coordination and initiative from the ranks, the temptation either to add global initiatives to existing portfolios (which can overwhelm officials from department chairs on up) or to oversimplify the response by entrusting too many responsibilities to a single agency. Global education conferences consistently highlight the extent to which even getting people responsible for the housing of international students together with those dealing with visas and with those dealing with academic advising remains a serious challenge at many institutions, and this can mean inadequate integration of the students and inadequate utilization of their presence for wider educational impact. Departmental activities can be recast, for example, with an influx of foreign students whose perspectives are truly valuable but who also require some special attention, quite apart from the demands of actually setting up a program at an overseas branch. Science and technology units at least have a long experience with international clientele; the more recent involvement of economics or management, though educationally salutary in the long run, challenges workloads and prior orientations alike. Learning curves for major outreach efforts can be steep—from infrastructure demands back home to cultural sensitivities in dealing with foreign partners. Simply freeing up time to entertain delegations and maintain suitable presence abroad can be onerous. Global education adds a significant chunk to the functions of senior university officials, as well as to many staffing areas, if the effort is at all serious, whatever organizational mechanisms emerge.

It is not surprising, in this context, that institutional responses vary, with some schools placing much higher priority on a wider range of global activities than others. It is impossible, yet, to say that a school without this or that global factor is going to suffer—even the general education conversion, from Western history to world history remains incomplete, not to mention the extremely varied appetites for more ambitious undertakings like joint degrees or foreign branches. For most colleges, global education is still a new frontier (whatever specific precedents may exist, as in earlier study abroad initiatives), and it's appropriate to experiment, defendable to be a bit cautious, inevitable to venture different degrees of commitment.

This said, the need to do more globally remains an inescapable responsibility, whether the institution is just dipping into the global waters or has a significant portfolio already. Collectively, American higher education should be reaching for more international students and utilizing them better; for more, and more imaginative and curricularly integrated study abroad; for more global components to curricula generally; for more collaborative activities with foreign partners. Cost and effort are real, but the mounting obligation has even more pressing reality.

The fundamental reasons for the global priority are clear-cut, but they bear repeating in conclusion. Americans, in whatever walk of life, are surrounded by global issues. Any college student, who graduates today without some understanding of the current economic connections between the United States and China, or without some knowledge of the relationships between Islam and Christianity, is insufficiently prepared for effective citizenship—American OR global. The list of essential points can, I admit, easily grow too long, in the hands of a devoted globalist; but even when kept to a manageable minimum, there is a list. And, as we have seen, more than data points are involved. Students must gain some facility in mental habits such as comparison and the capacity to relate the local and the global, if they are to operate effectively, as citizens and often as workers, in the world they will live in.

American institutions of higher education have a special obligation here, and while some of us welcome the challenge there is also a burden involved. Universities across the world are upping the ante on global connections, and while U.S. schools are not behind, there is every reason to respond to this growing pressure. As we have seen, study abroad efforts, international recruitment and branch campuses are not the American province that we once imagined. We owe it to our students, if nothing else, to keep pace with the range and innovation that many international institutions now display. Beyond this, of course, is the accelerating pace of globalization itself (with its complex mix of gains and losses and an equally complicated set of regional responses). More and more students, whether they anticipate this or not, will find themselves in situations where their work, their voting, their leisure interests depend on some awareness of global and comparative history and trends, and American higher education—like its counterparts elsewhere—simply must keep abreast, which means further curricular change and further program innovation.

But there is more, which is where the compensatory challenge comes in— not exactly a new one, but increasingly pressing. While some secondary schools are moving a bit in a global direction, with some new foreign languages and serious world history, most are largely locked into a more conventional framework; and as we have seen, exposure to global issues at the primary level actually retreats. One can hope for change; and indeed a university responsibility, through schools of education and beyond, is to assist in teacher training and curriculum development at all grade levels and also to promote appropriate school district policies and commitments. Even in high school world history, we still have too many teachers thrown into courses for which they have no college training and too many courses that are badly defined in the first place; and the shortage of trained teachers in Chinese or Arabic, for the schools, is already palpable. For the foreseeable future, though, much of what students ideally ought to learn about the wider world—do learn, at least with regard to foreign languages, in the systems of many other nations—before college, have to be addressed, in the United States, at the college level. This means that universities must expect to need segments of general education to bring students more fully up to speed on basic global contexts, and it means (this is not new, just newly urgent) that they need to find ways to motivate more effective foreign language learning, now in languages additional to the standard European array.

More than compensation for K-12 limitations is involved. A national deficiency in foreign affairs knowledge remains troubling. Media coverage has increased after the parochial withdrawal of the 1990s, but it continues to focus mainly on a few trouble spots, mainly those involving the most immediate U.S. interests, rather than the changing global landscape more generally. The 2008 presidential campaign, in its intense early stages, was noteworthy for a lack of coverage for candidates' foreign policy positions beyond the issue of Iraq—despite the fact that several contenders put forth detailed statements, there was little echo in the media or in the seemingly endless parade of debates. Reporters themselves, and presumably the public as well, simply could not escape the habits of seizing on domestic woes, real or imagined—immigration, the economy—rather than balancing them with foreign policy concerns or even, very carefully, putting these issues themselves in international context. (Virtually nothing was heard about balance of payment issues, for example.) Even though the Bush presidency had been dominated by foreign policy issues, assumptions, and mistakes, the United States seemed still eager to retreat to a national framework as quickly as possible. It is not, of course, the responsibility of higher educational institutions to inject themselves directly into political discussions, save as individual faculty and student groups seek to encourage analysis; over time, however, they do need to help prepare a public that is more attuned to the international issues that will continue to shape the American future.

This in turn involves more than providing better information, through world history efforts and global requirements in general education. It involves working on some deeply rooted mindsets. The manner of the American invasion of Iraq in 2003 constituted among other things a sad failure for American education, to the extent that it reflected so little learning, at either the policy or the public levels, from what had happened in Vietnam less than 40 years before. It is not the fact of invasion that is in question here: obviously, different people could have different views on whether we should have moved in against Saddam Hussein, with the same levels of international awareness. What is so deeply troubling was the assumption that American presence and values would quickly win over a different people with their own history, their own experience of outside intervention and colonialism; here is where blithe optimism, easily sold to the American public, suggests a set of beliefs about the national role in the world that must be opened to examination and discussion. Reliance on easy American superiority, and I would add ongoing beliefs in a cold war mentality in which we must assume that those who are not with us on all major issues are therefore determined enemies, simply will not position us well for the global opportunities and challenges of the coming years. Higher education must obviously avoid blind partisanship, whatever the views of individual faculty members or administrators; but it must help growing numbers of Americans open some almost knee-jerk mindsets to serious and critical analysis. Here too, compensation is essential.

Many recent reports, particularly from some of the higher education associations, have called for global education programs that might transform the mentality of the American undergraduate. The term can seem grandiose. Its challenge is unmistakable. What the mission involves centers on the kind of compensation needed in the American public, as well as in the preparation of future leaders—whether the issue is sensitivity to the ironically heightened role of foreign languages even amid a sea of English, or the conceptual approach to present and likely future claimants on American foreign policy.[1]

The needs, from several vantage points, are considerable. Few institutions can or should feel comfortable with the global education array thus far developed. The sense of further challenge is unavoidable, and not just for schools newly entering the arena, given the need not just to keep pace with global connections and developments but to address some specifically national deficiencies as well.

Furthermore this is, as we have argued in several chapters, a vital time for the intelligent and imaginative commitment of American colleges and universities to a wider global education agenda, using and extending familiar components, like study abroad, but building new facets as well. Widespread eagerness for American education invites further response; the openness will not last forever, but long-term as well as short-term gains, in terms of student connections and institutional collaborations, can be generated in the meantime. There is also, without starry-eyed idealism, the chance to help certain regions of the world, if the American approaches are carefully and mutually interactive. Certainly, the chance to build an American image different from that shaped by recent policy moves and consumer blandishments is clearly in the national interest. The moment is defined as well by new barriers set up by the more fearful aspects of contemporary American culture and by narrow policies with regard to the entry of foreign scholars and students. Innovation, in the form of new types of outreach, is essential both to counter the disruption to international ties and, again, to provide a different American face to the wider world. Quite apart from urging more schools to catch up with the leaders in global education—at community college, liberal arts unit, and research university alike, with a special plea to some of the comprehensive public institutions—we need further experimentation and initiative even from the bellwethers.

During the Cold War, after its 1950s intensity began to yield a bit, American institutions of higher education played a vital role in forging new contacts with scholars "behind the curtain," in the process helping to defuse tensions and promote greater mutual understanding. The challenge and opportunity are at least as great today, in using education and research to forge new links—with the many parts of the world now dubious about elements of American policy—and to promote reciprocal clarifications. Dependence on institutional initiative is greater than was the case 40 years ago, at least in terms of current federal leadership, but the opportunities are all the brighter for this fact. It is a high calling, and colleges and universities at various levels can participate in the response.

The domestic mission is vital as well. I believe—cannot prove, of course, and there will be some worthy scholarly dissenters—that 50 or 100 years from now, historians will look back on our period as a time of crucial readjustment between the Cold War and a new, multilateral balance among major powers—with the fling of the United States as sole superpower a brief interlude. The rise of China, India, probably Brazil, along with the maturation of the European Union and, possibly, the revival of Russia all constitute significant markers that do not displace tremendous American strength but increasingly complicate national assertiveness, with terrorism an important but ultimately perhaps less significant concurrent development that serves to distract from broader patterns. There are those, of course, who believe that Western economic values will still prove transcendent, that the abundant vulnerabilities in Chinese or Indian political and economic frameworks will constrain their competitiveness. But if the rebalancing theme is at least plausible, as I think is incontestably the case, we need an active educational effort to make sure that Americans understand the nature of change and do not so emphasize parochial positions that the nation's global standing is needlessly weakened by global ignorance or inability—by global *in*competence in short. The same active effort must help Americans distinguish between new complexities and rooted enmities, so that the nation does not greet inevitable changes and competitive challenges as acts of belligerence. The transition, if this is what the current moment turns out to be, is not a simple one, and Americans might well mishandle it. Education, broadly construed, including of course debate about the plausibilities of key scenarios for the global future, has a vital role to play in encouraging the most constructive reactions to change. This is why, beyond the specifics of visa regulations or even global public opinion, we need to extend and deepen the global initiatives in American colleges and universities.

It is imperative as well to involve a wider range of the academy than has previously been brought into global endeavors. We require specialists, of course. Global education in the United States has progressed on the backs of devoted study abroad offices and international recruiters. We need more of these, and probably additional professional training opportunities for their preparation. We certainly need particularly devoted faculty, from areas studies programs, the languages, international relations, and increasingly now from global environmentalism and global health as well, to spur collaborative projects and to anchor curricular discussions from general education on up. Arguably, as already discussed, we need to grow another expert area, the global studies coordinator or high-level international affairs administrator who can consolidate specific facets of the larger effort, so that study abroad has more contact with joint degree efforts and other outreach, and both with the management of international students. Hopefully, this survey of key aspects of global education will facilitate this kind of larger coordination, by focusing on the whole field rather than on individual operations. But it is increasingly obvious that global education is too complex and too important to be left to specialists alone, however well consolidated and interactive. Global education impinges increasingly on business offices, on registrars, obviously on admissions programs and housing operations. It involves teaching in the sciences and engineering and nursing, and increasingly even in law. Staff and faculty in these areas need a sense of what the global mission is all about, some sense of what some of its key expressions and key issues are. This is why we need efforts to summarize the field in ways that can be used in higher education training and workshops, to bring others into at least serious acquaintance with the global education arena and into a position where their ideas and interests can contribute actively to its further development. Global education must become part of the common currency of academic administration, along with tuition and scholarships or retention or assessment. Here too, the preparation of higher education professionals must play a key role.

* * *

Needs and obligations are very real, but they are only part of the main point. The field of global education highlights the excitement of learning about distant places and global systems. Its progress must be measured not simply in terms of global competency assessments or numbers of students going abroad, though these form part of the story. The excitement comes through in the student, unsure of direction when he came to college, whose exposure to studies of central Asia brought him to spend internship time in the region, before coming home to pursue graduate work that will lead him to NGO involvement in the same area; or the freshman who brings with her to college impressive experience in raising funds for the school system in Sierra Leone, and then parlays this into further international study as an undergraduate; or the student in conflict analysis, undistinguished though adequate as a freshman, who finds the prospect of a community service program in the Philippines after his junior year a potential turning point in his life. The excitement comes through, in other words, in the growing number of students who are taking every advantage of what global education currently has to offer and who are racing ahead, often carving out their own initiatives with global organizations or regional programs literally around the world. It comes through, if less dramatically, in the basketball player who decides to take Arabic, not as a professional commitment but because he knows it will equip him to know more about what's going on internationally. Or the business student or engineer who adds a global affairs minor from a mixed sense of sheer interest and potential career advantage. Our job, as participants in global education, is to keep up with these students and to challenge them further. And if the excitement of global inquiry has not captured us already, it will surely move and motivate as we work to keep American higher education apace with global change.

Notes

Chapter 1

1. *2006 Mapping of Internationalization* (Washington, D.C: American Council on Education (ACE), 2008).
2. ACE *Mapping*.
3. Jane V. Wellman, *Apples and Oranges in the Flat World: A Layperson's Guide to International Comparisons of Postsecondary Education* (Washington D.C.: ACE, 2007).

Chapter 2

1. Charlotte Crabtree and Gary Nash, *National Standards for World History: Exploring Paths to the Present* (Los Angeles, CA: National Center for History in the Schools, 1994).

Chapter 3

1. Madeleine Green, "Joining the World: the challenge of internationalizing undergraduate education," *Change*, 34 (3) (May–June, 2002): 13–21; Fred Hayward and Laura Siaya, *Public Experience, Attitude, and Knowledge: A Report on Two National Surveys about International Education* (Washington D.C.: ACE, 2001).
2. Patrick O'Meara, Howard D. Mehlinger, and Roxana Ma Newman, eds., *Changing Perspectives on International Education* (Indiana: Indiana University Press, 2001).
3. Green, "Joining the World."
4. President's Commission on Foreign Language and International Studies, *Strength Through Wisdom: A Critique of U.S. Capability* (Washington, D.C.: Superintendent of Documents, U.S. Government Printing Office, 1979).
5. Green, "Joining the World."
6. Gary Nash, Charlotte Crabtree, and Ross Dunn, *History on Trial: Culture Wars and the Teaching of the Past* (New York: Vintage, 1977).
7. Robert Marquand, "Stanford's CIV Course Sparks Controversy," *Christian Science Monitor*, January 25, 1989, p. 13; "Bennett Draws Fire in Stanford Talk Assailing Course Change," *Los Angeles Times*, April 19, 1988.
8. Ann I. Schneider, *Internationalizing Teacher Education: What Can Be Done? A Research Report On the Undergraduate Training of Secondary School Teachers*, retrieved from http://iienetwork.org/?p=27433, April 15, 2008; Merry Merryfield, Elaine Jarchow, and Sarah Pickert, eds., *Preparing Teachers to Teach Global Perspectives* (California: Corwin Press, 1997).
9. K. Masuyama, "Foreign Language Education at High School Level in the United States and Japan," in John Hawkins and William K. Cummings, eds., *Transnational Competence* (New York: State University of New York Press, 2000); President's Commission on Foreign Language and International Studies, *Strength Through Wisdom: A Critique of U.S. Capability* (Washington D.C.: Superintendent of Documents, U.S. Government Printing Office, 1979); *What We Can't Say Can Hurt Us—A Call for Foreign Language Competence by the Year 2000* (Washington D.C.: ACE, 1989); Green, "Joining the World."

10. Dorothy Jones, "The Impact on Higher Education of Standards for Foreign Language Learning," (Alexandria, VA: American Council of Teachers of Foreign Language, 1999); Carol Hernon, "Foreign Language and International Studies High Schools," retrieved August 2008 from www.ericdigests.org/pre-825/high.htm. See also http://www.cal.org/projects/flsurvey/html. The Center for Applied Linguistics works with the Department of Education every ten years to conduct a national survey of foreign language instruction (K-12). Each survey period is three years long. The most recent survey period began in 2007. Thus, the most current, nationally based data we have are from 1997, which can be found at http://www.cal.org/topics/fl/flsurvey97executivesummary.pdf.

11. S. Groenning and D.S. Wiley, eds., *Group Portrait: Internationalizing the Disciplines* (New York: American Forum, 1990); G. Grosvenor, "Americans Get Low Grades in Gallup Geography Test" (Washington D.C.: National Geographic Society, 1998).

12. Hayward and Siaya, *Public Experience.*

Chapter 4

1. JoAnn McCarthy, "Continuing and Emerging National Needs for the Internationalization of Undergraduate Education," in *International Education in the New Global Era: Proceedings of National Policy Conference on the Higher Education Act, Title VI, and Fulbright-Hays Programs* (Los Angeles: International Studies and Overseas Programs, 1998); Craufurd Goodwin and Michael Nacht, *Missing the Boat: The Failure to Internationalize American Higher Education* (Cambridge, England: Cambridge University Press, 1991); James B. Henson, Jan C. Noel, Thomas E. Gillard-Byers, and Marcus D. Ingle, *Internationalizing U.S. Universities: A Preliminary Summary of a National Study* (Pullman, WA: Washington State University, 1991); Richard D. Lambert, *International Studies and the Undergraduate* (Washington D.C.: ACE, 1989).

2. Daniel Segal, " 'Western Civ' and the Staging of History in American Higher Education," *American Historical Review* 106 (2000): 770–805; Gilbert Allardyce, "The Rise and Fall of the Western Civilization Course," *American Historical Review* 87 (1982): 695–725.

3. Peter N. Stearns, *Western Civilization in World History* (London: Routledge, 2003).

4. Patrick Manning, *Navigating World History: Historians Create A Global Past* (London: Palgrave Macmillan, 2003).

5. Association of American Colleges and Universities, "Shared Futures: narratives:" http://www.aacu.org/SharedFutures/gened_global_learning/models.cfm.

6. *Foreign Languages and Higher Education: New Structures for a Changed World* (Washington D.C.: Modern Language Association, 2007).

7. Nelly Furman, David Goldberg, and Natalia Lusin, *Enrollments in Languages Other than English in United States Institutions of Higher Education* (New York: CATJ Presentation, June 1, 2008).

8. Noralee Frankel and Peter N. Stearns, eds., *Globalizing American History* (Washington D.C.: American Historical Association, 2008).

9. Karin Fischer, " 'Flat World' Lessons for Real-world Students," *Chronicle of Higher Education*, November 2, 2007.

10. "Community Colleges Take on Global Challenges," *Chronicle of Higher Education*, April 7, 2007.

11. Elizabeth Redden, "Growing—and Defining—'Global Studies'," *Inside Higher Ed*, February 21, 2008. For global studies programs in community colleges—typically, more diffuse than global affairs majors—see Robert Frost, "Global Studies in

the Community College Curriculum," *Community College Enterprise* (Fall, 2007); L.S. Levin, *Globalizing the Community College* (New York: Palgrave Macmillan, 2002).

12. Redden, "Growing."

13. Ibid.

14. *Global Perspectives on Graduate Education* (Washington D.C.: Council of Graduate Schools, 2008).

15. Madeleine Green, "Joining the World: the challenge of internationalizing undergraduate education," *Change*, 34 (3) (May–June, 2002): 12–21.

16. Peter N. Stearns, *Meaning Over Memory: Recasting the Teaching of Culture and History* (North Carolina: University of North Carolina Press, 1994).

17. Green, "Joining the World."

18. "A Call to Leadership: The presidential role in internationalizing the university," A Report of the NASULGC Task Force on International Education (Washington D.C.: NASULGC, 2004).

19. Green, "Joining the World"; Madeleine F. Green and Christa Olson, *Internationalizing the Campus: A User's Guide* (Washington D.C.: ACE, 2003).

20. Lisa K. Childress, "Faculty Engagement in the Internationalization of Higher Education Institutions," presented to Fourteenth International Conference on Learning, Johannesburg, South Africa, June 26–29, 2007.

21. Paula Zeszorarski, "Issues in Global Education Initiatives in the Community College," *Community College Review* 29(1) (2008): 65–78.

Chapter 5

1. *Mapping Internationalization on U.S. Campuses* (Washington D.C.: ACE, 2008).

2. *Proceedings of the Forum on Study Abroad and Economic Competitiveness* (Washington D.C.: National Press Club, 2007).

3. Ibid, p. 11.

4. Mark Rennella and Whitney Walton, "Planned Serendipity: American Travelers and the Transatlantic Voyage in the Nineteenth and Twentieth Centuries," *Journal of Social History* 38 (2004): 365–84. See also http://www.Forumea.org/dialogue-resources-callforauthorshistory2.htm, for an ongoing history project.

5. Rennella and Walton, "Planned Serendipity," p. 380.

6. Walter Hullihen, "Undergraduate Foreign Study for Credit toward the American Baccalaureate Degree," *The Educational Record* 5 (January 1924): 45; Horatio Krans, "L'American University Union à Paris et son nouveau domicile," *Revue international de l'enseignement* 78 (1924): 242.

7. Letter of Mary Louise Chaill, 1936, cited in Rennella and Walton, "Planned Serendipity," p. 382.

8. Neil Howe and William Strauss, *Millennials Go to College 2* (New York: Howe and Strauss, 2007).

9. From the Institute of International Education, *Open Doors* 2007 Fast Facts, http://www.opendoors.iienetwork.org.

10. "A Semester in Ghana, $4,725. A year in Beijing, $35,150. Experience Abroad: Priceless?" *New York Times*, November 4, 2007.

11. Alan Dessoff, "Who's NOT Going Abroad?" *International Educator* (March–April, 2007).

12. Marilyn Jack, "Study Abroad for Students of Color," IIE *Networker* (Fall, 2005), 16–18; Pat Lemay Burr, "Building Study Abroad Acceptance among Hispanic Students," IIE *Networker* (Fall, 2005): 36–8.

13. "Information for Multicultural Students Studying Abroad: scholarships for multicultural students," http://studyabroad.mus.edu/people/studentsofcolor/scholarships/html.
14. From the Institute of International Education, *Open Doors* 2007 Fast Facts, http://www.opendoors.iienetwork.org.
15. IIE Network, "American Students Studying Abroad at Record Levels," news release, November 13, 2007.
16. J. Carlson, B. Burn, J. Ussem, and D. Yachimowica, *Study Abroad: The Experience of American Undergraduates in Western Europe and the U.S.* (Westport, CT: Greenwood, 1990).
17. On assessment, Associated Colleges of the Midwest, Associated Colleges of the South, Great Lakes College Association, *Liberal Education and Study Abroad: Assessing Learning Outcomes to Improve Program Quality* (New York: The Treagle Foundation, November 2005); Mell Bolen, ed., *A Guide to Outcomes Assessment in Education Abroad* (Austin, Texas: The Forum on Education Abroad, 2007); Richard Sutton and Donald Rubin, "The GLOSSARI Project: initial findings from a system-wide research initiative on study abroad learning outcomes," *Frontiers: The Interdisciplinary Journal of Study Abroad* X (2004): 45–82; Benjamin Haddis, "Gauging the Impact of Study Abroad," *Assessment & Evaluation in Higher Education* 30 (February 2005): 3–19.
18. Barbara Freed, ed., *Second Language Acquisition in a Study Abroad Context* (Philadelphia: John Benjamins North America, 1995), pp. 26, 27.
19. Sally Sieloff Magnan and Michele Back, "Social Interaction and Linguistic Gain during Study Abroad," *Foreign Language Annals* 40 (1) (Spring, 2007): 43–59.
20. Ewa Golonka, "Predictors Revised: linguistic knowledge and metalinguistic awareness in second language gain in Russian," *Modern Language Journal* 90 (2006): 496–505.
21. Freed, *Second Language Acquisition*, p. 26.
22. H. Tyrone Black and David Duhon, "Assessing the Impact of Business Study Abroad Programs on Cultural Awareness and Personal Development," *Journal of Education for Business* (January–February, 2006): 140–4.
23. Haddis, "Gauging," pp. 10–14.
24. Carlson et al., *Study Abroad.*
25. Nadine Dolby, "Globalization, Identity and Nation: Australian and American undergraduates abroad," *Australian Educational Researcher* 32 (2005): 101–7.
26. *Experiences That Matter: Enhancing Student Learning and Success, Annual Report* (NSE, 2007), pp. 17, 21.
27. Diana Jean Schemo, "In Study Abroad, Gifts and Money for Universities," *New York Times*, August 13, 2007.
28. Ibid.
29. On particularly well-developed foreign internship programs, see (in addition to Mt. Holyoke) http://ie3global.ous.edu (Oregon State); http://world.yale.edu/abroad/intl_internships.html; http://www.princeton.edu/-iip and (from Canada) http://international.yorku.ca/internships/index.htm.
30. Mt. Holyoke College, McCulloch Center for Global Initiatives, "Global Education for All Students: innovation and integration in expanding learning abroad," White Paper, August, 2007. See also Forum on Education Abroad, "A Baseline Survey of Curriculum Integration in Education Abroad," www.forumea.org/documents/surveyfinal.pdf.

Chapter 6

1. *Fall 2007 International Student Enrollment Survey*, retrieved from *www.opendoors. iienetwork.org/file_depot/0-10000000/0-10000/3390/folder/67124/Fall+2007+ Survey+Report+Final1.pdf*
2. *Internationalization of Higher Education* (Paris: International Association of Universities, 2003).
3. Jack Yanz and Ching-Mei Hsiao, "Educational Marketing of Transnational Education in Asia," *Journal of American Academy of Business* 9 (September, 2006): 72–4.
4. Ellen Knickneyer, "Structure in U.S. Prompts Arabs to Study Elsewhere," *Washington Post*, December 18, 2006, A20, 26.
5. Sandra Merras, "International Education in Australian Universities," *Journal of Higher Education Policy and Management* 26 (November 2004): 371–80.
6. Deanna de Zilwa, "Using Entrepreneurial Activities as a Means of Survival: examining the processes used by Australian universities to diversify their revenue streams," *High Education* 50 (2005): 287–411.
7. "Looking Out for Foreign Students," http://www.channelnewsasia.com/stories/ singaporelocalnews/view/244650/1/html. Retrieved December 1, 2006.
8. International Institute of Education Operators, 2006 Fast Facts.
9. Liping Bu, *Making the World Like Us: Education, Cultural Expansion, and the American Century* (Westport, CT: Praeger 2003).
10. H. Koh Chin and R. Bhandari, *Open Doors 2006: Report on International Educational Exchange* (New York: Institute of International Education, 2006); Fall, 2007 International Student Enrollment Survey.
11. 2007 International Student Enrollment Survey.
12. IIE, *Open Doors* 2006.
13. 2007 International Student Enrollment Survey, Fig. 6.
14. 2007 International Student Enrollment Survey.
15. Ibid.
16. NAFSA: Association of International Education website, Code of Ethics, http://www.nafsa.org/publication/sec/documentlibrary.dlib/students_coming_ the/guidelenes_for_ethical.
17. www.educationusa.state.gov on the visa process.
18. U.S. Classroom Culture pamphlet (New York: NAFSA: Association of International Education, 2004). See also J. F. Anderson and R. Powell, "Intercultural Communication and the Classroom," in L.A. Samovar and R.W. Porter, eds., *Intercultural Communication: A Reader*, 6th ed. (Belmont, CA: Wadsworth Publishing Company, 1991), pp. 208–14; J. Dunphy, "Teaching in the Multicultural Classroom," *NAFSA Newsletter* 50(3) (March–April, 1999): 1–8; A.J. Eland, "Intersection of Academics and Culture: The Academic Experience of International Graduate Students, unpublished dissertation (Minneapolis, MN: University of Minnesota, 2001); H. Fox, "And Never the Twain Shall Meet: International Students Writing for a U.S. University Audience," presented in March, 1996 at the Annual Meeting of the Conference on College Composition and Communication, Milwaukee, WI; and M. B. Smithee, "Factors Related to the Development and Implementation of a University-wide Teaching Assistant Program," unpublished dissertation (Syracuse University, NY: 1990).
19. Eland, "Intersection of Academics and Culture."
20. http://www.ets.org/portal/site/ets/menuitem.435c0b5cc7bd0ae7015d9510c 3921509/?vgnextoid=4876be3a864f4010VgnVCM10000022f95190RCRD; also Eric Kronenvelter, "TOEFL: the Next Generation," *International Educator* (October, 2005):18–22.

21. http://www.ets.org/portal/site/ets/menuitem.fab2360b1645alde9b3a0779fl751509/?vgnextoid=06cfd898c84f4010VgnVCM10000022f95190RCRD; http://www.free-english.com/TOEFL-iBT-practice-test.aspx#overview; and http://www.ielts.org/.

22. http://www.ets.org/portal/site/ets/menuitem.fab2360b1645alde9b3a0779fl751509/?vgnextoid=06cfd898c84f4010VgnVCM10000022f95190RCRD; http://www.free-english.com/TOEFL-iBT-practice-test.aspx#overview; and http://www.ielts.org/.

23. http://www.ets.org/portal/site/ets/menuitem.435c0b5cc7bd0ae7015d9510c3921509/?vgnextoid=4876be3a864f4010VgnVCM10000022f95190RCRD; see also http://www. ets.org/portal/site/ets/menuitem.1488512ecfd568849a77b on TOEFL reporting.

24. Commission on English Language Program Association Standards, www.cea-accredit.org. See also Mary Ann Christison, ed., *Handbook for Language Program Administrators* (San Francisco, CA: Alta Professional Series, 1997).

25. Typical is a Minnesota requirement, demanding that all non-native English-speaking teaching assistants demonstrate "proficiency in spoken English appropriate to the demands of their teaching assistantship," assessed by a Spoken Proficiency in English Assessment Kit (SPEAK) test, the Test of Spoken English (TSE) or an English Language Proficiency rating earned through the University's Center for Teaching and Learning. Score requirements are specific for each type, with some work assignments possible along with continued English communication coursework for students with middling results, but with low-result students excluded. See http://wwwl.umn.edu/ohr/policies/performance/language.html and http://ase.ufl.edu/testing.html (for Florida).

26. U.S. Immigration and Customs Enforcement, SEVIS I-901 Free Frequently Asked Questions, http://www.ice.gov/sevis/i901/faq2.htm.

27. International Student Enrollment Survey, 2007.

28. Dave Hart, "Global Flows of Talent: benchmarking the U.S.," Information Technology and Innovation Foundation policy brief, November 17, 2006. An impressive percentage of foreign, largely Asian, nationals who receive American doctorate degrees stay in the United States at least for some time, winning formal employment, particularly in engineering. Two-thirds of all foreign Ph.D. degrees in science and engineering with degrees from 2003 were still in the country two years later. On the other hand, there are small signs that the "stay rate" is declining just a bit, at least for brief stays; five-year stay rates continue to rise very slightly. But stay rates from some countries, like Korea and Taiwan, are noticeably lower than those from places like China and India. See "Foreign Science and Engineering Presence in U.S. Institutions and the Labor Force," retrieved August 11, 2008 from www.fas.org/sgp/crs/misc/97–746.pdf; and Michael G. Finn, "Stay Rates of Foreign Doctorate Recipients from U.S. Universities, 2005," *Science and Engineering Education*, 2007.

29. Personal communication, Curtis H. Porter, Vice Chancellor for International Affairs, Troy University, January 7, 2008. My thanks for Dr. Porter's valuable time and insights.

30. "Internationalization Collaborative: Community Colleges: Northern Virginia Community College" retrieved August 1, 2008 from http://www.acenet.edu/AM/Template.cfm?Section=Home&Template=/CM/HTMLDisplay.cfm&ContentID=11804

Chapter 7

1. Beth McMurtrie, "The Global Campus: American colleges connect with the broader world," *Chronicle of Higher Education*, March 2, 2007.

2. For overviews, see: Tamar Lewin, "U.S. Universities Rush to Set Up Outposts Abroad," *New York Times*, February 10, 2008; Madeline Green, Peter Eckel, Lourdes Calderon, and Dao Luu, *Venturing Abroad: Delivering U.S. Degrees through Overseas Branch Campuses and Programs* (Washington D.C.: Society for College and University Planning, 2007); J. Knight, "Crossborder Education," in J.C. Smart, ed., *Higher Education: Handbook of Theory and Research* (Dordrecht, The Netherlands: Springer, 2006), pp. 345–95; S. Marginson, ed., *University Futures: Global Markets and the Public Good* (Dordrecht, The Netherlands: Springer, forthcoming); J. Kanwar Daniel and S. Uvalic-Trumbic, *Who's Afraid of Cross-border Higher Education? A Developing World Perspective*, presented at the Final Plenary Session: Quality Assurance in Transnational Issues Annual Conference (Wellington, New Zealand, April 1, 2005); L. Verbik and C. Merkley, "The International Branch Campus – models and trends," No. 46, Observatory on Borderless Higher Education (London: 2006) p. 14; Laura Rumbley and Philip Altbach, "International Branch Campus Issues," paper retrieved from *www.international.ac.uk/documents_library/index.cfm?pageNum*=9& July, 2007; W. Underhill, "Sowing Seeds: from Cornell in Qatar to Monash in Malaysia, satellite campuses are a booming business," *Newsweek International Edition*, August 21, 2006; Philip Altbach and Jane Knight, "The Internationalization of Higher Education: Motivations and Realities," Journal of Studies in International Education, Vol. 11, No. 3–4 (2007), 290–305; Burton Bollag, "America's Hot New Export: higher education," *Chronicle of Higher Education. p.* A44–47, Feb. 17, 2006; and Grant McBurnie and Christopher Ziguras, *Transnational Education: issues and trends in offshore higher education* (New York: Routledge, 2007).
3. J. Knight, *Higher Education Crossing Borders: A Guide to the Implications of the General Agreement on Trade in Services (GATS) for Cross-border Education* (Vancouver and Paris: UNESCO, 2006).
4. On American University in Beirut and American University in Cairo, useful historical summaries are available in Wikipedia.
5. Mark Ward, "The Importance of International Education to Development in the Middle East," *Liberal Education* 94 (2008): 36–41.
6. Shafeeq Ghabra with Margreet Arnold, "Studying the American Way: an assessment of American-style higher education in Arab countries" (Washington: The Washington Institute for Near East Policies, 2001).
7. Neil Swidey, "All the Rage: even as Middle Eastern students hotly denounce U.S. policies, they line up for an American-Style college education," *Boston Globe*, April 20, 2003.
8. Verbik and Merkley, "The International Branch Campus." See www.obhe.ac.uk— the *Observatory* issues a regular series of articles that provide vital information and evaluation of this new trend, with emphasis on U.K. initiatives but with more general coverage as well.
9. Lewin, "U.S. Universities Rush to Set Up Outposts Abroad."
10. "American Schools Abroad: subversive values," *The Economist*, June 20, 1998.
11. Sally Findlow, "International Networking in the United Arab Emirates Higher Education System: global–local tensions," *Compare* 35 (September, 2005): 285–302.
12. W. Michael Kemp, "Reflections on a Middle Eastern Higher Education Experience," *The Greentree Gazette*, September 2007.
13. Donald Hall, "Why Professors Should Teach Abroad," *Chronicle of Higher Education*, October 5, 2007.
14. American University of Sharjah website, www.aus.edu/.

15. "ABTI-American University of Nigeria Reaches Major Milestones," *American Weekly* (American University Newspaper), February 20, 2007.
16. Barbara Tedrow and R.O. Mabokela, "An Analysis of International Partnership Programs: the case of an historically disadvantaged institution in South Africa," *Higher Education* 54 (2007): 159–79.
17. Green et al., *Venturing Abroad*.
18. Michael Stopford, "Changing China: American universities lead the way," *Washington Times*, February 14, 2001.
19. Beth McMurtrie, "Culture and Unrealistic Expectations Challenge American Campuses in Japan," *Chronicle of Higher Education*, June 2, 2000.
20. "The Phantom Campus in China," *Inside Higher Education*, February 12, 2008.
21. Lewin, "U.S. Universities Rush to Set Up Outposts Abroad."
22. McMurtrie, "The Global Campus."
23. "Sharing Quality Education Across Borders: a statement on behalf of higher education institutions worldwide" (International Association of Universities (and others), January, 2005).
24. "The Phantom Campus in China."
25. M.A. Overland, "Foreign Universities in Vietnam Ordered to Teach Communist Ideology," *Chronicle of Higher Education*, June 24, 2005.
26. Aisha Labi, "World Bank Urges Sweeping Changes in Higher Education Across the Arab World," *Chronicle of Higher Education*, February 15, 2008.
27. Kemp, "Reflections on a Middle Eastern Higher Education Experience".
28. ibid.
29. Lewin, "U.S. Universities."
30. Sara Hebel, "On an American Campus in Greece, A Chorus of Critics," *Chronicle of Higher Education*, December 15, 2006.
31. Lewin, "U.S. Universities."

Chapter 8

1. Christa Olson, "Comprehensive Internationalization: an integrated approach for engaging faculty" (Association of Consortium Leadership webinar, March 21, 2007).
2. Karin Fischer, "Colleges May Face Challenges in Realizing Greater Internationalization," *Chronicle of Higher Education*, February 21, 2008.
3. Penn Compact: engaging globally, http://www.upenn.edu/compact/globally.html; The President's Council on Boston University and the Global Future, university report of September, 2006.
4. University of Delaware website, http://www.udel.edu/PR/UDaily/2008/sep/strategic091007.html, retrieved March 1, 2008.
5. *Building a Strategic Framework for Comprehensive Internationalization* (Washington D.C.: American Council on Education, 2005). See also the ACE networks, particularly the Leadership Network on International Education for Presidents and Provosts.
6. "A Call to Leadership: The presidential role in internationalizing the university," A Report of the NASULGC Task Force on International Education (Washington D.C.: NASULGC, 2004).
7. Association of International Educators, *Internationalizing the Campus 2007* (New York: NAFSA, 2007).
8. Patti Peterson, "Addressing the Challenge to Internationalize Our Academic

Institutions: how are we doing?" Council for the International Exchange of Scholars, http//www.iie.org/cies/articles/patt_internation.htm.

9. Roslind Latiner Raby and Edward Valeau, "Community College International Education: looking back to forecast the future," *New Directions for Community Colleges* 138 (Summer, 2007).

10. American Council on Education, Internationalization Collaborative: community colleges: Northern Virginia Community College, January 29, 2008, http://www.acenet.edu.

11. Joann McCarthy, "A Roadmap for Creating the Global Campus," *Chronicle of Higher Education*, June 29, 2007.

12. Arizona State University, Office of the Vice President for Global Engagement, http://ovpge.asu.edu/, March 1, 2008.

13. East Carolina University, www.jobs.ecu.edu, March 3, 2008.

14. Peterson, "Addressing the Challenge."

15. Thomas Barrow et al., *College Students' Knowledge and Beliefs: Survey of Global Understanding* (Princeton, NJ: Educational Testing Service, 1981); *What We Don't Know Can Hurt Us* (Washington D.C.: American Council on Education, 1984); Richard Lambert, *International Studies and the Undergraduate* (Washington D.C.: ACE, 1989); Charles Anderson, *International Studies for Undergraduates, 1987: Operations and Opinions*, Higher Education Panel Report No. 76 (Washington D.C.: ACE, 1988); *What We Can't Say Can Hurt Us—A Call for Foreign Language Competence by the Year 2000* (Washington D.C.: ACE, 1989); "Building the Global Community: The Next Step," Report of a conference sponsored by the American Council on International Intercultural Education and the Stanley Foundation, 1994; Louis W. Goodman, Kay King, and Nancy L. Ruther, *Undergraduate International Studies on the Eve of the Twenty-first Century* (College Park, MD: Association of Professional Schools of International Affairs, 1994); "Educating Americans for a World in Flux: Ten Ground Rules for Internationalizing Higher Education" (Washington D.C.: ACE, 1995); "A Research Agenda for the Internationalization of Higher Education in the United States" (Durham NC: Association of International Education Administrators, 1995); "Educating for Global Competence—America's Passport to the Future" (Washington D.C.: ACE, 1998); "Global Responsibility: Final Report of the AASCU Task Force on Global Responsibility" (Washington D.C.: American Association of State Colleges and Universities, 1998). (See also www.aascu.org/campus/global.htm).

16. "A Call to Leadership: The presidential role in internationalizing the university," A Report of the NASULGC Task Force on International Education (Washington D.C.: NASULGC, 2004).

17. McCarthy, "A Roadmap."

Chapter 9

1. John W. Creswell, *Educational Research: Planning, Conducting, and Evaluating Quantitative and Qualitative Research* (Upper Saddle River, NJ: Pearson Education, Inc., 2005).

2. Christa Olson, *Internationalizing the Campus: an integrated approach for addressing globalization* (Washington D.C.: ACE, October 12, 2007); Madeleine Green, "Joining the World: the challenge of internationalizing undergraduate education," *Change* 34 (3) (May–June, 2002): 13–21.

3. Green, "Joining the World"; "A Call to Leadership: The presidential role in internationalizing the university," A Report of the NASULGC Task Force on International Education (Washington D.C.: NASULGC, 2004).

4. Laura Siaya, "A Framework for Identifying International/Intercultural Competencies," prepared for the ACE Internationalisation Collaborative Annual Meeting, March 16–17, 2001 (Washington D.C.: ACE, 2001).

5. Michael Carpini and Scott Ketter, *What Americans Know about Politics and Why It Matters* (New Haven: Yale University Press, 1989); Norman Dinges, "Intercultural Competence," in D. Landis and R. Brislin, eds., *Handbook of Intercultural Training* (New York: Pergamon, 1983); *College Students' Knowledge and Beliefs: A Survey of Global Understanding* (New York: Educational Testing Service, 1981); S. Groenning and D.S. Wiley, eds., *Group Portrait: Internationalizing the Disciplines* (New York: American Forum, 1990); Josef Mestenhauser, "Portraits of an International Curriculum: an uncommon multidimensional perspective," in J.A. Mestenhauser and Brenda Ellingboe, eds., *Reforming the Higher Education Curriculum: Internationalizing the Campus* (Phoenix, AZ: Oryx Press, 1998), pp. 1–39. See also William D. Hunter, "Got Global Competency?" *International Educator*, 13:10 (Spring, 2004): 6–12; K. Curran, *Global Competencies that Facilitate Working Effectively Across Cultures*, 2003, from http://content.monster.com.sg/management/5808; R. Lambers, "Parsing the Concept of Global Competence," *Educational Exchange and Global Competence*, (New York, NY: Council on International Educational Exchange, 1996); *An International Education Agenda for the United States: Public Policy, Priorities Recommendations* (Washington D.C.: NAFSA, 2003); C.L. Olson and K.R. Kroeger, "Global Competency and Intercultural Sensitivity," *Journal of Studies in International Education* 5(2) (2001); C.B. Klasek, *Bridges to the Future: Strategies for Internationalizing Higher Education* (Carbondale, IL: Association of International Education Administrators, 1992).

6. G. Bonham, "Education and the Worldview," *Change* 12(4) (1980): 2–7.

7. Colleen Kelley and Judith Meyers, *The Cross-Cultural Adaptability Inventory* (Yarmouth, ME: National Computer Systems, 1987).

8. S. Lamy, "Defining Global Education," *Educational Research Quarterly* 8(1) (1987): 9–20; Brian Spitzberg, "A Model of Intercultural Communication Competence," in L.A. Samovar and R.E. Porter, eds., *Intercultural Communication: A Reader* (New York: Wadsworth Publishing, 2000), pp. 375–87.

9. Mitchell Hammer and Milton Bennett, *The Intercultural Development Inventory Manual* (Portland, OR: The Intercultural Communication Institute, 1998); Dale Stanley, *International Learning Outcomes: Report for the BC Centre for International Education* (Vancouver: British Columbia Centre for International Education, 1997).

10. See www.bentley.edu/.

11. W. Parker, A. Ninomiya, and J. Cogan, "Educating World Citizens: toward multinational curriculum development," *American Educational Research Journal* 36(2) (Summer, 1999): 117–45.

12. Peter N. Stearns, "Getting Specific About Training in Historical Analysis: a case study in world history," in Stearns, Peter Seixas, and Sam Wineburg, eds., *Knowing, Teaching and Learning History* (New York: NYU Press, 2000), pp. 419–36. Enhancing the comparative skill is an intriguing challenge, as students are much more comfortable juxtaposing data from two different cases than actually, actively comparing. In the global context they also tend much more readily to seize on differences than beneath-the-surface similarities, another challenge that explicit work on skill development can modify.

13. Robert Hanvey, *An Attainable Global Perspective* (New York: American Forum, 1979).

14. One such tool is posted on the American Council of Education website (2008).
15. Hunter, "Got Global Competency?"
16. University System of Georgia, "Recommended Minimal Global Competencies"; Kristen Renn and James Lucas, "Internationalizing the Student Experience: working group report," Michigan State University, July, 2007.
17. Thomas Matthews and Cheryl Hansen, "Ongoing Assessment of a University Foreign Language Program," 37(4) (2004): 630–40. The article references the growing literature both on portfolio work and on oral competency testing; *2005–2006 Guide to Educational Credit by Examination* (Yonkers, NY: American Council on the Teaching of Foreign Languages, 2006).

Chapter 10

1. Christa Olson, Rhodri Evans and Robert Shoenberg, *At Home in the World: Bridging the Gap between Internationalization and Multicultural Education* (Washington D.C.: ACE, 2007). This discussion continues at ACE: see the "Bridging the Gap" symposium, June 25–6, 2008.

Chapter 11

1. "A Call to Leadership: The presidential role in internationalizing the university," A Report of the NASULGC Task Force on International Education (Washington D.C.: NASULGC, 2004).

Further Reading

The suggestions that follow are not exhaustive, but they cover the major facets of global education and, largely recent, can lead to additional depth as desired. Consultations of regular or recurrent outlets, such as the ongoing publications of the American Council on Education or the IIE, are also warmly recommended.

The following journals, associations and websites also regularly provide articles of interest in the area of global education:

AAC&U—American Association of Colleges and Universities: *Liberal Education Higher Education Journal*
Issues in Integrative Studies Journal
Boston College Center for Higher Education: www.bc.edu/bc_org/avp/soe/cihe/
International Journal of Teaching & Learning in Higher Education (IJTLHE): www.isetl.org/ijtlhe/
NASPA—National Association of Student Personnel Administrators: *NASPA Journal*
ACPA—American College Personnel Association
Journal of College Student Development
Higher Education in Europe
Journal of Higher Education
Journal of Studies in International Education
Review of Higher Education
Studies in Higher Education
World Yearbook of Education

"A Baseline Survey of Curriculum Integration in Education Abroad," analysis of data from *The Forum on Education Abroad* 2003–2004 Survey of Curricular Integration, retrieved from www.umabroad.umn.edu/ci/impact/index.html on March 15, 2008.

"A Call to Leadership: The presidential role in internationalizing the university," A Report of the NASULGC Task Force on International Education (Washington D.C.: NASULGC, 2004).

Ahmed, Iftikhar, *Education for Democratic Citizenship and Peace* (Washington D.C.: Educational Resources Information Center, 2003).

Altbach, Philip G., ed., *International Higher Education: An Encyclopedia* (New York: Garland, 1991).

Altbach, Philip G., ed., *The International Academic Profession: Portraits of Fourteen Countries* (Princeton, NJ: The Carnegie Foundation for the Advancement of Teaching, 1996).

Altbach, Philip G., *Comparative Higher Education* (New York: Ablex, 1998).

Altbach, Philip G. and Jin Wang, eds., *Foreign Students and International Study* (New York: University Press of America, 1989).

American Council on Education (ACE), *What We Don't Know Can Hurt Us* (Washington, D.C.: ACE, 1984).

American Council on Education (ACE), *Survey of International Attitudes and Knowledge* (Washington, D.C.: ACE, 2000).

American Council on Education (ACE), *Public Experience, Attitudes and Knowledge: A Report on Two National Surveys about International Education* (Washington, D.C.: ACE, 2002).

American Council on Education (ACE), *Mapping Internationalization on U.S. Campuses* (Washington, D.C.: ACE, 2003).

American Council on Education (ACE), *Building a Strategic Framework for Comprehensive Internationalization* (Washington, D.C.: ACE, 2005). See also the ACE networks, particularly the Leadership Network on International Education for Presidents and Provosts.

American Council on Education (ACE) *2006 Mapping of Internationalization* (Washington, D.C.: ACE, 2008).

Andrzejewski, Julia and John Alessio, *Education for Global Citizenship and Social Responsibility*, John Dewey Project on Progressive Education (VT: University of Vermont Press, 1999).

Associated Colleges of the Midwest, Associated Colleges of the South, Great Lakes College

Association, *Liberal Education and Study Abroad: Assessing Learning Outcomes to Improve Program Quality* (New York: The Teagle Foundation, 2006).

The Academy in Transition: Globalizing Knowledge, Connecting International and Intercultural Studies (Washington, D.C.: AAC&U, 1999).

Avila, Joselyn Gacel, "The Internationalization of Higher Education: a paradigm for global citizenry," *Journal of Studies in International Education*, 9(2) (Summer, 2005).

Barrows, Leland C., ed., *Internationalisation of Higher Education: An Institutional Perspective* (Bucharest: UNESCO-CEPES, 2000).

Barrows, T.S., *College Student's Knowledge and Beliefs: A Survey of Global Understanding* (Princeton, NJ: Educational Testing Service, 1981).

Bolen, Mell, ed., *A Guide to Outcomes Assessment in Education Abroad*, The Forum on Education Abroad (Carlisle, PA: Dickenson College, 2007).

Bragaw, Don, "Schooling and Citizenship in a Global Age," *Issues in Global Education, 164* (2001).

Bremer, Darlene, "Global Workers," *International Educator*, May and June, 2006.

Brustein, William, I. "Paths to Global Competence: preparing American college students to meet the world," *IIE Networker: Internationalizing the Campus*, Spring, 2006.

Cabrera, Angel, "Emphasizing Global Citizenship for Business Leaders," *International Educator*, (Washington, D.C.: NAFSA, January and February, 2005).

Carlson, J., B. Burn, J. Ussem, and D. Yachimowica, *Study Abroad: The Experience of American Undergraduates in Western Europe and the U.S.* (Westport, CT: Greenwood, 1990).

Centre for Educational Research and Innovation, *Internationalisation of High Education* (Paris: Organisation for Economic Co-Operation and Development, 1996).

Chandler, Alice, *Paying the Bill for International Education: Programs, Partners and Possibilities at the Millennium* (Washington, D.C.: NAFSA and the Association of International Educators, 1999)

Chernotsky, Harry I. and Heidi H. Hobbs, *Preparing Students for Global Citizenship: The Challenge for International Studies*, Paper presented at the International Studies Association Annual Convention (San Diego, CA, 2006).

Clarke, Velta. "Students' Global Awareness and Attitudes to Internationalism in a World of Cultural Convergence," *Journal of Research in International Education* 3, pp. 51–70 (2004).

Colby, A., T. Ehrlich, E. Beaumont, and J. Stephens, *Educating Citizens: Preparing America's Undergraduates for Lives of Moral and Civic Responsibility* (San Francisco: Jossey-Bass, 2003).

Connell, Christopher, "Realizing 'Outrageous Ambitions,'" *International Educator*, July/August, 2005.

Creswell, John W., *Research Design: Qualitative, Quantitative, and Mixed Methods Approaches* (Thousand Oaks, CA: Sage Publications, 2003).

Creswell, John W., *Educational Research: Planning, Conducting and Evaluating Quantitative and Qualitative Research* (Upper Saddle River, NJ: Prentice Hall, 2005).

Cummings, William, *Current Challenges of International Education* (Washington, D.C.: Educational Resources Information Center, 2001).

Deardorff, Darla Kay Bowman *The Identification and Assessment of Intercultural Competence on a Student Outcome of Internationalization at Institutes of Higher Education in the United States* (unpublished doctoral dissertation, Raleigh, NC, 2004).

Deardorff, Darla Kay and William Hunter, "Educating Global-ready Graduates," *International Educator*, May–June, 2006.

Dessoff, Alan, "Who's NOT Going Abroad?" *International Educator*, March–April, 2007.

Dolby, Nadine, "Globalization, Identity and Nation: Australian and American undergraduates abroad," *Australian Educational Researcher* 32 (2005).

Dower, Nigel, *An Introduction to Global Citizenship* (Edinburgh, UK: Edinburgh University Press, 2003).

Dwyer, Mary and Courtney K. Peters, *The Benefits of Study Abroad*, retrieved from www.transitionsabroad.com/publications/magazine/0403/benefits_study_abroad.shtml (September, 2006).

Eckel, Peter, Madeleine Green, and Barbara Hill, *On Change V. Riding the Waves of Change: Insights from Transforming Institutions* (Washington D.C: ACE, 2006).

Fanton, Jonathan, *Guiding Students Toward Global Citizenship*, retrieved from www.macfound.org/site/apps/nl/content2.asp.

Fowler, Sandra M. and Judith M. Blohm, "An Analysis of Methods for Intercultural Training," in *Handbook of Intercultural Training* (Thousand Oaks, CA: Sage Publications, 2004).

Frankel, Noralee and Peter N. Stearns, eds., *Globalizing American History* (Washington, D.C.: American Historical Association, 2008).

Freed, Barbara, ed., *Second Language Acquisition in a Study Abroad Context* (Amsterdam and Philadelphia: John Benjamins North America, 1995).

Global Citizenship Definition, retrieved March 7, 2005 from www.oxfam.org.uk/coolplanet/teachers/globciti/whatis.htm.

"Global Competence & National Needs: one million Americans studying abroad," in *Commission on the Abraham Lincoln Study Abroad Fellowship Program* (Washington, D.C.: NAFSA, November 14, 2005).

Goodwin, Craufurd and Michael Nacht, *Missing the Boat: The Failure to Internationalize American Higher Education* (New York: Cambridge University Press, 1991).

Green, Madeleine, Peter Eckel, Lourdes Calderon, and Dao Luu *Venturing Abroad: Delivering U.S. Degrees through Overseas Branch Campuses and Programs* (Washington D.C., 2007).

Green, Madeleine, "Joining the World: the challenge of internationalizing undergraduate education," *Change* 34 (May/June, 2002).

Green, Madeleine and Christa Olson, *Internationalizing the Campus: A User's Guide* (Washington, D.C.: ACE, 2003).

Groening, S. and D.S. Wiley, eds., *Group Portrait: Internationalizing the Disciplines* (New York: The American Forum for Global Education, 1990).

Grosvenor, G., *Americans Get Low Grades in Gallup Geography Test*, (Washington D.C.: National Geographic Society, 1998).

Grudzinski-Hall, Magdalena N., "How Do College and University Undergraduate Level Global Citizenship Programs Advance the Development and Experiences of Global Competencies?" (thesis submitted to the faculty of Drexel University, May, 2007).

Hall, Donald. "Why Professors Should Teach Abroad," *Chronicle of Higher Education*, October 5, 2007.

Hayward, Fred, *Internationalization of U.S. Higher Education, Preliminary Status Report 2000* (Washington, D.C.: ACE, 2000).

Hayward, Fred M. and Laura Siaya, *Public Experience, Attitudes and Knowledge: A Report on Two National Surveys about International Education, Executive Summary* (Washington, D.C.: ACE, International Initiatives Program, 2002).

Henson, James B., Jan C. Noel, Thomas E. Gillard-Byers, and Marcus D Ingle, "Internationalizing U.S. Universities: A Preliminary Summary of a National Study" in *Internationalizing U.S. Universities: A Time for Leadership*. Conference Proceedings (Spokane, Washington: Spokane University, 1991).

Hinchcliff, John, *The globalization of education*, in: Cross-Roads of the New Millennium Proceedings of the Technological Education and National Development (TEND) Conference (2nd April 8–10, 2000, Abu Dhabi, United Arab Emirates).

Hovland, Kevin, "Shared Futures: global learning and social responsibility," *Diversity Digest* 8(3), 2005.

Hovland, Kevin, "Shared Futures: global learning and liberal education" (Washington, D.C.: AAC&U, 2006).

Hunter, William D., "Got Global Competency?" *International Educator*, Spring, 2004.

Hunter, William, *Knowledge, Skills, Attitudes and Experiences Necessary to Become Globally Competent* (Lehigh, PA, 2004, unpublished doctoral dissertation).

Institute for International Education, *Fall 2007 International Student Enrollment Survey* (IIE, November, 2007).

International Association of Universities, *Internationalization of Higher Education* (Paris: UNESCO, 2003).

Johnson, Joseph and R. Edelsstein, *Beyond Borders: Profiles in International Education* (Washington D.C.: Association of American Colleges and American Assembly of Collegiate Schools of Business, 1993).

Johnson, Robert *The Not-so-hidden Agenda of Global Studies*, retrieved from http://hnn.us/articles/6678.html on March 7, 2005.

Kiernan, Henry and John Pyne, "National Standards and Education Reform," *Journal of the New Jersey Council for the Social Studies* (Spring, 1993).

Klasek, Charles B., ed., *Bridges to the Future: Strategies for Internationalization of Higher Education* (Carbondale, IL: Association of International Education Administrators, 1992).

Knight, Jane and Hans de Wit, eds., *Quality and Internationalisation in Higher Education* (Paris: Organisation for Economic Co-operation and Development, 1999).

Lambert, Richard D., *International Studies and the Undergraduate* (Washington D.C., 1989).

Latham, Andrew A., *Liberal Education for Global Citizenship: Reviewing Macalester's Traditions of Public Scholarship and Civic Learning* (St. Paul, MN: Macalester College, Project Pericles, 2003).

Latiner Raby, Roslind and Edward Valeau, "Community College International Education: looking back to forecast the future," *New Directions for Community Colleges* 138 (Summer, 2007).

Maki, Peggy, *Developing an Assessment Plan to Learn about Student Learning*, American Association for Higher Education, retrieved March 7, 2005 from www.sciencedirect.com/science?_ob=ArticleURL&_udi=B6W50-451NMXJ-3&_user=650615&_rdoc=1&_fmt=&_orig=search&_sort=d&view=c&_version=1&_urlVersion=0&_userid=650615&md5=5ff713c78a197e3e5e4c1dd66f1866e0.

McCarthy, JoAnn, "A Roadmap for Creating the Global Campus," *Chronicle of Higher Education*, June 29, 2007.

McCarthy, JoAnn, "Continuing and Emerging National Needs for the Internationalization of Undergraduate Education," in *International Education in the New Global Era: Proceedings of National Policy Conference on the Higher Education Act, Title VI, and Fulbright-Hays Program* (Los Angeles: International Studies and Overseas Programs, 1998).

McIntosh, Peggy, "Gender Perspectives on Educating for Global Citizenship," in *Educating Citizens for Global Awareness* (New York: Teachers College Press, 2005).

McMurtrie, Beth, "Culture and Unrealistic Expectations Challenge American Campuses in Japan," *Chronicle of Higher Education*, June 2, 2000.

Medina-Lopez-Portillo, Adriana, "Intercultural Learning Assessment: The link between program duration and the development of intercultural sensitivity," *Frontiers: The Interdisciplinary Journal of Study Abroad* Volume X (Fall, 2004).

Mestenhauser, Josef M. and Ellingboe, Brenda, *Reforming the Higher Education Curriculum: Internationalizing the Campus* (Phoenix, AZ: The Oryx Press, 1998).

NAFSA: Association of International Educators, *An International Education Agenda for the United States: Public Policy, Priorities Recommendations* (Washington, D.C.: NAFSA, Association of International Educators, 2003).

NAFSA: Association of International Educators, *Internationalizing the Campus 2007* (Washington, D.C.: NAFSA, Association of International Educators, 2007).

National Association of State Universities and Land Grant Collages, *National Action Agenda for Internationalizing Higher Education* (Washington, D.C.: The NASULGC Commission on International Programs, October 2007).

Nussbaum, Martha C., *For Love of Country?* (Boston, MA: Beacon Press, 1996).

Noddings, Nel, ed., *Educating Citizens for Global Awareness* (New York: Teachers College Press, 2005).

Olson, Christa, Madeleine Green, and Barbara Hill, *A Handbook for Advancing Comprehensive Internationalization: What Institutions Can Do and What Students Should Learn* (Washington, D.C.: ACE, (2006).

Olson, Christa, *Internationalizing the Campus: An Integrated Approach for Addressing Globalization* (Washington D.C.: ACE, October 12, 2007).

Olson, Christa, "Comprehensive Internationalization: an integrated approach for engaging faculty," (Washington, D.C.: ACE Webinar, March 21, 2007).

Opper, S., U. Teichler, and J. Carlson, *Impacts of Study Abroad Programmes on Students and Graduates* (London: Taylor and Francis, 1990).

Parker, W., A. Ninomiya, and J. Cogan, "Educating World Citizens: Toward multinational curriculum development," *American Educational Research Journal*, 36(2) (Summer, 1999).

Pickert, Sally and Turlington, Barbara, *Internationalizing the Undergraduate Curriculum: A Handbook for Campus Leaders* (Washington D.C.: ACE, 1992).

Schattle, Hans, "Global Education and Global Citizenship: Widening the Scope of civic education," paper submitted to *PS: Political Science and Politics*, 2004.

Siaya, Laura, "A Framework for Identifying International/Intercultural Competencies," (Washington, D.C.: ACE Internationalization Collaboration Annual Meeting, March 16–17, 2001).

Stanley, Dale, *International Learning Outcomes: Report for the BC Centre for International Education* (Vancouver: British Columbia Centre for International Education (BCCIE), 1997).

Stearns, Peter N., *Meaning over Memory: Recasting the Teaching of History and Culture* (Chapel Hill, NC: University of North Carolina Press, 1994).

Urias, David, Darla Deardorff, and John D. Heyl, "Standards of Quality for Master's Degree Level Programs in International Education: Ensuring Quality & Effectiveness," July 26, 2007, retrieved from www.iienetwork.org/page/109508/.

Whalley, Tom, *Best Practices for Internationalizing the Curriculum* (Victoria, B.C.: Centre for Curriculum, Transfer, and Technology, 2000).

Young, Ben, "Global Citizens Unite," *The Times Educational Supplement Section: Opinions*, September 3, 2004.

Zeszorarski, Paula, "Issues in Global Education Initiatives in the Community College," *Community College Review* 29(1) (2008).

About the Author

Peter N. Stearns is Provost and Professor of History at George Mason University. He has taught previously at Harvard, the University of Chicago, Rutgers, and Carnegie Mellon; he was educated at Harvard University. He has published widely in modern social history, including the history of emotions, and in world history. Representative works in world history include *World History: A Survey*, *The Industrial Revolution in World History*, *Gender in World History*, *Consumerism in World History* and *Growing Up: The History of Childhood in Global Context*. His publications in social history include *Old Age in Preindustrial Society*, *Anxious Parents: A History of Modern American Childrearing*, *American Cool: Developing the Twentieth-Century Emotional Style*, *Fat History: Bodies and Beauty in Western Society*, *The Battleground of Desire: The Struggle for Self-Control in Modern America*; *American Fear: The Causes and Consequences of High Anxiety*; *Revolutions in Sorrow: A History of American Experiences and Policies Toward Death in Global Context* and *From Alienation to Addiction: Modern American Work in Global Historical Perspective*. While under Dr. Stearns' leadership, George Mason University was awarded the 2006 Andrew Heiskell Award for Innovation in International Education. He has also edited encyclopedias of world and social history, and since 1967 has served as editor-in-chief of *The Journal of Social History*.

In most of his research and writing, Dr. Stearns pursues three main goals. First, as a social historian he is eager to explore aspects of the human experience that are not generally thought of in historical terms, and with attention to ordinary people as well as elites. Second, he seeks to use an understanding of historical change and continuity to explore patterns of behavior and social issues. Finally he is concerned with connecting new historical research with wider audiences, including of course classrooms. Dr. Stearns is also eager to promote comparative analysis and the assessment of modern global forces – for their own sake and as they illuminate the American experience and impact.

Index